D0076190

SPORT, VIOLENCE AND SOCIETY

- Is violence an intrinsic component of contemporary sport?
- How does violence within sport reflect upon the attitudes of wider society?

In this landmark study of violence in and around contemporary sport, Kevin Young offers the first comprehensive sociological analysis of an issue of central importance within sport studies. The book explores organized and spontaneous violence, both on the field and off, and calls for a much broader definition of 'sports-related violence,' to include issues as diverse as criminal behaviour by players, abuse within sport and exploitatory labour practices.

Offering a sophisticated new theoretical framework for understanding violence in a sporting context, and including a wide range of case studies and empirical data, from professional soccer in Europe to ice hockey in North America, the book establishes a benchmark for the study of violence within sport and wider society. Through close examination of often contradictory trends, from anti-violence initiatives in professional sports leagues to the role of the media in encouraging hyper-aggression, the book throws new light on our understanding of the socially-embedded character of sport and its fundamental ties to history, culture, politics, social class, gender and the law.

Kevin Young is a professor in the Department of Sociology at the University of Calgary, Canada. He has served on the editorial boards of several journals, including *International Review for the Sociology of Sport*, *Sociology of Sport Journal* and *Soccer and Society*. Young has also served on the executive board of the North American Society for the Sociology of Sport and as vice president of the International Sociology of Sport Association.

SPORT, VIOLENCE AND SOCIETY

Kevin Young

Routledge
Taylor & Francis Group

LONDON AND NEW YORK

First published 2012
by Routledge
2 Park Square, Milton Park, Abingdon, Oxon OX14 4RN

Simultaneously published in the USA and Canada
by Routledge
711 Third Avenue, New York, NY 10017

Routledge is an imprint of the Taylor & Francis Group, an informa business

© 2012 Kevin Young

The right of Kevin Young to be identified as author of this work has
been asserted by him in accordance with sections 77 and 78 of the
Copyright, Designs and Patents Act 1988.

All rights reserved. No part of this book may be reprinted or reproduced
or utilized in any form or by any electronic, mechanical, or other means,
now known or hereafter invented, including photocopying and recording,
or in any information storage or retrieval system, without permission in
writing from the publishers.

Trademark notice: Product or corporate names may be trademarks or
registered trademarks, and are used only for identification and
explanation without intent to infringe.

British Library Cataloguing in Publication Data
A catalogue record for this book is available from the British Library

Library of Congress Cataloging in Publication Data
Young, Kevin, 1959-
  Sport, violence and society / by Kevin Young.
  p. cm.
  1. Violence in sports. 2. Sports—Sociological aspects. I. Title.
  GV706.7.S655 2001
  306.483—dc23
  2011027401

ISBN: 978–0–415–54994–3 (hbk)
ISBN: 978–0–415–54995–0 (pbk)
ISBN: 978–0–203–87461–5 (ebk)

Typeset in Bembo by
by Swales & Willis Ltd, Exeter, Devon

Printed and bound in Great Britain by
TJ International Ltd, Padstow, Cornwall

This book is dedicated to the memory of
Michael Dewar Smith, whose pioneering
contributions to Canadian studies of
(sports) violence should never be underestimated.

CONTENTS

ILLUSTRATIONS

Figures

Tables

ACKNOWLEDGEMENTS

I would like to thank several people who have been instrumental in helping me complete this book. I am indebted to innumerable Criminology, Sociology and Sociology of Sport students at the University of Calgary who have helped me formulate, sharpen and test my thinking on violence in sport. This book is the outcome of years of lively classroom dialogue and debate; long may that continue. Several students in particular deserve thanks. For their enthusiastic research assistance, I am grateful to Donald McKeown, Krista McEwen, Daniel Christie and Sarah Harvey, all of whom helped at various points along the way. The guidance of so many colleagues at Routledge, UK has been indispensable from start to finish. In particular I would like to express my gratitude to Simon Whitmore, Joshua Wells, Sarah Willis, Richard Willis and Caroline Watson for their leadership, patience and support, and for so professionally steering me through this project. I am fortunate to have many friends in the academic community who have supported my work, but none more so than Michael Atkinson whose uncanny ability to keep on top of the literature and keen editorial eye are much appreciated. Thanks to my children, Niki and Stephen, for providing a daily reminder that while this book is important to me, its importance has limits. Finally, and above all, Ashley Weldon offered more time and insight than I had a right to expect. For her tireless generosity and support, I am deeply grateful.

PREFACE

The idea for this book, which has taken far too long for me to write, probably started in the late 1970s when, as an undergraduate university student in the UK, I was exposed to one of the first in-depth sociological investigations into 'football (soccer) hooliganism.' Even then, long before emigration and travel provided an opportunity to witness global sports violence first-hand, it seemed unlikely to me that the phenomenon was so unidimensional that it was limited to the aggressive proclivities of young British soccer supporters (a stereotypical view popular at the time, and one that continues to be espoused by many North Americans). After all, if sports violence, as with sport more broadly, was indeed *social* and *cultural* – 'lesson one' in the sociology of sport – then other societies and other cultures must forge their own versions of it. And of course they do. This book represents a long-standing fascination with the varied manifestations of violence in the sporting cultures of many countries, and the sociological threads that tie together and underpin those manifestations.

Aspects of both organized and spontaneous violence in sport have been seen as a serious social problem in many settings for some time, both on and off the field of play. Fans of European sport, particularly soccer, have gained notoriety for their xenophobic rituals inside and outside stadia. Violent sports crowd disturbances have also occurred with predictable frequency in Australia, Central and South America, Asia and North America. In most of these contexts, particular behaviours have prompted solicitous responses from politicians, police, sports officials and journalists. Apart from its most familiar, and most consistently reported, dimensions (the two most studied likely being soccer hooliganism and player violence in ice hockey), scholars have been relatively slow in turning their attention to the problem. Indeed, although thousands of books and articles have been written on sport, until recently, little serious attention has been paid to the disorderly behaviour, roles and rituals of spectators (again, with the notable exception of soccer 'hooligans' from Europe, and England in particular). This is even more true of athletes themselves, whose on-field 'aggro,' located within or outside the rules, has traditionally been rationalized as 'just part of the game.' As I will argue in this book, entire clusters of related and harmful dimensions of sports violence have been either under-studied or completely *un*studied.

Violent and disorderly incidents in sport have occurred in almost all settings where sport occupies cultural significance. A surprisingly wide range of sports are involved: baseball, golf, cricket, 'Aussie Rules' football, wrestling, ice hockey, boxing, horse racing, basketball, motorcycle and car racing, lacrosse, American and Canadian football, rugby and, of course, soccer. It is equally clear that such incidents are not only of recent origin, as historical accounts attest (Guttmann 1986).

While violence in sport is not new, then, what remains obvious and germane today is a degree of public and official urgency vis-à-vis 'getting to know' and 'coming to grips with' particular dimensions of the problem. Despite some clear contradictions in the way in that *sports violence* has traditionally been approached (for instance, authorities have been keen to police crowd disorder out of existence, but the often much more injurious forms of on-field aggression have been condoned), even the most staunch supporter of, and apologist for, sport can no longer deny that the positive attributes of sports are often compromised by a darker downside. Whether it is the havoc that crowd violence causes in the lives of innocent victims and entire communities as they prepare for game-day 'disruptions,' the willingness of sports organizers and players to contribute to a culture where almost everyone seems to get hurt (sometimes catastrophically) or the cynicism of sports promoters and the sports media in using violence and injury to 'sell copy' and make profit in a violence-approving climate, there are numerous ways in which we may begin to suspect that violence, far from being incidental to sport, appears to be one of its primary dimensions, organizing principles and attractions.

As an institution, sport is notoriously slow to change. But it is not static. Consider the following scenarios (which may also be seen in other sports and other contexts) in North American ice hockey: as professional, organized amateur and recreational versions of the game become increasingly litigious and the courts come to re-define traditionally acceptable sports behaviour as 'crime' (witness long sequences of players formally charged with assault), as workers' rights continue to prompt players' associations to critically evaluate the risky conditions of their employment (as may be seen in an increasing demand for safety and better equipment), as more and more official pressure is brought to bear on leagues to adopt anti-violence and anti-injury platforms (witness recent steps taken by the National Hockey League (NHL) to reduce 'high-hits' and concussions), as alternatives to traditionally aggressive models of sport are explored and adopted (witness the non-contact ice-hockey leagues throughout Canada) and as communities become increasingly 'green' and their accounting processes more transparent (as may be seen in the growing trend towards energy and waste efficiency in hockey arenas), processes of aggression, violence and victimization related to sport are taking on new levels of seriousness and poignancy in public debate. There is a sociological synchronicity here, of course, with decreasing tolerance towards other aspects of violence more broadly in society.

All of this is not to suggest that aggression, violence and victimization in sport are 'on the way out.' Simply put, things are far more complicated than this and, as this book will show, there are many examples of how sport continues to encourage, systematically and in patterned ways, hyper-aggressivity, forms of exploitation and abuse and injury-producing and community-compromising behaviours. But there is no doubt that sports violence (and its perceived causes and outcomes) is being taken as seriously today as it has ever been, and a critical sociological study examining international aspects of the phenomenon seems both important and timely. The time also seems right for an examination of violence in sport that does not represent an isolated snapshot of any single component of sports-related aggression, violence or victimization, but is, rather, sensitive to the fact that ostensibly *un*linked and apparently disparate behaviours share sociological things in common. These 'things' are better referred to as causes, manifestations and outcomes, and essentially derive from the stratifying elements (such as gender, race, social class, age etc.) that tie all societies together, as well as relations of power in every community and sport setting. In investigating and identifying these sociological layers and links, the primary purpose of this book, then, is to reconsider how best to define, think about and make sense of *sports-related violence* (SRV).

1

A HISTORY OF VIOLENCE

Definitions, theories and perspectives

Introduction

Even when Michael Smith published his seminal early volume, *Violence and Sport*, in 1983, it was the case that violence had been studied from, as he put it, 'the spectrum of academic disciplines from anatomy to zoology' (p. 1). While we are in the fortunate position today to benefit from a far greater, and still expanding, body of research on violence, most of it conducted within the disciplines of sociology, psychology and criminology, what remains baffling is that so little of it has attempted to define and explain violence related to *sport*. Almost all of the sociological research on sports violence emanates from the subdiscipline of the sociology of sport; the parent discipline has basically ignored it.

Where sociology and criminology are concerned, the predictable fascination with, for example, murder, gangs, delinquency, domestic violence, rape, drugs, riots and serial killers endures, but almost none of this colossal sociological/criminological literature even mentions the types of violence that may be done in sport contexts, and it certainly does not take the next step to examine whether violence in different social institutions shares commonalities in cause, expression or outcome. Admittedly, that sort of comparative approach would be ambitious, and it is not the express purpose here, but it does come 'into play' at many junctures of this book. Surely, even the most elementary sociological/criminological mind would suspect that the sorts of social dimensions that underpin any of the aforementioned behaviours may occur in another dominant social institution such as sport. Yet, only a cursory glance at the sociology of violence and criminology literatures is needed to see that the terms 'sport,' or 'sports violence,' are rarely mentioned. Another way of thinking about the phrase 'rarely mentioned' is 'rarely taken seriously.' This is a sociological book that attempts to take violence in sport seriously and, in so doing, brings together a cluster of sociological literatures to encourage a fresh way of thinking about *sports-related violence* (SRV).

Defining violence

One of the immediate problems anyone wanting to study 'sports violence' faces is the constellation of terms that has been used to define the subject matter, many of which have been used interchangeably and often carelessly. Put simply, and as Cashmore (2000: 436) has candidly observed, sports violence is 'difficult to pin down.' The sociology of sport literature contains extensive reviews of the meaning of a very long list of terms, most of which, confusingly, bear relevance and which, to be fair, also appear in this book. As Coakley and Donnelly note (2009: 187), this list includes, but is not limited to, terms such as 'physical, assertive, tough, rough, competitive, intense, intimidating, risky, aggressive, destructive, and violent.' It is understandable that these signifiers appear in the violence research – indeed, it would be difficult to imagine that research without them. All of them are relevant, but none more so than 'aggression' and 'violence.'

At this stage, and before moving on to a review of theories of causes of aggression and violence, it is important to define these two salient terms. To this end, Coakley and Donnelly (2009: 187–188), who have been as succinct on the matter as anyone, define *aggression* as 'verbal or physical actions grounded in an intent to dominate, control, or do harm to another person,' while *violence* is understood by them to refer to 'the use of excessive physical force, which causes or has the potential to cause harm or destruction.' As with all such attempts, these definitions are not entirely satisfactory and inevitably contain ambiguities and contradictions. But Coakley and Donnelly are correct to suggest that aggression is normally regarded as a broader and more generic concept, while violence is typically used to refer to physical forms of aggression, and especially excessive and harmful physical forms of aggression. The adoption of these terms in this book is similarly based upon such a distinction.

Theories of violence

Disagreements and uncertainties about how the terms 'aggression' and 'violence' may be used are clearly visible in the theoretical literature. As with *definitions* of violence, researchers have attempted to *explain* violence (and related phenomena such as aggression and victimization) using a variety of theories and perspectives. Eller (2006: 31) correctly summarizes the main camps of a vast literature:

> The two most general perspectives are the 'internal' and the 'external' – that is, whether the cause or source of violence is 'inside' the violent individual (in his head or her 'mind' or personality or genes) or 'outside' the violent individual (in the social situations, values, or structures in which he or she acts). These two overarching perspectives correspond roughly to biology and psychology on the one hand and sociology and anthropology on the other . . .

While this chapter reviews both theoretical camps, and respects the broad and complex landscape of existing work and the varied academic disciplines it represents, it privileges thinking (i.e. defining and theorizing) about violence in sport *sociologically*. What follows is not an exhaustive review of *all* theories of violence but, rather, a selective review whose purpose is to showcase the perspectives that have been, and continue to be, most adopted and helpful in making sense of violence as it occurs in the world of sport (see Tables 1.1 and 1.2).

Biological and psychological approaches

Instinct theory

Following some of the classic early thinkers, such as Aristotle (Berczeller 1967), and the seventeenth-century English political-philosopher Thomas Hobbes (1957), all of whom believed that humans were violent 'by nature,' instinct theorists

TABLE 1.1 Biological and psychological approaches to aggression and violence

Approach		Three key arguments
Instinct theory	1	Humans are naturally aggressive; aggression is an innate biological drive.
	2	Humans lack a natural mechanism for inhibiting aggression.
	3	It is possible to extrapolate from physical appearance to a propensity to aggress.
Frustration–aggression hypothesis	1	Aggression is a consequence of frustration.
	2	The likelihood and level of aggression are related to the type and level of frustration.
	3	Once the source of aggression is countered, frustration, and thus aggression, subsides.
Hostile and instrumental aggression	1	Humans use aggression to achieve specific goals.
	2	Hostile aggression (or 'angry' aggression) is used intentionally to inflict harm or damage.
	3	Instrumental aggression is used strategically to achieve a goal other than harming the individual or target.
Catharsis	1	In routine, everyday life, humans accumulate frustrations.
	2	Societies contain channels through which frustrations may be purged responsibly.
	3	In the absence of a socially tolerated 'safety valve', aggression may worsen and manifest itself more dangerously.
Reversal theory	1	Human behaviour is comprised of four motivational states or conditions: telic-paratelic, conformity-negativism, mastery-sympathy and autic-alloic.
	2	Frustration and satiation determine whether the response will be aggressive or passive.
	3	The four 'meta-motivational' states can occur simultaneously and be 'switched' from one to another depending on arousal.

TABLE 1.2 Sociological approaches to aggression and violence

Approach	*Three key arguments*	
Social learning theory	1	Aggression derives not from biological cues, but from observing, and modelling, the behaviour of others.
	2	Through observation, humans learn how aggression may be used to perform roles, to construct and confirm identity, and to promote rewards.
	3	Aggression does not serve 'safety valve', or cathartic, functions for society.
Techniques of neutralization	1	Sociological theory must explain not only the structural causes of crime and violence, but also show how these causes are translated into action by individuals.
	2	Learning how to justify social behaviour is as important as learning how to do it.
	3	Offenders may deny responsibility, injury or victimization, condemn the condemners, or appeal to higher loyalties.
Subculture of violence	1	Societies contain sub-groups (subcultures) governed by their own unique rules, norms and values.
	2	Pro-violent subcultures may develop in the general society or in specific workplaces.
	3	Subcultural rules, norms and values are restricted to, and contained within, the subcultural setting.
Figurational ('process') sociology	1	Social action is the outcome of complex webs of power-imbued interdependency chains between individuals and groups.
	2	Since societies generally pacify over time, some forms of aggression may be understood in terms of the 'quest for excitement in relatively unexciting societies.'
	3	Sport represents a socially acceptable forum for the 'controlled de-controlling' of emotions.
Victimology	1	Victimization is not only caused by individual actors, but also by institutions, including workplaces and governments.
	2	Society shows a high tolerance for victimization when it occurs in autonomous social institutions, such as the home, work or sport.
	3	Professional athletes should be considered as 'workers' and provided the sorts of legal protections and benefits other workplaces offer.
Sports ethic	1	Athletes and those assessing athletes (e.g. coaches, administrators, sponsors and fans) both respect and reward task-commitment in sport.
	2	Identity and status are related to making sacrifices, striving for distinction, accepting risks and refusing to accept limits in the pursuit of winning.
	3	Over-conformity to the sports ethic stems from a widespread sense of anxiety and self-doubt among athletes.

argue that, since our 'pre-human' ancestors were 'naturally' aggressive, modern day humans share the same trait and lack, in Goldstein's terms, 'a well-developed mechanism for the inhibition of aggression' (1986: 5). The theory was brought to life in the twentieth century by scholars interested in tracing the biological genesis of social behaviour, such as ethologists Konrad Lorenz (1966) and Desmond Morris (1967), but it has its embryonic criminological roots in Lombrosian logic that, among other things, extrapolates from physical features, such as facial characteristics (physiognomy), skull shape (phrenology) and body type (somatology) to criminal propensity (Deutschmann 2007).

In addition to representing a clearly reductionist view of society, and viewing humans as little more than a hodgepodge of genomes waiting to be provoked, instinct theory is also unable to address the different ways in which, and the relative degrees to which, violence is acted out, such as the myriad forms that violence assumes both within the rules of sport (e.g. body checking in ice hockey) and outside the rules of sport (e.g. fist-fighting in ice hockey), and the fact that aggressive behaviour varies enormously by individual (e.g. exposed to the same cues, not all ice-hockey players aggress, retaliate or fight).

The frustration–aggression hypothesis (FAH)

Central to the frustration–aggression hypothesis (FAH) is the definition of frustration as 'interference with the occurrence of an instigated goal-response at its proper time in the behaviour sequence' (Berkowitz 1978: 692). Popularized by a group of researchers at Yale University in the 1930s (Dollard et al. 1939), the FAH was broken down into three simple arguments: (1) aggression is always a result of frustration; (2) frustration always leads to aggression; and, (3) there is an inclination towards aggression when the aggressive act is disallowed, but this decreases once an object or person (i.e. the source of frustration) is confronted (Berkowitz 1978: 692). The FAH was later modified slightly to acknowledge that aggression is not *always* the response to frustration and that frustration may lead to 'a number of different responses, [only] one of which is an instigation to some form of aggression' (Miller 1941: 338). The approach was used to explain aspects of sports crowd disorder in the 1970s (Russell and Drewry 1976) and, more recently, soccer hooliganism in Scandinavia (Pirks 2010).

The FAH perspective is minimally useful in underlining the relationship between frustration and aggression, but sport is filled with episodes where frustration does not lead to aggression, and where aggression takes place, either inside or outside the rules of the game, where there is little frustration or none at all. Stated simply, frustration does not always cause or provoke aggression and, again, can be mitigated by any number of game-specific factors (i.e. instructions from coaches, time of occurrence etc.), as well as wider sociological factors (i.e. education, gender, role etc.), including 'choice' (i.e. choosing not to aggress).

The hostile and instrumental aggression approach

Predicated upon the view that aggression is a behaviour that attempts to achieve a specific goal, the hostile and instrumental aggression approach is based on a 'dichot-omous outcome' understanding of why aggression occurs. In the first case, instru-mental aggression does not pursue the goal of personal hurt or injury (although personal hurt or injury may result); rather, it aims to achieve an external, or related, goal (Berkowitz 1993: 11). For instance, a police officer who shoots a suspect may intend to prevent him from fleeing or protect innocent bystanders rather than seek masochistic satisfaction from the act itself. In the same way, in sport, a baseball pitcher may throw a 'brush-off' pitch not to injure the batsman but to decrease his/her confidence 'at the plate.' Thus, instrumental aggression is rational and planned, and obtaining the desired goal reinforces the legitimacy of the act (Berkowitz 1993: 11). Conversely, the goal of hostile aggression is to inflict damage (to an object or person) for the express purpose of harming it/them. Also known as 'emotional,' 'angry' or 'reactive' aggression, and sharing obvious overlaps with FAH, it is assumed that this type of action is taken without much planning (Berkowitz 1993: 11). In sport, spontaneously 'cleating' (or raking, i.e. the deliberate scraping of boot cleats [studs] against skin to cause pain or injury) an opponent in soccer, throwing a 'scrum punch' in rugby or elbowing an opponent under the net in basketball are examples of actions intended to make targets suffer by inflicting pain.

Although it is sometimes given lip-service in the sociology of sport research, and has obvious potential for application to any number of aggressive acts and strate-gies within sport, the hostile and instrumental aggression approach may, again, be found largely in psychological accounts of sport behaviour (e.g. Mintah et al. 1999). But here, too, it has generally been rejected for being overly simplistic (Bush-man and Anderson 2001). Most critics point out that the logic of the hostile–instrumental dichotomy could be completely reversed, with instrumental aggression involving anger and hostile aggression being executed coldly and in a pre-determined way.

Catharsis theory

Again, the role of frustration features centrally here. Proponents of 'catharsis' believe that humans accumulate frustrations in daily life that can potentially lead to aggressive behaviour, but that can also be discharged ('purged' or 'vented') by participating in tension-relieving activities, or through observing others participate in such activities. In one of the earliest renditions of sport as a social 'safety valve,' Brill (1929: 434) celebrated the 'rewards' of sport spectating for men: 'He will purge himself of impulses which, too dammed up, would lead to private broils and public disorder. He would achieve exaltation, vicarious but real. He will be a better individual, a better citizen, a better husband and father.' This view remained popu-lar throughout much of the twentieth century, as Beisser (1967: 183) indicated in the 1960s:

There can be little doubt about the advantages of confining violence to the athletic field if it frees man to act in humane manner at other times. Certainly, to compete in a symbolic way in sports and thus to avoid wanton killing is consistent with the highest goals of civilization.

Perhaps best known for their adoption of the catharsis perspective was the 1970s research of Peter Marsh and his colleagues (1978) in the UK who argued that soccer hooliganism on the part of young English men could best be understood as a constructive, and relatively harmless, way of ritually reducing aggressive drives that might otherwise be manifested more dangerously outside the sport milieu (see Chapter 3). Thus, shooting a deer, watching a boxer pummel his or her opponent or yelling abuse at officials thus became construed as a socially useful and acceptable means of releasing naturally pent-up hostilities. (Certain recreational activities, such as 'war games,' 'paint ball' and video games have frequently been rationalized using similar 'catharsis' logic.)

An almost unanimous lack of empirical support for the 'safety valve' position has led, over time, to a widespread rejection of catharsis theory. As one of its main advocates noted in the 1970s: 'Nowadays, I have strong doubts whether watching aggressive behaviour even in the guise of sport has any cathartic benefits at all' (Lorenz, cited in Evans 1974: 93). Around the same time, a sizeable cluster of violence studies actually began to show that participating in sport, either directly as a participant or indirectly as a fan, was far more likely to *enhance* rather than *reduce* aggressive drives and to have a '*dis*-inhibition' effect (e.g. Goldstein and Arms 1971; Sipes 1973; Atyeo 1979; Arms et al. 1979a).

Despite the fact that the catharsis view has been refuted in far more academic studies than it has been validated, the alleged benefits of catharsis continue to be propounded by 'applied' professionals (e.g. physical educators, kinesiologists and coaches) and remain widely accepted in lay circles, including recreational athletes, many of whom remain convinced that, for instance, thrashing a ball around a squash court for 40 minutes leaves them feeling less aggressive. The bulk of the existing scientific research rejects this popular belief, instead arguing that the aggressive act (such as a hard fought game of squash) serves to put time between the individual and the source of frustration rather than eliminating that source altogether.

Reversal theory

By far the most contemporary of the psychological approaches to explaining violence (Apter 1989; Kerr and de Kock 2002; Kerr 2004; Shepherd et al. 2006), reversal theory explains why athletes and/or spectators may conform to rule expectations in one context, but 'revert' to aggression and violence in others. Perhaps the most recognized advocate of this approach in sport studies, Kerr outlines a number of bi-polar 'meta-motivational states' that determine passive or aggressive behaviour in sports settings and that can be 'switched' in response to factors such as frustration or satiation. Using language not always warmly received by sociologists (e.g. Dunning and his colleagues (2002a: 15) dismiss it as 'psychological jargon'), Kerr identifies his four meta-motivational states as 'telic-paratelic,' 'conformity-negativism,' 'mastery-sympathy' and 'autic-alloic.'

Kerr (2004) explains violence in sport by arguing that aggressors spend more time in a certain combination of meta-motivational states than in any other combination; namely, they spend more time in paratelic (risk-taking), negativism (norm-violating), mastery (dominance) and autic (self-concerned) states. The crucial point for Kerr is how such states are cognitively and physiologically experienced when combined with arousal and what he calls the 'hedonic tone.' To be relaxed is to be in the telic state with low arousal and a high hedonic tone. For Kerr, the combination of meta-motivational states and the feelings they create explains the trigger behind aggressive or violent acts in sport. Indeed, he explains soccer hooliganism and nuances of the coach–athlete relationship in this way.

Unsurprisingly, sociologists are sceptical of the 'reversal' approach. Among other limitations, it would be very difficult to empirically assess the 'mental state' of a fan or an athlete (as, according to the theory, these change quickly – Shepherd et al. 2006: 153). The 'dichotomous parallel states' position it advocates raises questions regarding the mutual exclusivity of each state and, moreover, how much one must experience one feeling or another before 'transitioning.' It also fails to take into account the rational choices an actor might make predicated upon notions of 'cost–reward.' For example, a fan may have (inward) feelings of aggression towards a rival fan, but may (outwardly) not manifest these feelings for any number of reasons. Finally, while the theory carries potential for explaining certain aggressive player-to-player exchanges, it hardly begins to tackle the structural issues of, for instance, sexism, racism or homophobia, which may also motivate aggression and violence in sport.

Sociological approaches

Social learning theory

Albert Bandura's (1973, 1977) popular and widely used social learning theory (SLT) rejects the centrality of biological drives in behaving aggressively and emphasizes how punishment and reward play an important role in the modelling of behaviour. Bandura argues that aggression and violence, like any other behaviours, are learned through observation and imitation, and depend upon the degree to which one 'emulates the behaviour of a role model' (Sellers et al. 2005: 381). While accepting the Skinnerian view that we learn through direct reinforcement of our responses to stimuli, Bandura adds that we also learn to aggress by observing the consequences of other people's actions. His theory, not entirely dissimilar to Sutherland's (1947) theory of differential association, suggests that people imitate aggressors who are similar to themselves, who are rewarded for their actions and who hold cultural prestige. For Bandura, aggressors use violent behaviour if it is perceived to lead to a positive self-evaluative reaction. Simply put, if aggression is defined as pleasurable, meaningful or rewarding, it will continue. Scholars of violence in Canadian ice hockey (e.g. Robidoux 2001) have contended that fist-fighting and forms of vicious body checking are learned in the social psychological manner Bandura outlined. Elsewhere, Kreager (2007) uses SLT to explain how violence in American school sports interfaces with forms of gender-learning, and Muir and Seitz (2004) use it to show how misogynistic rituals are learned and reproduced in collegiate rugby.

While human behaviour is clearly the outcome of imitation and complex forms of social learning at the hands of influential role models, critics of SLT have indicated that this approach underestimates people's choice-making abilities and that, in popular terms, 'watching is not the same thing as doing.' In other words, not all people who are raised around smokers smoke and not all athletes who are encouraged to hit by coaches and peers hit. In this way, social roles and statuses can be rejected and 'cycles of violence,' including those that occur in sport, can be modified or broken. Put simply, learning is a fundamental part of the social process, but it can be 'undone.'

The techniques of neutralization approach

Growing directly out of the famed 'Chicago School' of the early part of the twentieth century, the techniques of neutralization (TN) approach (Sykes and Matza 1957, 1989) focuses less on the social causes of behaviour and more on the ways in which structural conditions are translated into action by individuals, thus allowing them to perform certain tasks. As with all interactionist approaches, the TN approach focuses on micro-level relations, especially between the actor and those who require justifications for the act (such as the authorities). In this way, and building on C. Wright Mills' earlier notion of 'vocabularies of motive' (1940), Sykes and Matza (1957) offer a way of explaining behaviours such as delinquency, crime or violence by participating in five possible strategies (or 'techniques') of 'neutralizing' harm inflicted by the behaviour – denying responsibility, injury or victimization, 'condemning the condemners' and 'appealing to higher loyalties.' The TN approach has been most widely used in the deviancy and criminological research, in particular to explain the behaviour of young offenders, but it has also found a home in the research on deviance and violence in sport. For instance, with colleagues, I have found this approach helpful in explaining justificatory strategies used by injured athletes that allow them to accept pain and return to play (Young et al. 1994) and by persons involved in abusive practices in animal sports (Atkinson and Young 2005a).

Critics of the TN approach have correctly observed that this is far more a modest framework for making sense of certain episodes of, for instance, delinquent, deviant or violent behaviour than a fully-fledged 'theory' per se. However, as the classic differential association theorists (e.g. Sutherland 1947, 1973) indicated, doing crime and deviance is as much about the *sense-making* of the act (i.e. the motivations and rationalizations that allow it to take place), as it is about the techniques of *doing* the act itself (i.e. the performance of the act). Since athletes and other individuals behaving deviantly, aggressively or violently in the context of sport constantly rationalize their actions (both to themselves and to others), the TN approach contains real potential for explaining aspects of sports behaviour.

Violent subcultures

Also directly influenced by the Chicago School, and not entirely distinct from the TN approach (techniques of neutralization are frequently used by members of subcultural groups to justify pro-violence norms), the violent subcultures approach has been used to explain high rates of violence in certain socially definable groups, such as youth gangs or collectivities. As Smith (1983) noted, this two-pronged body of research tends to be splintered into assessments of a 'violent societal subculture hypothesis' (e.g. early US ethnographic work showed how youth gangs operationalize situation-specific behaviours, such as physical intimidation and fighting, that do not pervade all aspects of participants' lives – Wolfgang and Ferracuti 1967), and a 'violent occupational subculture hypothesis' (e.g. persons occupying work-settings develop unique value systems that guide their behaviours while in that setting). While both approaches have been used in the sociology of sport, and while the research on sport subcultures is now sizeable (Atkinson and Young 2008), it is the latter approach that has been most relevant for sports violence research thus far. In particular, a vibrant literature examining the pro-violence occupational culture of North American ice hockey now spans almost 40 years (e.g. from Faulkner (1973, 1974) and Vaz (1982) to Robidoux (2001) and Atkinson and Young (2008)). The subcultural research has been criticized for suggesting that the behaviours and values that characterize recreational- or work-settings are 'contained' only in those settings. As Chapter 4 and other chapters will show, it is quite clear that pro-aggression and pro-violence attitudes cultivated and revered in the world of sport neither develop solely from within those settings nor are restricted to them in their manifestation.

Figurational ('process') sociology

Based centrally upon the work of Norbert Elias (1994), figurational, or 'process' sociology, sets out to explain the 'complex chain of interdependencies and power relationships' that exist in, and across, human communities (Layder 1986: 370). At the core of this approach is a rejection of the traditionally dichotomous approach to understanding individuals and society existing independently of one another. Instead, figurationalists attempt to bridge the micro–macro divide and view human behaviour as sets of actions in broad interconnected webs of relationships between actors (Layder 1986: 374; Mouzelis 1993: 249) that are underpinned by power differentials between the actors (Layder 1986: 370).

A central theme in Elias's (1994, 1996) research on long-term civilizing processes is that Western societies have become relatively 'unexciting' social environments.

With the general pacification of cultures over time, a collective need to devise and institutionalize cultural activities that strike a balance between personal pleasure and restraint occurs. As outward displays of emotion become less socially acceptable (Elias 1994), individuals pursue a range of activities that elicit exciting significance in highly controlled contexts of interaction.

Where sport is concerned, Elias and Dunning (1986) and Dunning (1999) have examined the relationship between violence and aggression in arousing 'exciting significance' for spectators. They argue that sports involving a moderate degree of violence (even rule-violating forms) are generally tolerable and allow individuals to participate (either as competitors or spectators) in practices that are taboo in other social spheres. In the language of figurational sociology, sports contests represent interactive scenarios that legitimate a 'controlled decontrolling' of emotions (Elias and Dunning 1986). Sport is described as 'mimetic' because it resembles war-like competition – it is socially and emotionally significant to individuals because it promotes excitement through controlled violence in a contest that is not as harmful as actual war (Goodger and Goodger 1989; Sheard 1999). Using this approach, Atkinson (2002) examines spectator enjoyment of relatively 'safe' violence in North American professional wrestling.

For years popular only in Europe, figurational sociology is now widely adopted by sociologists across the globe, but it is not without shortcomings (Layder 1986). For instance, critics argue that, for a theory that advocates a dynamic interaction between psychological and sociological determinants of behaviour, empirical work validating the 'psycho-genesis' argument is far less available than (the more plentiful) 'socio-genesis' research, and that elements of figurational sociology (such as its notions of 'established/outsider' relations) may represent a reorganization of familiar ideas found in existing theories. But this theory offers rich potential for explaining sport, and violent behaviour in sport, as will be evident from its re-appearance in several of the chapters that follow.

Victimology

An obvious departure from existing thinking about violence in sport, victimology was introduced by criminologists concerned that, in the offender–victim dyad, the experiences of the victim were being overlooked (Karmen 2004: 8). Thus, victimological perspectives began to focus on those who are harmed in situations of conflict or violence (Elias 1986: 3–4). Originally applied to offences such as rape and street crimes such as mugging, it is also possible to conceive of aspects of the offender–victim relationship in sport. In this connection, victimology may be understood as an approach rooted in the idea that people who participate in potentially dangerous institutional settings, such as sport, hold inherent rights to freedom, safety and personal welfare (Young 1993; Young and Reasons 1989). Moreover, athletes who are paid to participate in sport and are members of complex economic organizations should be viewed as 'workers' and deserve formal and legal protections for the risks they endure. Early victimological research in the sociology of sport displayed Marxist and cultural studies leanings, addressing the multiple ways athletes, or other sports participants, are systematically 'victimized' (e.g. physically, socially, economically, psychologically) by exploitative and corporate sports structures.

In brief, victimologists shift attention from the causes of violence per se to the sources of suffering and its treatment in social institutions. Victimological studies of sports violence (e.g. Young 1993; Young and Reasons 1989) challenge labour officials and courts to view the exploitation of athletes as a type of business or 'white collar' crime. Practices such as pressuring athletes to play while injured, or informally threatening their job security if they refuse to play in pain, should be considered exploitative and a violation of athletes' basic rights to personal safety.

The victimological approach is not heavily, or explicitly, utilized in the sociology of sport, but psychologists and sociologists of sport do study groups of abused athletes from quasi-victimological perspectives. For example, studies of the sexual victimization of athletes by coaches have been conducted using feminist approaches (e.g. Brackenridge 1996, 2001) and, describing how he dropped out of professional soccer due to 'overt and covert institutionalized racism' (Moran 2000: 190), Moran examines racism in English sport from a 'victim's perspective.' David (2005: 12) refers to the sexual and physical abuse of children in sport as a theoretical 'black hole.' He argues that the abuse of children in local and global sports cultures has been ignored and that sports personnel in highly competitive athletic circles rarely question whether things like intensive training, ideological indoctrination into winning-at-all-costs, isolation from non-athletes, emotional manipulation, dietary control, sexualization and corporal punishment for performance failure are reasonable, or victimizing, elements of the sports process.

The sports ethic perspective

Rooted in the symbolic interactionist tradition (e.g. Goffman 1974), Hughes and Coakley (1991) describe how athletes in competitive amateur and professional sports learn 'interpretive frames' and use these frames to gauge commitment to the group and sport. They describe how athletes are taught to strive for distinction, accept no limits as players, make sacrifices for their sports and play through pain and injury as part of an overarching 'sport ethic.' While not all athletes in sport are socialized quite so completely or assess all social interactions and athletic performances in relation to this ethic, this maxim is so pervasive that most athletes encounter it, and must reconcile themselves to it, at some point in their sport careers.

Hughes and Coakley (1991) suggest that the bulk of athlete behaviour during competition or training, or in social settings outside of sport, is in accordance with with the requisites of the sport ethic. They illustrate athlete behaviour on a statistical 'normal curve,' locating everyday athlete behaviour at the heart of the curve and behaviour that deviates from the sport ethic at either tail of the curve. On the one tail, they place a category of behaviours they called 'positive' deviance. These are athlete behaviours that pursue the principles of the sport ethic to an unhealthy extent. An example of positive deviance is dangerous weight loss (for instance, through dehydration strategies) in order to make a weight category in boxing or wrestling, or in order to please judges in so-called 'appearance' sports such as gymnastics or figure skating. On the other tail, Hughes and Coakley describe 'negative' deviance. Negative deviance involves athlete behaviours that reject the importance of the sport ethic. Disobeying a coach's instruction to attend every practice session, or to work hard in training, are examples of negative deviance.

Similar to the subculture perspective described above, the main conceptual contribution of Hughes and Coakley's (1991) typology is the idea that sports insiders decipher rule violation using group-specific codes and categories. In sport settings, deviance is defined and controlled by *situated* actors who understand the unique principles of their own sport ethic. The sport ethic 'tool' thus allows us to understand how decisions about positive and negative deviance are negotiated and how athletes are taught to rationalize rule-breaking, or excessive, behaviour as a normal and acceptable part of sports culture through a set of 'neutralizing techniques' (Sykes and Matza 1957) in specific settings. However, Hughes and Coakley's typology seems far better suited to explain the behaviours and values of high-performance athletes and less suited to explain those at the recreational or junior levels. Moreover, its ability to explain violent acts by non-athletes that occur in the context of sport (such as coaching abuse – see Chapter 4), or player violence that occurs away from the game (such as partner abuse – see Chapter 4), is unclear.

A fresh perspective on violence in sport: introducing SRV

Clearly, theories of violence that may be used to explain problem behaviour in sport are numerous and diverse and represent several academic disciplines. The preceding review is neither exhaustive nor covers all of the explanatory perspectives that are used in this book to make sense of the subject matter. Other approaches appear at relevant junctures, such as theories of crowd violence (see Chapter 3), theories of risk (see Chapter 5), theories of media treatment (see Chapter 7) and theories of gender (see Chapter 8). The empirical research on violence in sport is also impressive in volume, but sociologists of sport have usually limited their enquiries, as suggested by the layout of this book, to two principal dimensions of the subject matter – violence among athletes, or player violence, and violence among fans, or crowd violence. Most monographs and textbooks reflect this convention, especially with respect to crowd violence interpreted as an example of collective behaviour (e.g. Smith 1983; McPherson et al. 1989; Snyder and Spreitzer 1989; Leonard 1998; Wann et al. 2001).

However, if, using an amalgam of existing definitions of violence reviewed above, the customary parameters of 'sports violence' are broadened to include aggressive, threatening, harmful or otherwise unjust practices enacted within the context of sport, it becomes evident that the subject matter may be far more expansive and varied than commonly assumed. For example, other forms of SRV might include players being harassed, stalked or attacked away from the game, athletes involved in felonious 'street crimes', neophyte players being coerced by veteran team-mates into abusive initiation ('hazing') rituals against their will, animals being treated in a cruel and inhumane way, exploitative labour practices in the production of sport merchandise and forms of environmental damage in the preparation and hosting of large-scale venues and sport events. Cases such as these are not normally thought of as 'sports violence,' but they represent concretely or potentially harmful acts that cannot be separated from the sports process and that only begin to make sense when the socially embedded character of sport is closely scrutinized. Crucially, none of them suggest that aggression and violence occur 'naturally,' as the psychological theories reviewed above argue. Rather, all of them suggest that these practices are caused and manifested *socially*.

This book makes the case that it is sociologically useful, indeed sociologically *necessary*, to approach the full range of the subject matter as SRV rather than 'sports violence' per se. It aims to move beyond the de-contextualizing inclination of existing research – that tends to view types of sports violence as separate episodes of social action, unrelated to other types or to broader social structures and processes – and highlights the links and associations that underpin many, if not all, forms of SRV.

In moving towards an expansive definition of SRV, and in addition to definitions and theories woven through the existing body of research on violence in sport, this book is influenced by two existing definitions of aggression and violence. The first comes from a likely source. One of the most recognized, cited and respected sociologists of sport, Jay Coakley (1998: 199), defines aggression in the following way:

> Aggression originates in some combination of (1) frustration coupled with anger, opportunities, stimulus cues, and social support; (2) strategies used by athletes and encouraged by peers, parents, coaches, spectators, and sponsors; and (3) definitions of masculinity emphasizing violence as a basis for becoming a man and superior to a woman.

This definition is careful and thorough, and is sufficient on its own to sustain ongoing empirical and theoretical work. But, in addition to overlooking the many and complex ways that females also contribute to aggression and violence in sport (see Chapters 4 and 8), it lacks the victimological, social justice and community health trajectory that, coming from a more criminological perspective, I prefer. In this respect, a second definitional influence is 'less likely,' but impacting. The World Health Organization defines violence as:

> [T]he intentional use of physical force or power, threatened or actual, against oneself, another person, or against a group or community, that either results in or has a high likelihood of resulting in injury, death, psychological harm, maldevelopment, or deprivation.[1]

Here, then, the focus shifts from how the process of aggression takes place to the damage and harm it causes for individuals and communities, as well as to questions of social justice.

For the purposes of this book, and sensitive to the concerns implicit in both of these definitions, SRV, which encompasses notions of both aggression and violence, is defined in a twofold fashion:

1   direct acts of physical violence contained within or outside the rules of the game that result in injury to persons, animals or property; and
2   harmful or potentially harmful acts conducted in the context of sport that threaten or produce injury or that violate human justices and civil liberties.

Following this definition, the varied manifestations of SRV may be collated into a 'matrix of cells,' with each cell representing one specific *formation* of the phenomenon (see Chapter 4). As you will see, formations of SRV have included not only episodes of collective disorder by sports crowds and the aggressive practices of athletes who incur pain and impose injury on others on the field of play, but also a far broader landscape of harmful, or abusive, behaviours. However, the fact that the bulk of the existing research has so far focused on the first two cells is reflected in the relative weight of the discussions in this book (see Chapters 2 and 3). Shorter summaries of the remaining 16 cells are designed to provide the reader with a sense of the aforementioned 'broader landscape' of SRV and the research that has been committed to this broader landscape to date.

The shape of things to come

Having introduced some of the principal definitional, conceptual and explanatory tools and approaches that underpin violence and sports violence research, the remainder of this book is comprised of seven chapters and a Conclusion. Each chapter represents a component part of the violence-in-sport process. There are doubtless other components that could be explored, but are not. Rather than offering, or claiming, an exhaustive review of the subject matter, the book charts a path through some of the main issues and themes that strike me as most relevant in studying, and teaching about, violence in sport.

Chapters 2 and 3 deal separately with the two most studied aspects of sports violence to date – violence among participants, or player violence, and violence among fans, or crowd violence. These chapters initially describe the multiple and varied cultures of aggression that are acted out on and off the field of play and then critically survey existing approaches to explaining those cultures. Chapter 2 adopts a socio-legal approach and considers what appears to be an increasing presence by the authorities in policing player violence, while Chapter 3 summarizes what we know so far about transatlantic crowd violence. While these chapters seek to be as broad and international as possible in scope, the fact of the matter is that the bulk of the research pertains to North America and Europe. This trend is reflected in the content of Chapters 2 and 3.

Because it projects individual episodes of aggression and violence in sport onto a larger sociological canvas, Chapter 4 is the axial chapter of the book. If anything is distinctive about this book, it is this chapter. The goal of this chapter is twofold: (1) to demonstrate that sports violence is far more diverse and encompassing than scholars have typically acknowledged to date; and (2) to introduce and explain new ways of conceptual thinking about the full landscape of behaviours that is now seen as SRV. The sociological imperative here is to acknowledge the limitations of conventional approaches to studying sports violence that typically conceive of individual manifestations of the phenomena in terms of isolated empirical moments and settings without considering the links and associations they share.

Chapter 5 focuses on behaviours and values that, until relatively recently, had little presence in the sociological study of sport but were subsumed under the general rubric of 'sports violence.' Despite coming to this area later than other disciplines, things have changed, and now the sociological study of risk, pain and injury represents one of the most burgeoning research areas in the sociology of sport. This chapter explores what the research has taught us about risk, pain and injury, and how this alliance interfaces with sports violence.

Historically, sports violence, both on and off the field of play, has operated as a relatively autonomous process, poorly hidden by a social institution that clearly protects it but largely unpoliced from the outside. Almost everywhere, sport has been given the authority, as the saying goes, to 'keep its own house in order.' In so many obvious ways, it has done a bad job, and evidence of how abusive and violent practices grow out of, and are protected by, the sports industry is not hard to find. Again, things have changed, and while still often considered the last bastion of legitimate violence, there is abundant evidence to suggest that the contemporary world of sport is more controlled, accountable and intervened on than it has ever been. 'Big Brother' is definitely watching, at multiple levels, from varied vantage points, and assuming diverse guises, and sport's most stoic protectionists are engaged in an uphill battle to ensure that sport does not become fully 'panopticonic' (Foucault 1977). Chapter 6 reviews the ways in which sport has become a matter of surveillance, regulation, discipline and control, and introduces some of the multi-level bureaucracies that are now involved.

Any serious examination of sports violence must consider the role played by the mass media. Using Canadian data on media treatment of the subject matter, including an in-depth assessment of how media personnel rationalize the choices they make and the representations they privilege, Chapter 7 makes the case that the media's involvement in sports violence is far more active than passive and, overall, contributes to a climate of violence-approval.

While Chapter 8 ostensibly examines the central role played by gender in the sports violence process, it is actually a chapter that engages with the sociological obligation towards understanding the broader social stratification of behaviour. In this respect, while the gender implications for sports violence feature centrally in this chapter, there is also a consideration of how SRV is 'ordered' by other stratifying factors such as race, religion, social class and age. Needless to say, sociologists do not conceive of forms of social stratification as working independently of one another; rather, they interface and share interacting effects. How this may be true of SRV is considered.

Finally, the book comes 'full-circle' and draws together some of the major themes and issues covered in the preceding eight chapters. The Conclusion reviews the current status of sports violence research, summarizes the disparities in a field characterized by, on the one hand, an excess of information in some respects and, on the other, relative absences, and sometimes even gaping holes, in our knowledge, and considers what future work might involve. This final section acknowledges the not-insignificant methodological point that SRV research is not always easy to conduct, and that, in so many disturbing respects, tackling sports violence (and especially tackling its protectors and apologists) head-on remains a matter of stepping into the den of the dinosaur and challenging robust and revered values in sport. On this point, observations on how studying sports violence comes with certain 'occupational dangers' are made. But we live in a changing political climate where transparency, ethics and safety are concerned. As such, the book concludes with some reasons to feel positive and optimistic about the future of SRV.

2

PLAYER VIOLENCE

The drift to criminalization

Introduction

Player violence, involving behaviours encompassed both within, as well as outside, the rules of sport, has traditionally been condoned in many settings as 'part of the game,' and rationalized as ritualistic or harmless. This may be witnessed in the way in which aggressive, high-risk or injurious practices that would be socially or legally intolerable away from sport are encouraged, and even expected, to occur in sport. In many countries, sport is immersed in fervent cultures of aggression, hubris and risk, which compromise participant safety and, ultimately, limit the possibility of safe sport. These cultures may have influenced research on sport, since sociologists have paid far less attention to player violence than to crowd violence.

Most sociologists agree that while there is no single cause of player violence, understanding the phenomenon requires examining socialization processes associated with many sports and, indeed, with the institution of sport in general, where athletes learn from an early age that behaviours such as hitting and being hit, and conceiving of violence as a vehicle to resolve conflicts, are acceptable and protected 'strategies' (Coakley and Donnelly 2009). Combined with a strongly gendered component (Messner 1990; Robinson 1998; Burstyn 1999), and an emphasis in commercialized sports on heroic values, physical dominance and winning-at-all-costs, thinking and behaving aggressively is simply part of the learning that individuals and groups undertake in sport. Player violence is one outgrowth of this learning.

Like Smith (1983), adopting a socio-legal approach to the subject matter, this chapter begins by introducing a framework that can help us understand the various strands of player aggression and violence, and goes on to explore the expanding presence of the courts in legally assessing player behaviour. It reviews recent 'sports crimes' and explains the currently contradictory position in many contexts (especially Canada) for 'offenders' where, on the one hand, they are more at risk of being litigated than ever before but, on the other hand, evidence of 'preferential treatment' prevails. The chapter concludes by explaining how sociological theory can help us understand aspects of player violence and the responses by the courts.

A framework for understanding player violence

Several typologies of player violence exist, but none more popular, or useful, than the approach developed by Smith (1983), who classified player violence into four basic categories: the first two being 'relatively legitimate' and the last two 'relatively illegitimate' in the eyes of both sports administrators and the law. While the typology has been summarized many times in the literature, it remains pertinent to sport violence research, and to the legal implications of player violence, and is worth briefly revisiting here:

- *Brutal body contact* includes what Smith called the 'meat and potatoes' of our most popular sports, such as tackles, blocks, body checks, collisions, hits and jabs. Depending on the sport under scrutiny, these are all acts that can be found within the official rules of a given sport, and to which most would agree that consent is given or, at the very least, implied.
- *Borderline violence* involves acts prohibited by the official rules of a given sport but that occur routinely, and are more or less accepted by many people connected with the game. Examples might include: the fist-fight in ice hockey; the late hit and personal foul in US and Canadian football; the 'wandering' elbow in basketball, soccer and road racing; the high tackle, 'rake' and scrum punch in rugby; and, the 'beanball' (a pitch aimed deliberately at a batsman's head) in baseball. Importantly, all of these actions carry potential for causing injury as well as prompting further conflict between players, such as the bench-clearing brawl in ice hockey, players charging the mound in baseball or retaliatory fighting in any of these other sports. Historically speaking, sanctions imposed by sports leagues and administrators for borderline violence have been notoriously light, and the clubs themselves have done all they can to protect their players, especially their 'star' players.
- *Quasi-criminal violence* violates the formal rules of a given sport, the law and, to a significant degree, the informal norms of players. This type of violence usually results in serious injury, which, in turn, precipitates considerable official and public attention. Quasi-criminal violence in ice hockey may include 'cheap shots,' 'sucker punches' or dangerous high-stick work, all of which can cause severe injury, and which often elicit in-house suspensions and fines.
- *Criminal violence* includes behaviours so seriously and obviously outside of the boundaries of acceptability of both the sport and the wider community that they are treated formally by the criminal justice system from the outset. The Canadian case used by Smith is that of a Toronto teenage hockey player who, in 1973, assaulted and killed an opponent in the arena parking lot following a heated community game.

Smith's typology addresses what criminologists (e.g. Ball-Rokeach 1971, 1980) would call the question of the 'legitimacy of violence'; that is, the legitimation/de-legitimation process with regard to what is perceived as acceptable violence and what is not. In this way, the typology is illuminating, but it has one obvious limitation – keeping up with the times. As we will see below, since the late 1960s and the early 1970s there has been a shift in what may be categorized as 'legitimate' and 'illegitimate' player violence, no doubt prompted by shifting scales of public and legal tolerance when it comes to forms of interpersonal violence in general.[1] Using Smith's categories, incidents previously considered as *quasi-criminal violence, borderline violence* or even *brutal body contact* are being more closely scrutinized in some quarters today and, where litigated, may be dealt with under criminal rather than civil law. In this respect, there has been some collapsing of Smith's categories, and the typology requires updating to fit a dynamic socio-legal climate.

It thus becomes possible to conceive of aggression and violence among athletes, including at times, and confusingly, behaviour prized and protected within the subculture of the sport, as sports 'crime.' In-depth assessments of how player violence and sports injury cases are adjudicated by the courts, and the sorts of legal defences available to prosecuted athletes, have been advanced in a number of countries (e.g. USA – Horrow 1980; UK – Gardiner et al. 1998; Canada – Fogel 2009). How this literature can help us in understanding changing legal climates for athletes in trouble with the law is considered below.

Icing the goons: from 'sports violence' to 'sports crime'

As with sports crowd disorder (e.g. Elias and Dunning 1971), we can go back a long way to explore legal interventions into violent athlete behaviour. There is some early twentieth-century evidence that player violence (and its often injury-producing outcomes) occasionally troubled the authorities (Young and Wamsley 1996). In 1905, for instance, US President, Teddy Roosevelt, initiated a presidential commission to investigate brutality in the sport of football following a season where, according to one report, 18 players died from injuries sustained in the game.[2] In general, however, aspects of player violence, even those causing severe injury, have either been tolerated as part of the game or side-stepped by the authorities altogether and, until recently, the courts have shown a clear reluctance to intervene in player injury and player violence cases. The control of on-field violence has been viewed as the jurisdiction of the world of sport itself – coaches, teams, leagues, and regional, national and international governing bodies. Statistically speaking, the courts, and especially the criminal courts, have seldom been resorted to. As such, and as a number of late twentieth-century studies have underlined (cf. Horrow 1980; Reasons 1992; Young 1993; Young and Wamsley 1996; Fogel 2009), sport has enjoyed relative immunity from the law, despite the routine, and sometimes horrific, injuries that have been inflicted.

Evidence suggests that, transatlantically at least, and certainly in the US and Canada, consistent legal intervention into injury cases is a relatively recent phenomenon. For instance, Reasons (1992) argues that the Canadian courts became willing to hear sports injury cases in large numbers in the 1970s and, speaking of the US, Lubell (1989: 240) contends that 'the age of sports litigation was inaugurated in the mid-1960s when a New Jersey court awarded a gymnast more than $1 million in a negligence action and a California court awarded a[n injured] football player over $300,000.' While Reasons and Lubell are correct to point to a late twentieth-century 'surge' in legal intervention, and Reasons is, arguably, also correct to contextualize these changes in broader political movements concerned with social justice, civil liberties and personal rights during a relatively counter-cultural phase of the post-war era, the implication that player violence case law cannot be found prior to this time is misleading, as may be witnessed in several substantial historical reviews, some of which trace player violence and injury case law back to the start of the twentieth century (Barnes 1988; Grayson 1988; Moriarty et al. 1994; Young and Wamsley 1996; Gardiner et al. 1998).

Recent sports 'crimes'

Of course, not all player violence results in legal outcomes. The majority does not, but evidence from a number of countries suggests that player violence is increasingly being dealt with in a formally litigious way. Shifting scales of public and official tolerance have recently been emphasized by several highly publicized instances of player 'crimes' that suggest something of a global trend towards legal intervention into, and the criminalization of, sports violence, certainly in some Western countries.

A reliable quantitative, or longitudinal, study of such shifts in the nature and extent of legal intervention does not exist, but even a glimpse at the case law is indicative of significant change. Twenty years ago, Reasons argued that 'Canada leads the common law world in criminally prosecuting its athletes for criminal violence [and the injuries it causes]' (1992: 8). Table 2.1 provides some evidence for the ongoing validity of Reasons' claim, while Table 2.2 shows that criminalizing player violence is not restricted to Canada or, indeed, to ice hockey. Drawn from a combination of professional and amateur sports, these are all examples of player violence entering the jurisdiction of either civil or criminal law. Over the same time period, literally hundreds of similar incidents at the amateur and recreational level, including college and high school, have resulted in charges (usually of assault), litigation and prosecution across North America; other countries (such as Australia, New Zealand and England) are following suit. But, while they may be posted as news on the Internet, relatively few people hear about these cases; any media reports that do take place tend to be restricted to local news only.

Litigious sports climates and the role of consent

At the root of historical and contemporary legal wrangles regarding player violence is the thorny notion of *consent*. Used traditionally to exempt owners in risky labour

TABLE 2.1 Athlete 'crimes': North American ice hockey

Date	Athlete	Location	Incident	Source
February 2010	Name N/A under Canada's Youth Criminal Justice Act (YCJA) (Minor Hockey)	Leduc, Alberta	During a Midget game, a 17-year old player speared opponent, Austin Hoekstra, causing his bowel to tear, and requiring him to have major surgery. The offending player was charged with aggravated assault.	CBC News, 18 February 2010
March 2008	Jonathan Roy, Quebec Remparts (Quebec Major Junior Hockey League)	Chicoutimi, Quebec	Roy skated the length of the ice to attack his opposing goalkeeper during a bench-clearing brawl. Punching repeatedly and without the opposing goalie retaliating, Roy was charged with assault, and pleaded guilty.	Calgary Herald, 8 October 2009
May 2007	Name N/A under YCJA (Minor Hockey)	Montreal, Quebec	Described as the first such case in Quebec's, and possibly Canada's, history, a 13-year old boy was sentenced to 18 months probation and 100 hours of community service for an attack (during which he swung his stick like an axe) that broke the leg of a female opponent.	Calgary Herald, 20 May 2007
October 2006	Robert Simard, Calgary Canucks (Junior B hockey)	Calgary, Alberta	At the end of a match a fight erupted on the way to the locker rooms. Linesman, Rory McCuaig, attempted to break up the fight but was attacked by Simard (and other players) leaving him unconscious. Charges of assault were filed against the 22-year old, who was given a maximum six-month prison sentence.	CBC News, 1 November 2007
August 2004	Alexander Perezhogin, Hamilton Bulldogs (American Hockey League)	Hamilton, Ontario	Retaliating to a hit to from opponent Garret Stafford, Perezhogin swung his stick at Stafford's head, knocking him unconscious and causing a laceration that needed 20 stitches to close. The Hamilton Bulldogs forward was charged with assault causing bodily harm.	ESPN, 26 August 2004
March 2004	Todd Bertuzzi, Vancouver Canucks (NHL)	Vancouver, British Columbia	Near the end of a game against Colorado, Bertuzzi punched opponent Steve Moore from behind and slammed him head-first into the ice. Moore suffered a broken neck and a concussion. Bertuzzi was charged with assault, and was sentenced to one year probation, and 80 hours of community service.	Bloomberg, 22 December 2004

February 2000	Marty McSorley, Boston Bruins (NHL)	Boston, MA	McSorley was found guilty of assault with a weapon after slashing Vancouver Canucks player, Donald Brashear, over the head with his stick at the end of the game. The Bruin was sentenced to an 18-month conditional discharge.	*Maclean's*, 16 October 2000
April 1998	Jesse Boulerice, Plymouth Whalers (Ontario Hockey League)	Plymouth, Michigan	The Whaler pleaded no contest to a charge of assault with intent to do bodily harm and was sentenced to a nine-month conditional release after slashing opponent, Andrew Long, in the head resulting in a broken nose, facial fractures and a concussion.	*Sports Illustrated*, 22 March 1999
January 1992	Jimmy Boni (Italian Hockey League)	Courtmayeur, Italy	Boni, a Canadian, responded to a punch from opponent, Miran Schrott, by slashing him across the chest. Schrott fell to the ice and never regained consciousness. Originally, Boni was charged with intentional homicide, but pleaded guilty to the lesser charge of manslaughter. He was ordered to pay an $1800 Cd fine.	*Maclean's*, 28 February 1994 *Globe and Mail*, 27 September 2005

Sources:

(February 2010 incident) Teen suspended after hockey spear. CBC News, 18 February 2010. Accessed from: http://www.cbc.ca/news/canada/edmonton/story/2010/02/18/edmonton-player-suspended.html.

(March 2008 incident) *Calgary Herald*, 8 October 2009: F2.

(May 2007 incident) *Calgary Herald*, 20 May 2007: A8.

(October 2006 incident) Former player convicted of assault in hockey brawl. CBC News, 1 November 2007. Accessed from: http://www.cbc.ca/news/canada/calgary/story/2007/11/01/simard-guilty.html.

(August 2004 incident) Perezhogin charged after baseball-like swing. ESPN, 26 August 2004. Accessed from: http://sports.espn.go.com/nhl/news/story?id=1868300.

(March 2004 incident) Buteau, M. Canucks forward Todd Bertuzzi avoids jail time in assault plea. *Bloomberg*, 22 December 2004. Accessed from: http://www.bloomberg.com/apps/news?pid=newsarchive&sid=aH7liltNqdy0&refer=canada.

(February 2000 incident) *Maclean's*, 16 October 2000: 17.

(April 1998 incident) MacGregor, J. Less than murder. *Sports Illustrated*, 22 March 1999. Accessed from: http://sportsillustrated.cnn.com/vault/article/magazine/MAG1015394/1/index.htm.

(January 1992 incident) *Maclean's*, 28 February 1994: 11.

TABLE 2.2 Athlete 'crimes': assorted professional and amateur sports

Date	Athlete and sport	Location	Incident	Source
May 2011	Devon Tanner (high school lacrosse)	Dexter, NY	Following the teams shaking hands at the close of a lacrosse match, the 17-year-old struck opponent, Lindsey Pound, in the face with his lacrosse stick, fracturing his right cheek. Tanner was charged with second-degree assault.	Fox, WNYF, 5 May 2011
October 2010	Andres Diaz (recreation adult soccer)	Edison, NJ	Diaz punched and kicked a 17-year-old referee after disagreeing with a penalty call, sending the referee to hospital. Diaz was charged with aggravated assault.	NJ News, 26 October 2010
September 2010	Leon Woods (semi-professional football)	Rochester, NY	Woods head-butted referee, Peter McCabe Jr, resulting in severe facial injuries. Having pleaded guilty to assault, Woods was sentenced to 10 years in prison.	Huffington Post, 3 September 2010
September 2010	Thor Theis (co-ed adult softball)	Mason City, IA	Losing his temper during a game, the 22-year-old began wildly swinging his bat at people. He was charged with assault, disorderly conduct and harassment.	Globe Gazette, 26 September 2010
July 2010	Name N/A (high school wrestling)	Fresno, CA	During a wrestling practice a 17-year-old male used a manoeuvre called a 'butt drag' to submit his opponent. Allegations of rectal penetration were made and charges of sexual battery were filed. No sentencing information is available as a gag order was placed on this trial.	CBS News, 9 December 2010
September 2009	James LaShoto (high school football)	Arlington, MA	After a play had ended, LaShoto (age 17) head-butted opponent Daniel Curtin, causing his helmet to fly off. Charges of assault and battery were laid.	Fox Boston, 27 November 2009
July 2008	Julio Castillo (Minor League Baseball)	Dayton, OH	In a game against the Dayton Dragons a fight broke out. During the fight, Castillo threw a baseball, sending an uninvolved fan to hospital. The Peoria Chiefs player was charged with felonious assault, sentenced to 30 days in jail and three years probation.	ESPN, 6 August 2009

Date	Name (sport)	Location	Description	Source
December 2007	Tripp Isenhour (golf)	Orlando, FL	While making an instructional video, the 39-year-old golfer intentionally hit a ball at a hawk to stop the animal from making noise. The ball killed the animal and the golfer was charged with animal cruelty.	ESPN, 6 March 2008
November 2004	Ron Artest, Jermaine O'Neal and Stephen Jackson (NBA)	Auburn Hills, MI	In the closing minutes of a heated NBA game, a fan threw a cup at Artest from the stands prompting Artest to chase into the stands and attack him. A fight involving several fans ensued prompting O'Neal and Jackson to race to help their team-mate. All three were charged with assault, and sentenced to one year probation, community service and fines.	CBS News, 23 September 2005
January 2001	Ian Powell (Welsh rugby)	Talgarth, Wales	Powell was charged with grievous bodily harm and sentenced to six months in jail after deliberately kicking opponent Ashley Barnett in the leg, resulting in a double fracture.	*Daily Telegraph*, 7 April 2001
February 1996	Simon Devereux (English rugby)	Rosslyn Park, Wandsworth, England	During a rugby match Devereux punched opposing team captain, Jamie Cowie, in the face, resulting in a broken jaw. The Gloucester player was found guilty of grievous bodily harm and was sentenced to nine months in jail.	*The Sun*, 23 February 1996
May 1995	Duncan Ferguson (Scottish soccer)	Glasgow, Scotland	Convicted for assault on three previous occasions, Ferguson was sentenced to jail for three months after head-butting an opponent. He served 44 days in prison for his charges.	*Calgary Herald*, 12 October 1995
February 1995	Eric Cantona (English Premier League soccer)	Manchester, England	Cantona was charged with common assault and sentenced to a week in jail after his 'kung-fu' style assault on a taunting Crystal Palace fan.	*Calgary Herald*, 24 March 1995
December 1994	Howard Collins (Welsh rugby)	Cardiff, Wales	During a match Collins stomped on the head of opponent, Christian Evans, resulting in gashes requiring ten stitches. Collins was sentenced to six months in jail.	*Calgary Herald*, 22 December 1994

TABLE 2.2 Continued

Sources:

(May 2011 incident) Lacrosse player charged with assault following post-game fight. Fox WNYF, 5 May 2011. http://www.wwnytv.com/news/local/Lacrosse-Player-Charged-With-Assault-Following-Post-Game-Fight-121324134.html.

(October 2010 incident) Johnson, B. Edison adult soccer league player is charged with assaulting 17-year-old referee. NJ News, 26 October 2010. http://www.nj.com/news/local/index.ssf/2010/10/player_in_adult_league_charged.html.

(September 2010 incident) Leon Woods imprisoned for referee attack. *Huffington Post*, 3 September 2010. http://www.huffingtonpost.com/2010/09/03/leon-woods-imprisoned-for_n_705445.html.

(September 2010 incident) Softball player charged after allegedly threatening others with a bat. Globalgazette.com, 26 September 2010. http://www.globegazette.com/news/local/article_33327810-c98-11df-b3db-001cc4c002e0.html.

(July 2010 incident) Fresno-area high school wrestler faces trail over 'butt drag' move. CBS News San Francisco, 9 December 2010. http://sanfrancisco.cbslocal.com/2010/12/09/fresno-area-high-school-wrestler-faces-trial-over-%E2%80%98butt-drag%E2%80%99-move/.

(September 2009 incident) Mass. football game head-butt gets assault charge. Fox Boston, 27 November 2009. http://www.myfoxboston.com/dpp/news/local/mass-football-game-headbutt-gets-assault-charge.

(July 2008 incident) Castillo gets jail, probation. ESPN, 6 August 2009. http://sports.espn.go.com/minorlbb/news/story?id=4381593.

(December 2007 incident) Isenhour, charged with killing bird, says 'I am an animal lover.' ESPN, 6 March 2008. http://sports.espn.go.com/golf/news/story?id=3279958.

(November 2004 incident) Todd, S.R. NBA players sentenced in brawl. CBS News, 23 September 2005. http://www.cbsnews.com/stories/2005/09/23/sportsline/main881281.html.

(January 2001 incident) *Daily Telegraph*, 7 April 2001: 7.

(February 1996 incident) *The Sun*, 23 February 1996: 16.

(May 1995 incident) *Calgary Herald*, 12 October 1995: C1.

(February 1995 incident) *Calgary Herald*, 24 March 1995: D3.

(December 1994 incident) *Calgary Herald*, 22 December 1994: D2.

settings from liability, the English common law notion of *volenti non fit injuria*, or voluntary assumption of risk, is based on the assumption of freedom of contract and assumes that all parties involved in a social contract – including sport – share equal knowledge in all areas including such things as hazards, risks and medical information. Given the physically forceful and risky nature of sport, this means that many athletes must consent to a certain amount of physical harm done both by them, and against them. Athletes such as boxers, Mixed Martial Arts (MMA) fighters, footballers, ice-hockey and rugby players, for instance, clearly *give*, or *imply*, consent to physically painful, and even potentially disabling, actions.

As essentially self-regulating organizations, much like those, for instance, of doctors, lawyers and university professors, sports leagues have clearly preferred to practise their own versions of common law in dealing with player misconduct and violence. This continues to include what can only be termed paths of non–action or even condonement (these are discussed below as forms of *non-enforcement* and *covert facilitation*), in addition to more punitive responses such as warnings, fines, suspensions and other forms of deterrence. Until the 1970s, such a process of self-regulation and in-house accountability met, more or less, with legal approval (Barnes 1988: 97). Where litigated, sports violence cases typically troubled judicial experts, and their treatment and outcomes were characterized by variation and, occasionally, contradiction.

Although much of the violence occurring in Canadian and American sport satisfies the requirements of *assault* set out in their respective criminal codes (such as the *Criminal Code of Canada* – 'A person commits an assault when . . . without the consent of another person, he applies force intentionally to that other person, directly or indirectly,' s. 265 of *Martin's Annual Criminal Code* [of Canada] 2011) – it is equally clear that assault in sport is, in principle at least, distinguished by a degree of immunity from criminal liability. For example, with respect to ice hockey, it is clear that the rubric of 'implied consent' is expanded to envelop some, or even most, of the physical contact that occurs in the sport, including behaviours that may injure: 'By agreeing to play the game, a hockey player consents to some forms of intentional bodily contact and to the risk of injury therefrom' (*Martin's Annual Criminal Code* [of Canada] 2011: 560). Evidence of inconsistent interpretation of legal jurisdiction over sports violence may be found in the now hundreds of investigations across North America collated in socio-legal research (Hechter 1976/1977; Horrow 1980, 1982; Reasons 1992; Fogel 2009). Many other examples remain scattered and hidden in case law annals.

In a review of litigated sports violence cases involving charges of some form of assault, Horrow (1982) details six common defences compromising judicial resolution in favour of the plaintiff:

1 the *battery and problem of establishing intent defence* requires the plaintiff to prove that the individual causing injury possessed the requisite *mens rea*, or harmful intent. This is especially difficult to do given that intimidation, pain and injury are viewed as ordinary and acceptable dimensions of sport;

2   the *assumption of risk defence* emphasizes that players assume knowledge of ordinary game risks and dangers, but not including extraordinary risks. On a case-by-case basis, courts must thus distinguish injury in terms of 'ordinary' and 'extra-ordinary' risks;

3   the *consent defence* argues that players consent to all contact occurring in a game, regardless of outcome, and has historically proven to be one of the most 'sure bet' defences for athletes who injure opponents;

4   the *provocation defence*, by contrast, is rarely taken seriously, partly because arguing that the defendant was provoked into retaliation undermines the basic dynamics of many sports, but it does appear in the player violence case law;

5   the *involuntary reflex defence* has successfully been used to argue that assaultive players acted without malicious intent 'in the heat of the game,' and that professional sport contexts are conducive to loss of emotional control;

6   and, the *self-defence* argument legitimizes the use of force by a defendant in situations where force is used against him or her. However, the defendant is limited, Horrow goes on to note, to use no more force that that used by the attacker.

This list is by no means exhaustive of all defences available or those applied, but it demonstrates the level of difficulty the courts have experienced distinguishing illegal from aggressive and harmful, but nevertheless acceptable, play. Assumptions of *volenti* are associated with most of them. Such is true in National Hockey League (NHL) case law (Reasons 1992). For example, the well-known and precedent-setting 1970 *R. v. Green* and *R. v. Maki* cases showed evidence that Ted Green of the Boston Bruins came off the boards and swiped his opponent Wayne Maki with the back of his glove. Maki retaliated by chopping Green on the head with his stick. In Horrow's (1980: 19) account, 'Green sustained a serious concussion and massive hemorrhaging. After two brain operations, he regained only partial sensation and . . . never recovered 100 percent.' While charges of assault were brought against both players, Green, having used a 'self-defence' argument, was acquitted with the following assessment:

> No hockey player enters onto the ice of the National Hockey League without consenting to and without knowledge of the possibility that he is going to be hit in one of many ways once he is on the ice . . . we can come to the conclusion that this is an ordinary happening in a hockey game and that players really think nothing of it. If you go behind the net of a defenceman, particularly one who is trying to defend his zone, and you are struck in the face by that player's glove, a penalty might be called against him, but you do not really think anything of it; it is one of the types of risks one assumes.
>
> (*Horrow 1980: 186*)

Predictably, fist-fighting-related injuries in ice hockey, and in the NHL specifically, have drawn much attention publicly, academically and legally. Courts have commonly responded to such injuries by acquitting defendants on similar grounds of consent. Horrow (1980: 186) cites the Ontario case, *R. v. Starratt* (1971), where the court argued that fist-fighting was so frequent in the NHL as to be viewed 'normal' as long as the force of the fight 'does not exceed that level authorized by the other players.' The significant point here is that the courts have simultaneously been willing to find aggressive player behaviour unacceptable, but also willing to consider pro-aggression norms that pervade the value systems of many sport sub-cultures as mitigating factors, even when they fall outside of the rules of the sport (Smith 1983). No other social institution enjoys this privilege, with the possible exception of the military.

In brief, however hurt and injured, athletes have traditionally been understood to either express, or imply, consent to certain levels of force used against them, except in cases of extraordinarily savage and injurious attacks. Thus, as tolerated as player violence cases have been historically, their presence in tort and criminal law, coupled with what appears to be a decreasing social tolerance towards aspects of violence generally in many Western societies, has led litigators to more stringently re-evaluate certain sports offences as excessive and unjustifiable (White 1986). Contrary to its legal conventions, *volenti* does not imply *absolute consent*, but consent only as *a matter of degree*. Overly literal interpretations of *volenti* are further diluted by acts of violence occurring outside the rules of the games, or after the play has stopped, neither of which are given direct or implied consent by players. This is also true of negligent supervisory and administrative circumstances giving rise to sports injury, or compromising safety, as is demonstrated below.

While there has been no systematic tally of litigated sports violence cases involving grievances initiated by players against other players, even 25 years ago White acknowledged that '[t]here is a clear trend that the criminal systems in Canada and the United States are becoming more and more willing to control illegal violence in sports' (1986: 1030–1034). Of the very few quantitative studies that do exist, Watson and MacLellan's Canadian study (1986) found 66 cases of player versus player assault charges related to ice-hockey injuries (including 6 civil suits and 60 criminal charges) between 1905 and 1982; 75 per cent of their cases occurred in the later phase of that period, between 1972 and 1982. Similarly, a review of the case law led Reasons (1992: 9) to identify what he called 'the emergence of a "hockey crime wave"' in the 1970s. The existence of this 'wave' was further validated by the Office of the Attorney-General of Ontario, which, in 1976, ordered a crackdown on player violence following a season that witnessed dozens of cases of ice-hockey-related assault charges being laid in that province (Cashmore 1998: 229). The case law indicates that charges and convictions for assault causing bodily harm are most widespread, although criminal charges of common assault, and even manslaughter and homicide, are being heard (Reasons 1992: 25). As is the case in so many areas of 'sports violence' research, this work needs updating.

Along with boxing, North American football and rugby, ice hockey appears most frequently in criminal reports, especially in Canada. While the amateur game seems particularly cluttered with 'hockey crimes,' similar cases may be found at the professional level. In one of the most documented late twentieth-century cases, Dino Ciccarelli of the Minnesota North Stars was convicted in an Ontario court. Among other evidence proving *mens rea*, Ciccarelli told the court that in using his stick violently, he was 'probably trying to intimidate' the plaintiff (*R. v. Ciccarelli*, 1989). Although the latter was not seriously hurt, Ciccarelli was convicted on charges of common assault. Many of the issues raised in the Ciccarelli case (i.e. consent, *mens rea* and whether the athlete acted alone or was prompted by others) were repeated in the first major litigated NHL cases of the twenty-first century – the 2000 case of *R. v. McSorley*, and the 2004 case of *R. v. Bertuzzi* (see Table 2.1). Atkinson and Young (2008) offer a thorough examination of the respective positions of the courts, the players, the teams, the NHL and the fans in these and other ice-hockey cases.

However, prosecuting athletes for the violence they do, and the injuries they cause, is not restricted to the sport of ice hockey, or to Canada. A cluster of sports has been affected – some surprising[3] – and a number of precedent-setting cases from other international contexts indicate a similar 'drift' towards legal intervention into, and criminalization of, participant violence.

Widening the circle of culpability

In an earlier paper (Young 1993), I used a victimological approach to examine how sports injury results not only from that nature of athletic acts, but also from their organization (i.e. their ownership, management and administration) and supervision (i.e. coaching) in an often hyper-masculine culture that places disproportionate emphasis on winning-at-all-costs and, in the professional setting, profit. While financial profit may not be a major motive for high-risk sports practices that can cause physical harm at the non-professional level, team, school and university kudos and reputation may be, as the notion of the 'sports ethic' introduced in Chapter 1 suggests. Over-training, playing while injured and improper coaching or tackling and hitting techniques, all of which are normally avoidable, represent examples of the conventional hazards of sport settings, at all levels.

This is not groundbreaking news – people willing to tell the truth about what actually happens 'inside sport' have known that these things have always characterized competitive sport cultures. What is new are the links that the courts seem to be increasingly making between player violence and injury and the sorts of *unreasonable* circumstances that render injury possible, likely or even inevitable. At the professional level, these sorts of complaints have been acknowledged for some time, but they are worth briefly reviewing. For instance, in a revealing 1970s interview, former NHL player, Eric Nesterenko, spoke of player cynicism towards coaches and owners as a way of coping with (sport) workplace exploitation:

> I have become disillusioned with the game not being the pure thing it was earlier in my life. I began to see the exploitation of the players by the owners. You realize owners don't really care for you. You're a piece of property.

They try to get as much out of you as they can. I remember once I had a torn shoulder. It was well in the process of healing. But I knew it wasn't right yet. They brought the doctor in. He said, 'You can play.' I played and ripped it completely. I was laid up. So I look at the owner. He shrugs his shoulders, walks away. He doesn't really hate me. He's impersonal.

(*Terkel 1974: 501*)

While many coaches and sports apologists are irked by such allegations of callousness (Remnick 1987), others provide corroborating evidence for Nesterenko's view. In the infamous words of George Allen, former coach and general manager of the Washington Redskins: '[N]obody is indispensable. If he can't play, we let him know he's not going to be with us' (Terkel 1974: 509).

Public revelations of such athlete exploitation first became widespread during the 1960s and 1970s with the publication of several provocative exposés of professional sport (Bouton 1970; Meggyesy 1971; Shaw 1972), but these indictments are ongoing. More recently, while Remnick (1987: 46) speaks of 'sadistic coaches treating players like dray horses,' Adams et al. (1987: 4) discuss imprudent coaching techniques, Cruise and Griffiths (1991) decry the 'dog-eat-dog' business of the NHL, and Courson (1991) and Canseco (2005) argue that football and baseball coaches might just as well write prescriptions for drugs, and steroids in particular, when they advise players to appreciably gain weight and strength in the off-season.

It is precisely these underlying dynamics of competitive sport and, in particular, what I earlier called techniques of *non-enforcement* and *covert facilitation* (Young 1993: 378), that have resulted in the courts widening the circle of culpability where athlete injury is concerned. Legal actions are no longer limited to players themselves; they may also extend to cases against coaches, teams, owners, referees and governing sport bodies. For instance, in a 2001 Ontario case of a teenage ice-hockey player paralyzed in a high school tournament, Ian Strathern brought charges of negligence against the coach, the school, the hockey association, the city, the province and the Ministries of Education and of Tourism and Recreation. Interestingly, no charges were laid against the opposing player with whom Ian Strathern collided; the case revolved entirely around several parties who were viewed as indirectly responsible for the teenager's fate. After years of moving through the litigation process, the case settled prior to being heard by the Ontario Superior Court of Justice.

As such, in addition to player violence causing injury, the courts are also willing to hear cases of so-called 'vicarious liability.' Specifically, should players causing injury to themselves or others be penalized when it can be shown that they have followed coaching instructions, or when, as in the Ian Strathern case above, they have played under negligent conditions? Traditionally, cultural reverence for sport has meant that suing a coach has been considered heretical but, increasingly, coaches are being named in numerous lawsuits each year (Adams et al. 1987: 3). Connors (1981) argues that, at the amateur level in the US, physical educators and coaches represent those individuals most often sued in educational settings, and similar dynamics are currently being experienced in the UK. For instance, while widespread change is yet to be affected, a spate of serious injuries in school-based rugby, including some resulting from collapsing scrums, has led, as one news report put it, to several schools 'planning to drop rugby – partly because of the growing litigation culture over injuries' (http://news.bbc.co.uk/hi/english/education/newsid_2053000/2053233.stm).

If it can be proven that a violent player acts in accordance with his or her role requirements, that player may not be solely responsible for his or her conduct. This is especially resonant, of course, where cases of younger and child athletes are concerned. Young athletes are, after all, more likely to accept coaching advice uncritically, and be more vulnerable to potentially harmful advice coming from adults in coaching or mentoring positions. At the professional level, and in a well-known NBA case, the Los Angeles Lakers were found to be negligent when their player, Kermit Washington, punched his opponent, Rudy Tomjanovich of the Houston Rockets, during a 1977 game. The punch resulted in serious injury to Tomjanovich, including 'a fractured jaw, nose, and skull, severe lacerations, [and] a cerebral concussion' (Smith 1987: 12). Deemed negligent in not adequately training and supervising Washington, the Lakers were required to pay over $3 million in damages.

American and Canadian law holds anyone criminally responsible who 'counsels . . . or commands another to commit a crime' (Hechter 1976/1977: 426). This rests uneasily against the fact that coaches in football, ice hockey, rugby, soccer, lacrosse and other sports routinely require their players not only to physically overwhelm opponents, but to ensure, often by 'stretching' the rules of the sport (such as in the use of so-called 'professional fouls' and the like), that their opponents are 'taken out' of the game. Adams (1987: 3) cites several cases of such coaching techniques at elite amateur levels. The following, for instance, is an eminently dangerous football scenario giving rise to liability:

> Coaches denied players water breaks, even on extremely hot and humid days to teach mental toughness. Football coaches employ dangerous drills such as a 'suicide' drill where 5 to 6 players would tackle an unprotected lineman because he missed a block.

The dangers inherent in tyrannical or negligent coaching regimes in American football have been illuminated over the past several seasons as players have suffered, sometimes fatally, from heat stroke. As a 2002 Associated Press news story reported:

> Heat-related football deaths at all levels have steadily increased, replacing direct fatal injuries as the sport's biggest on-field safety concern. Eight football players died nationwide last year because of injuries, and another three died from heat stroke . . . Twelve more deaths were by natural causes aggravated by exercise, such as a heart attack. The number of injury deaths reflected a substantial drop since stricter rules about tackling and blocking were enacted

in the mid-1970s, when fatalities regularly reached double digits . . . Minnesota Vikings tackle Korey Stringer collapsed during practice July 31 and died the next day, as did Travis Stowers, a high school player near Michigantown, Ind. . . . Less than a week earlier, Eraste Autin, an incoming freshman at the University of Florida, died of complications of heatstroke. He collapsed at the end of a voluntary summer conditioning session and was in a coma for six days.

(*http://www.newsday.com/sports/unc-study-heat-related-deaths-steadily-rising-1.446105*)

Changing times, and shifts in legal thinking where sport is concerned, have thus required that coaches become more legally attuned to notions of 'foreseeability' (Adams 1987: 5). Coaches, teams and game officials are increasingly required to make all possible dangers or warning signs of injuries or accidents not just known to players, but fully understood. The message is increasingly clear – be negligent and run the risk of being sued (e.g. 'Crippled rugby lad sues ref for £1 million: scrums "were not safe."' *The Sun*, 16 April 2001: 15). The way certainly seems open, then, for sports owners, administrators and authorities to become more liable, both civilly and criminally, for the perceived negligent treatment of players, who become hurt and injured under circumstances deemed by the courts to represent, once again, 'unreasonable' risk.

At the time of writing, a fascinating NHL case of vicarious liability is in process linked to *R. v. Bertuzzi* (2004). Former Vancouver Canucks ice-hockey player Todd Bertuzzi, originally charged with assault and given a sentence of one-year probation in a Canadian criminal court for attacking Steve Moore of the Colorado Avalanche in a March 2004 game, continues to await the outcome of a civil case against his former coach, Marc Crawford. In the case, which seeks $38 million in damages, Bertuzzi alleges that, in dishing out what has been tagged as 'one of hockey's worst cheap shots' (Farber 2005: 20), he took 'direction from Crawford in all matters related to his role or function as a player,' including making Moore 'pay the price' for previously injuring one of Bertuzzi's team-mates (*Vancouver Sun*, 9 March 2004: E3; *Calgary Herald*, 29 March 2008: A6). When Bertuzzi slammed Moore's head into the ice, effectively ending his career, few might have guessed that the circle of culpability for Bertuzzi's actions might spread to his coach, who now awaits the outcome of being sued for lost income and aggravated and punitive damages (http://www.cbc.ca/sports/hockey/story/2008/03/28/bertuzzi-crawford.html).

Reluctance to prosecute: an update to Smith

While there is clear evidence of a late twentieth-century drift towards legal intervention into sports violence (and sports injury) cases in a number of countries, the evidence for increases in criminal prosecutions is less compelling. An early, but now outdated, attempt to account for the reluctance of the courts to prosecute and punish sports violence cases was offered again by Smith (1987), who identified seven key explanations for the relative immunity to prosecution of players criminally charged with injuring opponents. According to Smith, these reasons included the following concerns:

1   the courts have more important things to do like prosecuting 'real' criminals;
2   the leagues themselves are in the best position to effectively control player misbehaviour;
3   civil law proceedings are better suited than criminal proceedings for dealing with an injured player's grievances;
4   it is unfair to prosecute an individual player while ignoring those who may have aided, abetted or counselled;
5   it is unfair to prosecute a player when the law is unclear as to what sorts of injurious acts it would define as 'unreasonable';
6   it is almost impossible to reach a guilty verdict in sports violence or sports injury cases; and
7   prosecuting athletes does little to solve the wider social causes of sports violence and injuries.

It is likely that these views will continue to reflect popular thinking in the world of sport, in the public at large, and perhaps also in the courtroom. The role of the media in 'framing' sports violence and sports injury issues for the public is also noteworthy here, especially when it contributes to the view that violence and injury are ordinary, and even desirable, features of the sports process (see Chapter 7). Despite the prevalence of these views, more punitive attitudes on the part of both sports authorities and the law seem to be emerging. A process of *de-legitimation* of some aspects of sport that culminate in injury seems to be underway.

The following observations on this trend towards de-legitimation serve to update Smith's socio-legal explanations for the traditional reluctance of the courts to prosecute player violence:

1   In countries such as Canada, the US and the UK, justice systems are predisposed to policing so-called 'street crime.' While it may be some time before large sections of the public are willing to view athletes behaving violently in the same light as such 'real' criminals (i.e. persons involved in crimes outside of sport), whose behaviour (i.e. assault) may have the same outcomes (i.e. injury, paralysis, death), it seems reasonable to argue that the sheer numbers of athletes being charged with assault represent a discernable, if difficult to measure, shift in legal thinking regarding 'criminals' in sport.
2   The view that 'in-house' policing is the most effective means to monitor player violence remains controversial. On the one hand, it seems reasonable to argue that the leagues and clubs are in the most nuanced positions to judge the magnitude of an offence relative to the rules and traditions of the game. On the other hand, we know from the criminological literature that professional

organizations entrusted with policing themselves (such as lawyers, doctors and the police themselves) sometimes abuse that privilege by meting out only tokenistic sanctions, or none at all. Likewise, sociological research has uncovered processes of *non-enforcement, covert facilitation* and *cover-ups* with respect to sports violence and injury cases (Young 1993). We know, further, that there are numerous ways in which violent practices causing injury are rewarded in sport – financially, occupationally and subculturally. In other words, the institution of sport may not be willing, or able, as the phrase goes, to 'get its own house in order.'

3   The courts have traditionally viewed civil law proceedings as more appropriate than criminal proceedings in dealing with the grievances of injured athletes. Again, this approach stems from the view that a certain amount of physical damage should be expected in sport and from the previously discussed notion of *volenti non fit injuria*. While it may be true that most injury cases are dealt with in civil law, criminal law is also being viewed as an appropriate venue, as an already large number of cases on both sides of the Atlantic suggests.

4   The view that it is unfair to prosecute individual players for their *directly* violent or injurious actions while ignoring those who may have assisted in the teaching or promotion of those acts (i.e. coaches, trainers, managers etc.) remains relevant. Courts continue to invoke the philosophy of legal individualism that tends to shift the onus of criminal responsibility from an organization (i.e. a sports team or a league) to a particular player. However, sport has already witnessed numerous precedent-setting cases where American and Canadian courts have decided against sports teams rather than against an individual player, and the legal systems of many countries seem willing to continue to widen the circle of culpability.

5   Legal systems on both sides of the Atlantic continue to approach sports injury cases inconsistently and with variability. Despite recent pressures on sports organizations and the courts to examine more closely, and define more clearly, other aspects of 'risky' sports-related behaviour such as sexual harassment (Donnelly 1999) and hazing (Bryshun and Young 1999), it is probably fair to argue that definitions of what constitutes 'unreasonable' and 'negligent' behaviour related to sport remain less than clear. This seems as true for the courts as it does for the public and sports organizations, including, for instance, colleges and universities.

6   The argument that one should avoid sports violence or injury litigation because it is impossible to reach a guilty verdict may strike the reader as missing the point. However disagreeable one finds this logic, it is nevertheless true that the decision to litigate is often premised on the perceived odds of receiving a favourable decision in court. In this sense, it remains likely that, at the level of the aggrieved player or the prosecution, courts may be avoided due to the perception that the justice system would not be sympathetic to the case. However, it is also true that many cases *have* reached the courts and *have* resulted in guilty verdicts. In other words, where sports 'crimes' or 'assaults' are concerned, there are already many precedents in law in several countries. To

date, we have no up-to-date quantitative, longitudinal or reliable record of the extent to which these cases are growing but, again, anecdotal evidence seems to point in this direction – at least for countries such as Canada, England and the US.

7 The argument that prosecuting violent athletes represents a 'Band-Aid' solution to the problem because it does little to solve wider causes of violence is hard to contest. Player violence and sports-related injury are certainly socially and culturally embedded and, as with crime intervention more generally, criminalizing individual sports cases is likely to achieve very little unless anti-violence or anti-injury intervention and education takes place in a meaningful way throughout sport, as well as elsewhere in the wider community.

In sum, a socio-legal approach uncovers a paradox on the matter of player violence – while there seems to be an increasing degree of social and legal intolerance to forms of player violence causing injury, there remains an ongoing reluctance on the part of the courts to fully sanction athletes for assault, dangerous play and for other sports 'crimes' inflicting harm. In general, player violence is still defined ambiguously at best, and there remains little agreement among sports administrators and legal authorities as to the acceptable limits of aggressive, injurious or otherwise risky sports behaviour. Also, while civil and criminal charges against athletes may be on the increase, charges are commonly reduced, and prosecutions remain rare and sentences light. The world of ice hockey is littered with examples, but one recent Canadian case is particularly illustrative. In 2008, Jonathan Roy, the son of an NHL Hall-of-Famer (Patrick Roy) who also acted as his coach, skated the length of the ice and punched his opposing goalkeeper repeatedly in the head while his opponent lay on the ground refusing to retaliate. Originally charged with assault, the younger Roy was given an absolute discharge in a court in Quebec, a province where his father is an ice-hockey icon (*Calgary Herald*, 8 October 2009: F2). Such legal decisions illustrate not only the preferential treatment that violent athletes receive at the hands of the legal system, but also hint strongly at the continuing privileged status of sport and the still-reticent position of the courts, even in the face of apparent social change.

How theory plays in

In addition to the socio-legal and victimological approaches implemented so far in this chapter, there are numerous explanatory perspectives that could be used to make sense of questions like 'how and why does player violence in sport happen and with what implications?' For instance, building on Chapter 1:

• SLT (Bandura 1973, 1977) helps us understand how aggressive player styles, roles and identities are emulated and prized in sport, as well as how violence comes to be understood as a 'strategy' for accomplishing certain goals (Coakley and Donnelly 2009);

- the 'violent subculture' approach helps explain how sport groups operate as insular cultures that develop their own norms and rationalizations, and how, specifically, professional sports such as ice hockey operate as Goffmanian 'total institutions' in encouraging, and protecting, their particular brand of violence (Atkinson and Young 2008);
- the TN perspective (Sykes and Matza 1957) shows how social structures and patterns are translated into action by players who learn not only how to 'do' violence to opponents but, just as importantly, how to justify and neutralize it; and
- the 'sports ethic' approach of Hughes and Coakley (1991) reminds us that one of the most important axioms of many sports is that players should accept no limits in the pursuit of winning, even if this means hurting others, hurting oneself, playing outside the rules or cheating.

In casting light on the varied dimensions of player violence, these perspectives are all helpful. However, where the doing, and the policing, of player violence are concerned, three further sociological approaches seem particularly relevant and useful: namely, gender perspectives; figurational sociology; and 'wanted' and 'unwanted' violence.

Gender perspectives

Attempting to explain player violence, and player violence litigation, requires attention to gender dynamics, first, to account for why so many male athletes have traditionally been willing to risk health and safety in accepting physically brutal sport norms and, second, to explain the complicity of legal structures in defining player violence not only as legally tolerable but also as socially valuable.

Only a glimpse at early Canadian player violence case law is needed to validate these claims. For example, in the 1911 Ontario case, *R. v. Wildfong and Lang*, in which two men were charged with engaging in a prizefight, Judge Snider was unequivocal in his views on the value of sports being used as a physical and social training ground for males:

> I wish to make it clear that I am as much opposed to prize fighting and brutal and intentional injury in boxing, football, hockey or lacrosse, as any person can be. At the same time I feel confident that it will be a long time before Parliament will think it wise to so hedge in young men and boys by legislation that all sports that are rough and strenuous or even dangerous must be given up. Virility in young men would soon be lessened and self-reliant manliness be a thing of the past.
>
> (*Cited in Young and Wamsley 1996: 56*)

As disconnected from the current world of sport as these century-old legal views appear, their trappings may be seen throughout twentieth-century sports violence cases. In this sense, it can be argued that the state, early and modern, has been implicated in the management of gender relations through sport and, specifically, in helping construct what Donaldson (1993: 646) has called 'the public face of hegemonic masculinity.'

Prompted by the more gender-sensitive and, perhaps, more 'politically correct' social climate today, the explicitly gendered underpinnings of early sports 'assault' litigation have been toned down, but the traditionally chauvinist trappings of law may now be articulated in more subtle (though still impacting) ways. For instance, it may be speculated that the courts would be less tolerant of female-to-female player violence on the grounds that aggression and femininity are still viewed as mutually exclusive entities. In a slightly different area (i.e. the areas of player *deviance* as opposed to player *violence*), we know that while large numbers of well-known male athletes have used performance-enhancing drugs, and lied about their use to panels and investigators, one of the most punitive drug-related sanctions was recently given to a female athlete (Marion Jones of the US), who, in 2008, was sentenced to six months in jail for admitting to lying to two grand juries in steroid investigations (Atkinson and Young 2008). And, in a provocative indictment of the Canadian legal system ostensibly unrelated to sport but, in fact, germane for the 'gender' argument being summarized here, the former Governor General of Canada, Adrienne Clarkson, argued that 'the legal profession has been built by men, for men, in a man's world' (Cooper et al. 2004). In each of these ways, it is clear that not only is sport buttressed by gendered ideologies and discourses, but also systems of law may be, too.

As Chapter 8 will show, feminist work on sport and gender urges us to understand male tolerance of violence, risk and injury linked to sport not only as a passive social process, but also as a deliberate process through which doling out violence and even getting injured becomes reframed as *masculinizing*. Clarkson's comments, coupled with the obviously patriarchal legal views that have been emerged in sports violence cases, hint strongly at how the 'gendering' of sports violence goes well beyond the field of play.

Figurational sociology

A valuable approach to explaining the existence of, and some of the shifts in, levels of tolerance to player violence may be found in the work of Norbert Elias (see Elias and Dunning 1986) emphasizing long-term processes of social development. In particular, Eliasian notions of what Elias and Dunning call 'civilizing spurts,' 'thresholds of repugnance' and 'regressive spurts' are especially helpful.

First, civilizing spurts occur as part of the process of state control – that is, the way in which acceptable levels of violence gradually drop, and are policed, more tightly as the state increasingly comes to control the manifestation, rate and extent of violence in society. From this position, we can begin to make sense of the fact that most forms of interpersonal violence have come to be seen as unacceptable while sport (which, after all, interfaces with the state in a number of obvious ways – it makes money for the state and it underscores the power of the state to 'step in' when it feels necessary) remains one of the last *protected* and *celebrated* bastions of tolerated violence in many societies. Second, using the notion of 'thresholds of repugnance,' Elias pointed to the way in which our limits for violence decrease as part of the civilizing process. This may be seen in the introduction of 'safer' sports around the world such as non-contact ice-hockey leagues in Canada, consciously designed to oppose more mainstream versions of sport that hurt, injure and threaten participants' health. Third, and crucially, because the so-called 'civilizing process' is far from linear, uncontested, complete or irreversible, there are complexities in the relationship between communities and tolerated violence. Elias thus left room for what he called 'regressive' or 'de-civilizing spurts,' which can be witnessed in the fact that certain aspects of sports violence (such as fist-fighting in ice hockey) remain hugely popular among fans, despite simultaneous waves of criminalization. The precipitous advances in many countries of 'fight' and 'cage' sports, such as MMA, and organizations such as the Ultimate Fighting Championship (UFC), represent exactly the sort of social ambivalence and contradiction Elias suggested accompanies wider processes of 'civilization' (van Bottenburg and Heilbron 2006; Downey 2007; Harris 2009: A3; Garcia and Malcolm 2010). The potential applicability of such an approach to the growth of brutally violent (but increasingly controlled) sports at a time of apparent decreases in social tolerance to violence in general, and to the contradictory role of the courts in policing player violence, is obvious.

Wanted and unwanted violence

Picking up on the notions of 'legitimate' and 'illegitimate' violence used by Smith (1983) and Ball-Rokeach (1971, 1980), Atkinson and Young (2008) distinguish between 'wanted' and 'unwanted' behaviours (such as interpersonal violence) occurring in autonomous social institutions. Emphasizing that what is seen as valuable and positive outside of sport is not necessarily viewed the same way inside, or between different sports, or even between different levels of sport, they describe 'wanted' behaviour as an action, 'thought, or symbol that violates an accepted social or cultural standard . . . [it] tends not to be defined as proper or just and is generally understood by perpetrators to be controversial' (p. 6). They go on to underline the complex nature of forms of 'wanted violence,' suggesting that '[w]hen they are relatively controlled, predictable, and rationalized, they are not seen as being emblematic of pathological cultural or structural condition – yet, neither are they viewed as fully socially acceptable' (p. 6).

Using this definition, 'wanted violence' in sport might include many of the behaviours that have been reviewed in this chapter, such as fist-fighting in the NHL, and the broader, and clearly institutionalized, system of pro-violence and pro-fighting values ('the code' – Atkinson and Young 2011) instantly recognizable to hockey aficionados but 'unwanted' by many outsiders. However, part of the complexity of 'wanted' behaviours is that actors are not given an unchecked licence to perform them in excessive ways, or to embarrass organizations by performing them. The latter would constitute 'unwanted behaviour.' Examples of the uneasy, and often contradictory, relationship between 'wanted' and 'unwanted' sport behaviour may be seen in the ways that certain drugs (such as recreational drugs such as marijuana and cocaine) are heavily policed in sport while other drugs also associated with criminal activity (such as steroids and other 'performance enhancers') are condoned, rationalized or ignored. When the action is excessive, or excessively embarrassing, for sport organizations, the level of support offered to offending players by those organizations tends to diminish. Using case studies of criminalized ice-hockey violence, Atkinson and Young describe how episodes of 'rink rage' may be understood using this 'wanted and unwanted violence' approach.

Crucially for this chapter, this approach may be used to understand processes of social control. Specifically, when violent incidents occur, social controllers (from parent organizations, to leagues, to the law of the land) adopt what seem like firm stances on the action and its outcomes. But, while appearing as though tough measures are being applied, these trusted stakeholders effectively allow high-risk player behaviour, and recidivist offenders, to return to the game and contribute to recurring patterns of 'legitimate' (i.e. 'wanted') violence.

Conclusion

The main purpose of this chapter has been to demonstrate a drift over the course of the twentieth century towards criminalizing athlete violence, and to explore some of the legal complications that ensue as sports settings become more litigious. Despite the commonly held view that the courts are the wrong place to deliberate on player violence,[4] there is increasing evidence that the courts in a number of countries are more willing to hear player violence cases (often perceived and treated as 'sports injury' cases). Litigation of sport assault, or what has provocatively been tagged 'sports crime' not only by critics but, fascinatingly enough, by the government of Canada,[5] appears to be on the rise in Canada and elsewhere. What Michael Smith defined as *brutal body contact* and *borderline violence* close to three decades ago is increasingly prompting injured athletes to initiate not only civil, but also criminal, charges and proceedings. At the same time, non-legal forms of intervention (such as fines, suspensions and generally closer policing practices) based on principles of deterrence are also being adopted by sports clubs, leagues and organizations. In British rugby, for instance, media reportage of such interventions is not uncommon (e.g. 'Violent players face clampdown,' *The Guardian*, 12 December 1994: 17; 'Prop banned until 21st century,' *The Guardian*, 10 May 1995: 21). But, for all of this, it would be a mistake to assume that legal intervention into sports violence and sports injury cases has been uncomplicated, homogeneous or linear; this is not true. In general, 'sports violence' and 'sports injury' are still defined ambiguously at best, and there remains little agreement among sports leagues and authorities as to the limits of aggressive, injurious or otherwise risky sports conduct.

Despite some high-profile sports violence and injury cases proving that players do not always freely consent to injurious or negligent conditions, including negligent coaching, the notion of *volenti non fit injuria* endures at the centre of public and legal tolerance of even the most horrifying of sport injury cases. In other words, one of the main causes of the still-widespread tendency to excuse and accept injury, catastrophe and even death in sport is the concept of *implied consent*. From this position, it comes as no great surprise that when player conduct inflicting harm becomes redefined as 'assault,' a series of commonsense rationalizations (and, as we saw earlier, readily available legal defences) kick-in to protect the harmful dimensions of sport, and the violence 'doer.' As former England rugby 'hard man,' Mike Burton, proclaimed in his overly literal interpretation of the Simon Devereux incident described in Table 2.2, 'Every tackle in a game of rugby is a common assault' (*The Sun*, 23 February 1996: 42). It is equally clear that this sort of logic, found in both masculinist sport cultures as well as, ironically, in the institution of law itself (Young 1993; Young and Wamsley 1996; Atkinson and Young 2008), is founded on deeply gendered undercurrents that likely conflate to compromise the chances of punitive legal outcomes. Along with other factors, perhaps this explains why the growing number of charges brought against sports parties for injuring participants has not been matched by similarly stiff, or consistent, prosecution trends?

Where the role of the courts in player violence is concerned, then, there are several things that we know. We know, for instance, that throughout much of the twentieth century, the courts preferred not to hear such cases, 'bouncing' them back to the world of sport itself to adjudicate, or reaching 'acquittal' decisions quickly. On the basis of what socio-legal and criminological scholars tell us, we know that this began to change in Canada, the US and the UK in the final third of the twentieth century, and that, since that time, player violence case law has grown into a voluminous body of material on both sides of the Atlantic. We know that, when litigated, the notions of voluntary assumption of risk and consent have been instrumental in judicial logic and decision-making. We know, concomitantly, that sports law is a growing professional field, and we know that what has been called a 'litigation explosion' (Hans and Lofquist 1992) related to sport and its numerous compensation claims has expanded insurance costs and threatened sports programmes at many levels in many countries (e.g. 'Injury pay out puts soccer on the spot,' *The Guardian*, 15 October 1997: 9; '£1.5 million injury claim threatens football,' *Sunday Times*, 12 October 1997: 5). And, finally, we know that, in the drift towards player violence criminalization, the authorities remain uncertain as to how to act and how to act consistently, as may be witnessed in the apparent dissonance between the number of cases in which charges are laid and the still relatively lenient way such cases are treated when they finally 'get to court.'

3

CROWD VIOLENCE

From hooliganism to post-event riots

Introduction

Building on the definition of SRV offered in Chapter 1, sports crowd violence is best understood as acts of verbal or physical aggression (threatened or actual), perpetrated by partisan fans at, or away from, the sports arena that may result in injury to persons or damage to property. Crowd violence might also include forms of identity violence (see Chapter 4), such as xenophobia and jingoism – expressed as racially motivated threats, harassment and attacks. Unlike acts of violence among players, crowd violence has, for many decades, elicited anxious responses from the authorities and remains closely policed. The recurrence of injurious, and sometimes deadly, crowd episodes in many countries has sensitized social controllers and sports administrators to the need for careful regulation and planning. Indeed, in many settings, crowd violence is seen as a serious problem and policing concern for communities as a whole, and strict measures, including new laws, have been introduced to address this issue (see Chapter 6). Fans of British and European soccer have gained notoriety for their violent rituals and practices but, in fact, violent soccer crowd disturbances occur worldwide – so much so that Dunning et al. (2002b) view hooliganism as a 'world phenomenon.' Since sports crowd disorder goes beyond the sport of soccer (many sports have been affected, some more consistently than others), and assumes varying forms across the globe, this may be an overstatement, but it is certainly important to think about crowd violence globally. This chapter critically reviews existing knowledge of, and perspectives on, crowd violence, particularly with respect to the UK and North America, and concludes by identifying common denominators and variations both in the phenomenon itself and in the research.

United Kingdom

While disorderly behaviours associated with the game of soccer do not represent the only sports crowd violence that occurs in the UK (violent episodes have also occurred, but with much less frequency, at rugby and cricket matches – e.g. Harris 2002), the term 'hooliganism' has become closely aligned with the sport of soccer, and especially English soccer. There are stereotypes and mistakes at work in this relationship that have been hotly contested, but it seems fair to argue that the literature on soccer hooliganism (both as it applies to the UK as well as to other countries) represents the largest, most dense and most fractious in the entire 'sports violence' literature. Claims that the phenomenon has been 'over studied' have also been made (Moorhouse 2000: 1464). Itself contentious, and often imprecise, the term 'hooliganism' is used generically to refer to behaviours such as public drunkenness, threats, obscenity, vandalism and fighting and assault perpetrated in connection to, and in the vicinity of, soccer games. However, it is important to distinguish between spontaneous and episodic fan violence occurring at soccer games and the far more institutionalized version that involves organized groups of fans fighting against rival groups.

Manifestations

Because the 1980s are generally seen to represent a watershed period in the relationship between soccer and its fans, and for the purposes of surveying the literature, the following discussion splinters hooliganism into three broad periods.

The pre-1980s: the emergence of 'landscapes of fear'[1]

While the use of the term 'hooliganism' to refer to British soccer culture increased at the hands of an actively exaggerating media in the 1960s (see Chapter 7), and led to the identification of the problem and its perpetrators in terms of 'folks devils and moral panics' (Cohen 1973), Dunning and his colleagues (Elias and Dunning 1971; Dunning et al. 1988) found evidence that crowd disorders could be traced back to before the start of the twentieth century, and indeed far earlier. In fact, there is evidence that, with occasional fluctuations in frequency and force, crowd violence runs, as Cashmore (2000: 177) puts it, 'like a ribbon through the history of soccer.' Following loosely organized rival supporter clashes in the earlier decades of the twentieth century, often expressed along religious lines (i.e. fans of Catholic teams fighting fans of Protestant teams), aggressive behaviour ('aggro') by more coordinated fans began to be reported in deeply hyperbolized ways in the 1960s, and it quickly became difficult to distinguish between what was happening and what was being reported. Indeed, much of the early sociological research set out to disentangle the myth and the reality of hooliganism (Hall 1978; Williams et al. 1984; Young 1986).

There is no doubt that a significant increase in reported episodes of crowd violence occurred at approximately that time, and that much of it interfaced with burgeoning concerns regarding deviant youth subcultures (Cohen 1973). The local club and its stadium and, in particular, the sections behind the respective goals (the 'ends'), came to represent a source of identity, pride and reputation for young, working-class, male supporters. Conversely, attempting, through fighting and physical confrontations, to prove dominance by 'taking the ends' of rival supporters also became paramount (Marsh et al. 1978). The outcome was a combination of both ritualized and violent exchanges at soccer matches, with fighting and missile throwing often spilling out on to the field of play, eventually prompting the widespread installment of perimeter fencing. The latter would later come to be seen as a dangerous mistake. Around this time, and as a marker of their growing organization and identity, groups of hooligan fans began to assume nicknames and, eventually, a group of fans with such a label attached itself to almost every professional team, becoming recognized among the authorities and the soccer community for their label, size, reputation and, of course, practices.

From its inception in the 1960s and 1970s, the scholarly research showed that 'hooligan' soccer gangs derived from local (typically working-class) areas, were almost exclusively male and were stratified by age hierarchies, with veteran and central members playing leadership roles 'on the front lines' and younger recruits performing menial tasks on the periphery (Marsh et al. 1978; Williams et al. 1984). Initially, the action was restricted to the traditionally scheduled Saturday afternoon games, though this was to change. Soccer matches became the context for the acting out of increasingly complicated manoeuvres between rival supporters, and between supporters and the police. Throughout the 1970s, hundreds of violent clashes, including field invasions, took place. These have been systematically recorded in an extensive literature (e.g. Harrington 1968; Lang 1969; Dunning et al. 1988; Marsh et al. 1996).

In the rapidly transforming world of hooliganism, and as an unintended effect of increases in policing inside the stadia (including penning, fencing and other such means of segregating crowds), much of the violence that had traditionally taken place inside the grounds and during the game shifted to community locations less susceptible to police surveillance (e.g. petrol (gas) and train stations, pubs, city centres and public transport), and to the pre-game and post-game contexts (where over half of hooligan incidents take place today – Frosdick and Newton 2006: 403).

In this way, by the late 1970s, the relatively loosely organized world of soccer hooligans engaging in violent but predictable clashes in the soccer 'ends' had morphed into an increasingly complicated cat-and-mouse drama played out not only against opposing fans, but also against the authorities, both at home and overseas. In the lexicon of English football hooliganism, the once-violent but unsophisticated world of 'taking the ends' and avoiding 'the old bill' (the police) had now become a far more threatening and calculated world of 'firms,' 'crews' and 'plotting up' (Brimson and Brimson 1996). And around this time, the 'trouble on the terraces' was also being exported overseas and manifesting itself in the fan bases and experiences of many European clubs, which started to boast their own hard-core firms (such as the Ultras of Juventus, Turin). European games and international matches became the context for, as Williams et al. called it, 'Hooligans Abroad' (1984) – repeated and consistent episodes of violent, booze-filled, racially moti-vated clashes between fans of British (mostly English) clubs, or of the national team, and those of their European rivals. Despite frequent claims of hooliganism being an indigenously 'English disease,' the research from several countries, including Italy, Germany, the Netherlands, France and Austria, clearly demonstrated a wider problem, even at this point, prompting the introduction of numerous policing and social control initiatives throughout the continent.

The 1980s: a crisis period in English (and European) soccer violence?

The mid-to-late 1980s are widely considered to represent a pivotal crisis period in the history of English soccer but, crucially, not because of hooliganism alone. Several incidents occurred that highlighted the complicit roles played by the clubs and the police in football violence. On 11 May 1985, as Bradford City played at home against Lincoln City, a fire broke out in a wooden-framed stadium built almost a century earlier. An entire section of the stadium burned to the ground in less than 10 minutes, and 57 people were burned to death trying to escape the fire. The horrific scenes displayed on television and in the print media were made all the more disturbing by the fact that hundreds of fans had been trapped on the burning side of the stands by a tall and spiked perimeter fence intended, ironically, to keep fans from trespassing on the pitch (the playing surface being the safest refuge during the fire). Eighteen days later, on 29 May, the European Cup was due to be played between Liverpool of England and Juventus of Turin, Italy at Heysel Stadium in Brussels, Belgium. Approximately one hour before kick-off, and following a period of mutual taunting between rival groups of fans, a charge by the Liverpool fans into the Juventus 'end' resulted in a collapsing retainer wall and the injury of hundreds of fans. Thirty-nine (mostly Italian) fans died in the ensuing crush (Young 1986; Taylor 1987). Again, the scenes were broadcast live on television. Finally, on 15 April 1989, Liverpool fans were once more involved in a tragic incident prior to a domestic cup game against Nottingham Forrest, played at Hillsborough Stadium, Sheffield, although this time the incident was not caused by hooligan behaviour. After the police opened a gate to accommodate late-comers, as many as 3,000 Liverpool fans were channelled into the stadium, unaware that hundreds of fans inside the stadium were being crushed against a high steel control fence. Ninety-six fans were killed and hundreds of others injured (Taylor 1989; Scraton et al. 1995). Once again, the grizzly scenes were broadcast live to the world. A subsequent inquiry led by Lord Justice Taylor was heavily critical of the decisions made by the police on duty (Taylor 1990). Bradford, Heysel and Hillsborough continue to be viewed as axial moments in British sport. Not only do they endure as remind-ers of the potentially lethal risks related to fans behaving xenophobically (Spaaij

2006: 320), but they also represent stark reminders of the importance of providing safe environments for the public to gather and spectate, as well as the dangers of negligent policing.

After the 1980s storm: a 'post-hooligan' utopia?

When one factors in catastrophic violence and injury in European soccer throughout the 1970s and 1980s, the authorities introducing 'get tough' strategies (ranging from identity card schemes, to alcohol and travel bans, to jail terms), an increasingly savvy and exploitative media sending menacing images of European, and particularly English, soccer fans around the globe, and a transforming popular culture aimed at the young men typically involved in soccer offences, it comes as no great surprise that the 1990s represented a period of reflection and change for most involved in the game. Soccer hooliganism never stopped, nor has it since, but the research acknowledges that the cumulative impact of all these factors had a sobering, and transforming, effect on the game and those willing to re-think the relevance of 'football' in communities and in people's lives. But, despite occasional claims to the contrary, hooliganism never 'went away' (see Table 3.1).

Because sociology is correct in tracing the root causes of crowd violence to social structures and processes (or, what Dunning (2002b) and colleagues call 'fault lines' – such as gender, social class and jingoism), rather than situational factors (such as alcohol), it was always naive to think of hooliganism simply 'vanishing' or being 'policed out of existence' in a friendlier 'post-hooligan era.' It did neither, and can still be found, as Cashmore notes, 'lurking not too far beneath the surface' (2000: 179), bubbling up occasionally, though perhaps with less consistency than in the 'watershed' 1970s and 1980s.

By the turn of the millennium, the National Criminal Intelligence Service (NCIS), charged with overseeing the UK phenomenon, was again reporting major 'spikes' in incidents of disorder throughout the country. In 2008, a report by the Home Office noted that, while football-related arrests for offences of interpersonal violence (such as assault) had increased, arrests for missile throwing and racist chanting had dropped. Always difficult to interpret and trust (Frosdick and Newton 2006), official statistics from the UK suggested at this time that annual arrest rates had dropped from approximately 6,000 in the mid-1980s to 4,000 in 2009.[2]

By the turn of the century, dozens of anti-hooligan policing bodies had been assembled across Europe to investigate, control and anticipate hooliganism, and what started out as the most loosely organized, and loosely policed, of sports-related crowd problems had transformed into a matter of systematically coordinated and institutionalized criminal fan behaviour, sophisticated policing intelligence and deep cooperation between the clubs, their fan bases and the communities they represent. Today, hooliganism remains a problem and, clearly, racism, social class, sexism and other contributing social stimuli have not gone away. But there are positive changes. Among them, soccer hooligan discourse is as much about healthy, cooperative, sport-appreciating communities as it is about draconian and

TABLE 3.1 Recent cases of English soccer hooliganism

Date	Location	Incident/damage	Source
May 2011	Birmingham	Nine Aston Villa and Birmingham City fans were charged with violent disorder and jailed after taking part in disturbances following a derby game where police and police cars were pelted with bricks and bottles.	Birmingham Mail.net, 21 May 2011
May 2011	Doncaster	Approximately 35 fans of Doncaster Rovers and Leicester City fought two separate times on Hall Gate. Twelve men were arrested.	BBC News, 4 May 2011
December 2010	Birmingham	Following the conclusion of a Carling Cup match between Birmingham City and Aston Villa a riot broke out. City fans rushed the pitch after the game. Aston Villa fans ripped seats, threw flares, used CS gas against police and vandalized cars in the car park. A total of five people were arrested, and 27 people sustained injuries.	*Mail* online, 3 December 2010
August 2009	West Ham, London	Fan fighting and violent exchanges, involving hundreds of fans, broke out at Upton Park Tube Station when Millwall visited West Ham in the second round of the Carling Cup. Thirteen arrests were made. A 44-year-old man was stabbed at the London derby game attended by over 500 riot police.	Guardian. co.uk, 26 August 2009
May 2008	Manchester	The failure of a specially designed big screen area for ticketless Glasgow Rangers fans to watch the UEFA finals resulted in rioting between fans and police. Rangers fans destroyed a bus stop, damaged a bank and bounced a car across the road while clashing with police. A total of 15 people (including police) were hurt in the incident, and over 40 people were arrested.	BBC News, 15 May 2008
March 2007	Ipswich	A clash occurred between rivals Norwich City and Ipswich City at a train station. Ipswich fans lay in wait on the platform and ambushed the Norwich hooligans (returning from an unrelated match). Three people were injured and nine men were held in custody for conspiracy to cause violent disorder.	BBC News, 19 April 2007
February 2006	Stoke	Rival hooligans from Stoke City and Birmingham City attacked one another during and after the match. The altercation began when visiting fans ripped down the fence separating them. An undisclosed number of arrests were made.	BBC News, 20 February 2006

TABLE 3.1 *Continued*

Date	Location	Incident/damage	Source
July 2002	Burnley	Before a Division One match between Burnley and Nottingham Forest, a member of the so-called 'Suicide Youth Squad' (SYS) attacked a 17-year-old, smashing him over the head with a pint glass. The teenager died as a result of his injuries, and the member of the SYS was later charged with murder and sentenced to seven years in custody.	BBC News, 14 July 2002
May 2002	London	Following defeat by Birmingham in a Division One playoff match, Millwall fans clashed with police. Bricks, flares and various other missiles were launched at police. Seven people were arrested, while 100 police were injured, including three police horses.	BBC News, 13 September 2002

Sources:

(May 2011 incident) Aston Villa and Birmingham City hooligans jailed for mass battles. BirminghamMail. net, 21 May 2011. http://www.birminghammail.net/birmingham-sport/aston-villa-fc/aston-villa-news/2011/05/21/aston-villa-and-birmingham-city-football-hooligans-jailed-for-mass-battles-97319-28734905/.

(May 2011 incident) Doncaster versus Leicester football fight suspects held. BBC News, 4 May 2011. http://www.bbc.co.uk/news/uk-england-south-yorkshire-13287933.

(December 2010 incident) Have these mindless thugs put England's World Cup bid at risk? *Mail* online, 3 December 2010. http://www.dailymail.co.uk/news/article-1334849/Hooligans-hurled-flare-storming-pitch-putting-Englands-World-Cup-bid-risk.html.

(August 2009 incident) Hooliganism rears its head again to mar West Ham comeback. *The Guardian* online, 26 August 2009. Millwall v. West Ham game. http://www.guardian.co.uk/football/2009/aug/26/west-ham-millwall-report.

(May 2008 incident) UEFA fans clash with police. BBC News, 15 May 2008. http://news.bbc.co.uk/2/hi/7401814.stm.

(March 2007 incident) Hooligan suspects held in raids. BBC News, 19 April 2007. http://news.bbc.co.uk/2/hi/uk_news/england/nottinghamshire/6572069.stm.

(February 2006 incident) Football hooligans attack police. BBC News, 20 February 2006. http://news.bbc.co.uk/2/hi/uk_news/england/staffordshire/4730862.stm.

(July 2002 incident) Hooligan jailed for killing rival fan. BBC News, 14 July 2002. http://news.bbc.co.uk/2/hi/uk_news/england/lancashire/3065935.stm.

(May 2002 incident) Millwall riot stockbroker jailed. BBC News, 13 September 2002. http://news.bbc.co.uk/2/hi/uk_news/england/2256132.stm.

unidirectional policing. Fascinatingly, and likely critically, soccer fans themselves are routinely invited to participate in this multi-directional dialogue.

Explanations and perspectives

Once again, in terms of overall work produced, most sociological attention paid to sports violence, both empirically and theoretically speaking, has focused on forms and causes of British soccer hooliganism. In step with a popular, but inaccurate, perception that hooliganism began in the 1960s and 1970s (Dunning et al. 1988), with the publication of commissioned investigations (such as the Harrington (1968) and Lang (1969) Reports) and, as noted, with several tragic episodes resulting in multiple injuries and deaths at soccer games in the 1980s, the literature expanded rapidly during this period, though it has diminished somewhat since then. The debates between scholars on this issue have been complex and occasionally feisty, but certain strands within the research are identifiable and well-known.

The 'ethogenic' approach

One of the initial explanations of hooliganism was social psychological. Building on Lionel Tiger's (1969) study of aggression among *Men in Groups*, and on presumptions of the 'need' for male bonding, Peter Marsh et al. (1978) developed the 'Ritual of Soccer Violence Thesis' following observations at Oxford United FC. Employing a so-called 'ethogenic' method to explore the organization and motives of hooligan fans from, they claimed, an 'insider's' point of view, Marsh et al. (1978: 115) conceptualized aggression as a means of controlling the social world in the process of achieving certain outcomes. Therefore, crowd violence at soccer matches was viewed as a cultural adaptation to the working-class environment for male British adolescents – a 'ritual of teenage aggro.'

Emerging as it did in the mid–late 1970s, the Oxford School's work was precedent-setting, but it had several weaknesses that it has never been able to escape. For instance, the contention that hooliganism has ever represented a ritualistic 'fantasy' of violence has been heavily criticized, especially for failing to explain the regularity of serious injuries at soccer games, and for offering superficial explanations of the social class background of participants. There have always been, and remain, ritualistic elements to soccer 'aggro' in Britain and elsewhere (e.g. many of the crowd chants and gestures, and even aspects of inter-group provocation are certainly ritualistic), but to argue that the essence of hooliganism is ritualistic, and that actual violence seldom occurs, raises doubts about the potential of this approach, particularly when harmful hooligan encounters have been widely reported, routinely injurious and occasionally fatal.

The Marxist (social deprivation) approach

In the 1970s and 1980s, Marxist criminologist, Ian Taylor (e.g. 1971, 1987), offered a more macro-sociological, and class-sensitive, account of soccer violence. For Taylor, hooliganism was associated with two different phases in the development of the British game, and of British society, more generally. First, Taylor looked historically to the emergence of soccer in working-class communities, and to the disruptive effects of initial waves of commercialization on the game. Commercialization, he argued, fractured a formerly rich 'soccer subculture' that weaved its way through such communities. Practices such as the invasion of playing fields and vandalism were interpreted as attempts by the remnants of this subculture to reclaim a game that had become increasingly removed from its control. In the 1980s, and clearly moved by the tragic events at Bradford, Heysel and Hillsborough, Taylor revised portions of his earlier thesis to argue that contemporary manifestations of soccer hooliganism could be better understood if placed against crises of the British state. Specifically, he argued that an increasing dislocation within working-class communities and the development of an 'upper' working-class jingoism (or 'Little Englanderism') during the tenure of Prime Minister Margaret Thatcher's Conservative rule exacerbated Britain's hooliganism problem, and helped fuel a long sequence of xenophobically violent exchanges between fans of English club teams, and fans of the English national team and those of rival countries.

While sensitive to questions of history, social class and race, Taylor's work has been criticized for romanticizing any real 'control' working-class fans may ever have exerted over the game during its early phases, for ignoring very early 'hooligan' encounters (during, for instance, the early twentieth century and alleged 'soccer consciousness' phase), and for misidentifying the majority of hooligan fans as upper (and thus more educated, affluent and resourceful) working class. The fact that Taylor's ideas, while provocative, were never based on any acknowledged empirical programme has not helped their durability, although his attempts to offer a form of 'social deprivation thesis' has certainly influenced subsequent North American accounts of fan violence, as discussed below.

Theories of working-class subcultures

Taylor's approach to the effects of dynamic class culture on the development of the British game were echoed at approximately the same time by several writers at the Centre for Contemporary Cultural Studies at the University of Birmingham where, once again, soccer hooliganism was viewed as a reaction by young, working-class males to commercializing processes, such as the increasing presentation of soccer as a market commodity, emerging in what had traditionally been construed as 'the people's game.' Examining deep structural changes in working-class communities, Clarke (1978) and others added a rich subcultural and ethnographic component to their class analysis, allowing them to explain the presence in the 1960s and 1970s hooligan 'phases' of flamboyant skinhead groups combining traditional working-class values (such as the fierce defence of local and national identities, and a passion for soccer) with interests in commercial youth style.

Relating soccer hooliganism to the context of a culture in flux has proved a helpful framework of analysis (as enduring sociological threads are visible in the contemporary work on sport and youth culture – e.g. Redhead 1996, 2008), and the socio-historical approaches of Taylor, Clarke and others certainly offer considerably more explanatory insight into a complex social problem than the microsociological ventures of Marsh et al. However, as with Taylor's early work, Clarke and colleagues actually produced little concrete empirical data to support the argument that hooliganism was a response to changing working-class traditions and values. Stability of working-class social relations in an allegedly 'hooligan-free' past (i.e. in the pre-1960 era) was a view that both parties tended to assume too uncritically; this, again, has not gone unnoticed by critics.

The figurational approach

Perhaps the most recognized British approach emerged from the so-called 'Leicester School.' A group of sociologists (formerly based) at the University of Leicester examined the 'social roots' of British soccer hooliganism (cf. Williams et al. 1984; Dunning et al. 1988, 2002b; Murphy et al. 1990). Unlike Marsh and Taylor, however, the Eliasian/figurational work of the Leicester group was empirically grounded in comparisons of the phenomenon in its past and present 'figurations.' Essentially, Eric Dunning and his colleagues (Patrick Murphy, Ivan Waddington, John Williams and others) argue that aggressive standards of behaviour displayed by soccer hooligans are directly influenced by the social conditions and values inherent in the class-cultural background of those involved.

A predominant theme of their work, and one that represents a direct counterpoint to Taylor's 'Little England' thesis, is that hooligan groups are largely comprised of individuals from the 'roughest' (rather than 'upper') sectors of the working classes. They argue that the hooligan's relatively deprived social condition is instrumental in the production and reproduction of normative modes of behaviour, including strong emphases on notions of territory, male dominance and physicality. It is precisely the reproduction of this social condition that is seen to lead to the development of a specific violent masculine style manifested regularly in the context of soccer, and sport more generally. Notions of dynamic territoriality are also offered, which allow the Leicester researchers to account for the shifting allegiances of fan support (and thus shifting expressions of fan violence) at local, regional and international levels. While there are several unique features to the ideas of the 'Leicester School,' perhaps the most important is the adoption of a long-term Eliasian view regarding the development of soccer hooliganism, which allows them to demonstrate that forms of spectator disorder have existed for over a century, and to explain respective 'civilizing' and 'de-civilizing' phases in the phenomena. Figurational research has been heavily influential in Britain and internationally, both within the academy and with policy makers.

Other approaches

The first three of these approaches – ethogenic, Marxist and subcultural – are dated and their application to understanding British soccer violence today is questionable. Because it is more roundedly sociological (there is also, literally, much more of it to judge from), the figurational approach has more enduring appeal. But while all four approaches remain widely recognized and cited, none of them are fully satisfactory, and they do not represent the complete spectrum of work available on the phenomenon. Other studies that have contributed to the British 'hooligan debate' since the 1980s include: Murray's (1984, 1988) social histories of religious sectarianism in Scottish football; King's (1997, 1998) studies of sport as a historical outgrowth of spectator 'consumption'; Robins' (1984) account of the intersections between soccer violence and the popular cultural interests of young British men; Armstrong's

(1998) anthropological work on idealized masculinity and fan identity; Giulianotti's (1994, 1995, 1999) ethnographic studies of Scottish fans; Bairner's studies of soccer, violence and gender in Northern Ireland (1995, 1999); Redhead's (1996) postmodernist account of how hooliganism has been 'pacified' by market forces and commercial interests; and, Kerr's (2004) psychological perspective that explains crowd violence as an outcome of 'reversing' 'meta-motivational states,' such as boredom (see Chapter 1). Finally, existing 'knowledge' also derives (albeit less compellingly) from a dizzying cluster of speculative, journalistic and voyeuristic 'insider' accounts, often by former participants, that sometimes mock 'removed' sociological accounts (e.g. Buford 1991; Hornby 1992; Brimson and Brimson 1996; King 1996; Ward 1996; Francis and Walsh 1997; Kuper 1997; Brimson 1999).

North America

Manifestations

It has been several decades since *Newsweek* magazine proclaimed that 'the spectacle of the ugly American sports fan has been assuming increasingly frightful proportions' (17 June 1974: 93) and, similarly referring to 'increasingly brutal spectator outbursts and injuries to participants,' Yeager (1977) insisted that crowd disorder was 'the new violence in [North American] sports' (p. 161). In fact, neither claim was accurate. Fan violence in North America certainly did not begin in the 1970s. And, although there is evidence that particular manifestations of the phenomenon (such as missile throwing) were becoming more widely reported in the media and that they were being freshly constructed as 'new' social problems (Young 1988), there was, at that time, little hard evidence to suggest that they were escalating. There remains a startling lack of empirical research on crowd disorder in North America, and systematic quantitative work (which would provide a sense of scale and frequency) simply does not exist. But concern endures about what Winer (2011: 102) recently described as 'bleacher creatures, bottle-throwers, couch torchers, sexual harassers, projectile vomiters, and serially indifferent bandwagon-hoppers' throughout the world of (North) American sport. North American sports crowd problems may not be as institutionalized in shape, size and regularity as their European counterparts, or as ominous in their perceived threat, but they are real enough to the authorities, as Chapter 6 goes on to show.

Consider the following recent episodes from five of North America's most popular spectator sports:

- Amid scenes of vandalism and mass fighting, police use 'pepper guns' to disperse an unruly crowd, killing a college student who is struck in the eye by one of their 'bullets' (Major League Baseball (MLB), Boston, 2004).
- Fans pelting the field with thousands of bottles and other missiles prompt both teams and officials to take cover (National Football League (NFL), Cleveland, 2001).

- Male and female fans fight and one man attempts to strangle another, resulting in arrests and ejections (US Open, Pebble Beach, 2010).
- Following a play-off game, thousands of fans gather and fight on a downtown street. Two men in their twenties are stabbed and 49 arrests are made. To allow ambulances to reach the stabbing victims, police use tear gas to disperse the crowd (NHL, Edmonton, 2006).
- Fans throw bottles, vandalize over a dozen police cars and buses, start bonfires and loot a gas station. Over 20 fans are arrested and five police officers are injured (NBA, Los Angeles, 2009).

These incidents are not weekly occurrences, but neither are they rare. Although the research on fan violence in North America has often been impressionistic and the explanations frail (unlike the European scenario, ethnographies of North American fans are virtually non-existent), there is copious evidence to suggest that North American sports crowds have expressed their own versions of 'aggro' with regularity for many decades, although, again, in a far less institutionalized way. Whether one focuses on mêlées breaking out at 'prize fights' at the turn of the twentieth century, brawling baseball and football fans during the inter-war years, or destructive post-event outbursts throughout the last quarter of the twentieth century and now into the twenty-first century, it is clear that North American crowd violence is neither new nor uncommon (Atyeo 1979; Smith 1983; Guttmann 1986; Young 1988, 2002a; Dunning 1999). Indeed, those convinced that rambunctious North American sports crowds are very recent phenomena, or are restricted to any single sport, would do well to recall that one of the longest and most destructive of all North American sports riots followed an ice-hockey game in Montreal in the mid-1950s (Katz 1955; Duperrault 1981; Young 1988; Bélanger 1999), long before the contemporary trend in post-event rioting more typically associated with football, basketball and baseball emerged. The so-called 'Rocket Richard Riots' lasted two days, resulted in dozens of injuries and caused thousands of dollars in damage.[3]

Who riots?

Because in-depth empirical research is scarce (there is a modest psychological and sociological literature that is in need of updating – e.g. Smith 1975, 1976; Arms et al. 1979a, 1979b; Case and Boucher 1981; Lewis 1982; Smith 1983; Young 1988; Goldstein 1989; Wann et al. 2001; Russell 2008), information on the demographics of North American sports crowd disorder is limited to police, sports team and media reports, which are not always credible or accurate. Almost none of it is quantitative (Young 1988). Although the following characteristics repeatedly surface in crowd disorder episodes and are familiar to the authorities, they provide us with no more than a rudimentary outline of who is involved in certain articulations of the phenomenon.

While there are occasional cases of females involved in North American fan violence, most offenders tend to be young males. This suggests that, as with other forms of physical violence, North American sports crowd disorder is both gendered and, normally, a youthful activity. Both casual attendees and season-ticket holders have been involved in a variety of disorderly practices. Apart from Listiak's (1981) outdated case-specific study of class-related bar behaviour during the Canadian Football League's 'Grey Cup,' and preliminary thumbnail sketches offered by Lewis (1982), Smith (1983) and Wann et al. (2001), very little is known about the social class background of offenders. However, since some of the rowdiest crowds on the continent are, for example, US college football crowds,[4] a positive correlation between poor education and involvement in disorder should not be assumed, while a high level of education should not automatically be seen as preventing involvement in crowd disorder. Illustrating public perceptions of the role played by rowdy college crowds, CNN recently referred to fan violence as a 'campus craze' (CNN Education 2004), and USA Today estimated that there are between 10–15 seriously riotous college episodes annually (MacDonald 2004).

The scattered ejection report data that are available (Young 1988; Gramling 2001) indicate that among the varied occupational groups represented by ejected rowdy or abusive fans are middle-class professionals. For example, during the 1995 New York Giants' season finale, 'among those ejected were lawyers, doctors, teachers, firefighters [and] a middle-school principal' (Gramling 2001: 143). Similarly, a judge presiding over infractions at home games of the Philadelphia Eagles noted that '95 per cent of the people arrested live in the suburbs and the majority are college educated. I've had a US Senator's aide in my court, law enforcement people, [and] people in the business world' (Buckley 2002: 13).

Data from teams in four professional leagues (NBA, NFL, Canadian Football League (CFL), MLB) in the 1980s strongly indicated that the majority of offenders in crowd ejections and other stadium-based disturbances were white (Young 1988). However, there is also evidence that race and youth factors have coalesced in disorderly crowd behaviour in both Canada and the US, especially with respect to non-white street gang involvement in post-events conflicts (Johnson 1993; Nelson 1994).

The majority of incidents of fan-to-fan violence occurring at North American sports involve individuals or small groups of spectators participating in activities such as common assault, drunken and disorderly behaviour, and confrontations with authorities. Less frequently, larger episodes have occurred. These have taken place both inside as well as outside stadia and are often related to post-event 'celebrations.' Generally speaking, collective episodes of fan fighting, especially involving rival groups, are less common in North America than, for instance, at British soccer events, although certain teams have become well-known for the consistently hostile behaviour of their fans. This has prompted efforts to 'retake' stadium sections from chronically violent fans by temporarily closing them.

Fan violence in North America is not limited to any one behaviour. A number of practices have become familiar to the authorities. Far from mutually exclusive, these practices are often linked and manifested simultaneously.

Missile throwing

There is substantial evidence that North American fans have participated in missile throwing (i.e. the projection of objects onto the playing surface or at participants or fans) for many decades. Players as far back as the 1930s and 1940s have complained of being struck by cans, bottles, batteries, coins and other missiles launched from the bleachers (stands) (Runfola 1976; Greenberg 1977; Green 1984). As Gramling's (2001: 143) and Winer's (2011) more recent accounts suggest, the tradition continues.

The numerous missiles thrown from the stands onto the playing surface during the projectile-riddled 1996 World Series included batteries, cans, bottles and food (*Sports Illustrated*, 4 November 1996: 20). Several further incidents took place in 1999: at a college football game in Colorado in September, student fans threw bottles at police and sprayed them with mace when their attempts to destroy the goalposts were thwarted (*National Post*, 6 September 1999: B2); in October, a Denver Broncos player almost lost an eye after being struck by a ball of ice (*Sports Illustrated*, 13 December 1999: 27); and, in December, fans of the Vancouver Grizzlies pelted Houston Rockets rookie Steve Francis (who had previously declined an opportunity to play for the Grizzlies) with tennis balls and coins (*Sports Illustrated*, 13 December 1999: 27). At a 2001 Cleveland Browns NFL game, fans 'hurled snowballs at a TV cameraman because he was "blocking the view". The victim continued to be pelted as he lay unconscious in a snowdrift while receiving medical attention' (Gramling 2001: 142).

Numerous sports have been affected by missile throwing, but the evidence suggests that baseball and football have been particularly targeted. Missiles retrieved by ground staff at US college football stadia include flagrantly dangerous objects such as golf balls, and marshmallows weighted with coins and sharpened metal have been reported by game officials to have been thrown with some regularity by the often huge college football crowds (Herbert 1994; Riseling 1994). At the Oakland Coliseum, the home field of the NFL's Oakland Raiders, fans have 'hit players with nails, golf balls, bottle caps and coins' (Owen 2001: 16). Troublingly, the use of such objects by crowd members clearly hints at the preconceived, rather than the spontaneous, nature of the practice, for one hardly arrives at a football game with such objects 'accidentally.'

Although missiles have been a fairly common form of fan disorder in both North America and the UK in certain sports, a significant difference may lie in their intended targets. In the UK, the use of ammunition and missiles aimed by soccer hooligans at rival fan groups, players of the opposing team, and the police inside and outside the ground has been a recognizable aspect of hooligan deportment since the 1970s (Marsh et al. 1978; Murphy and Williams 1979) whereas, in North America, missiles appear to have been more commonly thrown at players – sometimes one's own – or with the possible intent of disrupting play. Incidents of one group of fans attacking a rival group with missiles exist, but they are infrequent. Also noteworthy, however, are missile assaults upon police by unruly fans in post-event incidents, such as the 1994 and 2011 Vancouver cases (British Columbia Police Commission 1994; City of Vancouver 1994; Vancouver Police Department 1995) and the 2000 Los Angeles case (*Daily Mail*, 21 June 2000: 27; Kane and Sinoski 2011: A1).

Use of weapons

Couched in terms of the wider concern about the place of weapons in North American, and particularly American, society, especially among young people, there has been much conjecture about the presence and use of weapons at North American sports events. No systematic research has been carried out on the matter, however. This is not to say that weapons are not smuggled into sports stadia. Confiscations show that, in fact, they are. The following examples provide a sense of the forms that weapon use assume:

- Crowd violence at Toronto high school basketball games in the 1990s became so persistent that security measures, including the hiring of armed guards, were significantly increased before, during and after games. One guard claimed that 'searches now routinely turn up small knives, scissors, and [other] makeshift weapons' (*Toronto Star*, 22 January 1995: A6).
- Gunfire erupted at a 1996 high school football game in Monrovia, California, wounding two people and sending terrified fans rushing from the bleachers (*Boston Globe*, 5 October 1996: 72).
- A man posing as part of the official 'Honour Guard' at a 2010 Michigan vs. Michigan State football game, where 113,000 people had collected, carried two concealed M16 rifles onto the field before being apprehended and removed by police (http://www.huffingtonpost.com/2010/10/21/m16toting-fan-got-inside-_n_771369.html).

The fact that weapons have been used in violent exchanges during post-event disorder again raises troubling questions for the authorities. First, as it has done with European soccer hooliganism, it forces us to ask what proportion of fans arrive at sports events armed, and to what extent an act, or threat, of sports crowd disorder involves premeditation and pre-planning (Murphy et al. 1990: 11). Second, since armed rioters in post-event incidents have been known to join the fray without actually attending the game, it seems inaccurate and misleading to attribute all of the damage and injury incurred in those contexts to sport spectators per se. In general, where the use of weapons is concerned, we can say that observational reports suggest that weapon use is an ongoing concern in some sports-related disorders. Many of the aforementioned missiles obviously qualify as 'weapons' in terms of the way that they are used, as do the mace and tear gas deployed by college football fans at the Colorado vs. Colorado State game in September 1999 (*National Post*, 6 September 1999: B2). However, the only valid way of summarizing the current state of knowledge on this issue is that we actually know very little in a definitive sense, and that no consistent patterns have been identified.

Field invasion

While field invasions are statistically uncommon in North American sports, there were nevertheless many citable cases throughout the second half of the twentieth century. Incidents have generally been associated with victory celebrations occurring on, and around, the playing areas of certain sports. In baseball, for instance, when the New York Mets won the World Series in 1969, jubilant fans burst onto the Shea Stadium field and proceeded to rip up the sod and home plate. Numerous championship victories in baseball and football since then have been followed by similar episodes.

However, not all field invasion cases have been related to victory celebrations, as the following widely documented examples illustrate:

- In the summer of 1974, the Cleveland Indians promoted a 'Nickel Beer Night' at a game due to be played against the Texas Rangers. The plan backfired when fans, many of whom were intoxicated, bombarded players and officials with bricks, cans and bottles. A riot ensued in which dozens of players and officials were injured, and the game was forfeited to Texas (*New York Times*, 6 June 1999: 35).
- In the summer of 1977, a promotional 'Disco Demolition Night' was hosted by the Chicago White Sox. Fans gained entry into the Comiskey Park 'double-header' with a disco record and 98 cents. The idea, which was to destroy the unpopular disco records on the field of play between games, backfired when up to 7,000 fans used them as missiles and started a riot in which bases, turf and the batting cage were destroyed. The second game was abandoned (Snyder and Spreitzer 1983: 202).

Though exclusively game-centred explanations for fan violence have justifiably received criticism for ignoring the larger sociological context giving rise to sports crowd disorder, the Chicago and Cleveland cases clearly show that the particulars of game contexts – what Smelser (1962) and other collective behaviour theorists have termed 'precipitating factors' – should not be overlooked. In the Chicago case, the club came under heavy criticism for not having the foresight to expect problems at a mid-summer's 'double-header' involving cheap beer, cheap tickets and a potentially dangerous hand-missile. Of course, the capacity for such events to backfire so embarrassingly also emphasizes the need for careful security preparations in hosting sports events. That said, it seems reasonable to argue that all the preparation in the world is insufficient at times. There was, for example, no way that, when painters caps were given away free at a New York Jets NFL game, the New York Sports and Exposition Authority could have anticipated that sections of the crowd would have responded by setting them on fire (Gramling 2001: 143).

As with other dimensions of North American sports crowd disorder, we simply do not know enough about the motives and expressions of field invasion. Furthermore, a cautious approach is important since it is easy to assume that field invasions are the result of fan frustrations or violent intent, which is not necessarily the case as, interestingly enough, Dunning et al. (1988: 102) previously found with 'pitch' invasions in British soccer. While the Chicago and Cleveland cases do suggest such motives, they are not statistically normative, and it must be said that North American incidents of encroachment onto the playing surface appear to be more celebratory than intentionally destructive to date.

Property destruction and vandalism

Once again, property destruction and vandalism at North American stadia have most commonly been associated with team victory revelry in play-off and other high-profile games (Gramling 2001: 142). Although these behaviours have usually been linked to post-event celebration and rioting, isolated incidents have occurred which demonstrate that this type of disorder can also be a response to team defeat or action involving the players. At the end of the 1986 baseball season, for example, the New York Mets' failure to clinch the National League East title in Philadelphia resulted in approximately 1,000 fans rioting. In a scene similar to some British hooligan scenarios and which suggests that such events can potentially happen in North America if the conditions are 'right,' dozens of seats were ripped from their moorings by Mets fans and used as ammunition against players, officials and police. More recently, two people were arrested and an official was injured when a chair-throwing mêlée broke out after a heavyweight boxing event in Atlantic City. According to press reports, over 50 people were involved in the disturbance, which occurred after one boxer was knocked out of the ring by his opponent (*Calgary Herald*, 8 November 1999: C8).

Further, fans of both collegiate and professional football have been associated with goalpost destruction, and even goalpost theft, for several decades. Most persons familiar with football culture would testify to this rather peculiar ritual, especially as it appears at the college level. Goalposts have been dismantled or removed at numerous college venues including several Canadian universities (*McMaster University Silhouette*, 28 October 1982: 5), Yale University (where an 18-year-old Harvard student was critically injured when a metal section of the posts fell on her head), Northwestern University, University of Illinois, and so frequently at Penn State University games in the 1980s that the Athletic Department 'offered $4,500, [then] the cost of new ones, to the Student Activities Fund if fans refrained from tearing down any more' (*Sports Illustrated*, 28 November 1983: 27). Dozens of other colleges and universities across the continent have experienced and continue to experience similar problems (*National Post*, 6 September 1999: B2). At the professional level, after a last-second-winning field goal in the 1998 season, hundreds of fans of the NFL's St Louis Cardinals yanked on the goalposts 'for half an hour to no avail before . . . giving up and settling for parading the netting down Mill Avenue outside the stadium' (Gramling 2001: 145).

As a result of these and other unruly fan practices, it is not uncommon for stadia personnel to smear goalposts with grease, and for playing areas to receive a significant police presence (replete with 'attack' dogs, horses and other protections) at the conclusion of games. One of the ugliest and most injurious pre-2000 field invasion episodes occurred at the University of Wisconsin-Madison in 1993. In a scene in some ways eerily reminiscent of the television pictures of the infamous 1985 Heysel Stadium (Young 1986; Taylor 1987) and 1989 Hillsborough (Taylor 1989) tragedies, organizers watched helplessly, making numerous announcements, as thousands of fans poured onto the playing area. In the Wisconsin case, dozens of fans dismantled the goalposts as injured fans receiving medical attention lay sprawled about them. Over 70 people were injured, six critically. Mounted police horses were brought in to enable ambulances to access the playing area (*Sports Illustrated*, 8 November 1993: 60–65; Beecher 1994: 24).[5]

Clearly, there are both ritualistic and dangerous aspects to the convention of goalpost destruction. The ratio of harmful-to-harmless incidents is not known, nor is the regularity with which injury is caused. But we do know that serious injuries have occurred and that stadium, college and city authorities have considered the practice a sufficient threat to tighten local policy and to protect against the potentially harmful outcomes of the practice. This has occurred on a widespread basis and at numerous levels at which football is played (e.g. school, college or professional).

Fan fighting

There is compelling evidence that crowd violence, such as fan fighting, has fundamentally sociological, as opposed to situational, causes (cf. Smith 1983; Dunning et al. 1988; Coakley 1998), and that parallel causes can be traced across various sports and geographic settings. However, this is neither to suggest that aspects of the phenomenon such as fighting are uni-causal, nor to deny the significance of 'situational' factors. For instance, perhaps partly due to the unique social and structural context of North American sport (e.g. travel on a huge continent is geographically and financially prohibitive; fan support between numerous sports and levels of sport is widely distributed; team franchises are extremely mobile; high season-ticket sales are normative etc.), fan fighting at North American sports has not expressed itself in terms of the ritualized rival gang episodes of British and European soccer, and certainly organized 'super crews' or 'firms' of fighters in the English sense have not appeared to date. No discernible or reliable pattern is known at this point with respect to involvement in fighting by season-ticket holders and casual attendees.

The majority of incidents of fan-to-fan aggression occurring at North American games involve individuals or small groups of supporters participating in activities such as common assault, drunken and disorderly behaviour, and confrontations with police (Young 1988). Less frequently, episodes of fighting involving larger numbers of fans have occurred (e.g. *Sports Illustrated*, 13 October 1980: 29; *Los Angeles Times*, 25 November 1986: 3). In 1985, over the course of three days of baseball between Toronto and Detroit, more than 200 fans were ejected for fighting and drunkenness and, at a 1996 boxing event at Madison Square Gardens, a post–contest riot involving dozens of fighting fans lasted 30 minutes and injured 22 people (*Sports Illustrated*, 19 August 1996: 58–63). More recently, and according to Gramling (2001: 142):

> So many fights broke out in the stands at [Philadelphia Eagles'] Veterans Stadium that in November 1997, the City of Philadelphia set up a municipal courtroom in the bowels of Veterans Stadium to dole out stiff penalties to the drunk and disorderly. The guilty had 60 days to pay fines of $150 to $300 or they went to jail.

Generally speaking, collective episodes of fan fighting, especially involving rival groups, are far more rare in North America than in, for instance, British soccer, although certain teams (such as the New York Yankees, the Philadelphia Eagles and Phillies, the Boston Red Sox and the Oakland Raiders) have become infamous for the consistently bellicose behaviour of some of their fans. In the latter case, the rowdiest Raiders fans congregate in a lower-deck, end-zone section known dauntingly as the 'Black Hole,' a section made all the more threatening to away players by the fact that it is closer to the field than any other end zone in the NFL (Owen 2001: 16). Fan 'aggro' has prompted, in the cases of several teams, efforts to 'retake' stadium sections from chronically violent fans by closing them. Similar attempts by British soccer clubs throughout the 1970s and 1980s to make stadia safer by closing sections of the 'ends' (areas of the stadium known for rowdy territorial fan behaviour) have been widely reported and critiqued (cf. Murphy et al. 1990: 90–91).[6]

Post-event riots

A major concern for colleges, universities and communities across the continent, and perhaps the most predictable and widely publicized form of North American fan disorder, is the 'post-event riot.' (Since these incidents can follow team victory *or* defeat, the broadly adopted term 'celebration riot' is misleading.) Mass inebriation, fighting, looting, vandalism, arson, vehicle destruction and physical and sexual assaults have occurred during these episodes.

Cases can be found throughout the twentieth century, with the period of the 1970s–1990s perhaps being worst in terms of frequency, damage toll to persons and property, and arrest rates. The locations of post-event riots following professional sports events include, but are not limited to: New York (1969), Pittsburgh (1971), Philadelphia (1980), Toronto (1983), Detroit (1984, 1990), San Francisco (1985), Chicago (1991, 1992, 1993, 1996, 1997), Dallas (1993, 1994), Montreal (1986, 1993, 2008, 2010), Vancouver (1994, 2011), Denver (1998, 1999), Boston (2004, 2007), Calgary (2004), Edmonton (2006) and Los Angeles (2000, 2010) (see Table 3.2). Probably the most catastrophic injury toll related to a post-event riot is eight deaths in Detroit in 1990 – in addition to dozens of arrests and injuries related directly to the behaviour of 'celebrating' fans, four people were killed by an errant driver. After three consecutive Chicago Bulls NBA World Championships

TABLE 3.2 Post-event riots in North America: select cases, 1971–2011

Date	Location	Event	Incident/damage	Source
June 2011	Vancouver	Canucks lose Stanley Cup Finals to Boston Bruins	Sections of a crowd of over 100,000 fans become involved in a stand-off with police, setting fifteen cars on fire (two of which were police cars), smashing windows of stores and businesses, and looting. Riot squads use tear gas and pepper spray to disperse the crowd. Over 100 arrests are made, and dozens of people are injured.	*Calgary Herald*, 16 June 2011
May 2010	Montreal	Canadiens win NHL play-off game against Pittsburgh Penguins	Stores are looted and windows smashed. Police resist missile-throwing fans using truncheons and tear gas.	*Toronto Star*, 1 June 2010
June 2006	Edmonton	Oilers beat Annaheim Mighty Ducks to advance to NHL Western Conference Final	Store windows are smashed, telephone booths overturned and multiple fires set on Whyte Ave. Over 10 arrests.	CBC News, 29 May 2006
October 2004	Boston	Red Sox win World Series	Firecrackers and small fires set during a riot, and restaurant windows smashed. Police use 'pepper ball guns,' resulting in the death of a 21-year old woman. Eight arrests and 16 minor injuries result.	*Boston Globe*, 22 October 2004
January 2003	Oakland	Raiders lose NFL Super Bowl to Tampa Bay Buccaneers	Police use rubber bullets and tear gas to disperse fans who smash windows and set cars on fire (including nine Fire Dept. vehicles and 12 police cars). Over 80 arrests, mostly for public drunkenness and disorder. Three firefighters injured.	*Calgary Herald*, 28 January 2003
February 2002	Salt Lake City	2002 Winter Olympics	In the fading hours of the Olympic Games, patrons are turned away from a beer garden. A stand-off ensues between them and police. Despite garnering little media attention, the incident is referred to locally as the 'Olympic beer riot.'	AlterNet, 25 February 2002
June 2000	Los Angeles	Lakers win NBA World Championship	Vandalism, arson, and fighting among fans provoke police into using rubber bullets and batons as players are detained inside the Staples Center for several hours until rioting subsides. Approximately 12	*The Observer*, 21 June 2000

TABLE 3.2 *Continued*

Date	Location	Event	Incident/damage	Source
			people are injured and same number arrested.	
June 1994	Vancouver	Canucks lose in NHL Stanley Cup Final	Police react to 70,000 disgruntled fans using tear gas and a fatal rubber bullet. One person is killed, 200 injured (including eight police officers). 50 arrests, and approximately $500,000 in damage.	*Maclean's*, 27 June 1994
June 1993	Chicago	Bulls win third consecutive NBA title	Two dead, 682 arrests, shops looted, cars burned, $150,000 in damage.	*Sports Illustrated*, 5 July 1993
June 1993	Montreal	Canadiens win NHL Stanley Cup	168 injured (including 49 police officers), over 100 arrests, cars and stores destroyed and $5 million in damage.	*Maclean's*, 21 June 1993
February 1993	Dallas	Cowboys win NFL Super Bowl	Fighting, vandalism and looting results in 26 injured, 25 arrests and $150,000 property damage.	Dallas Police Dept. (personal communication)
June 1992	Chicago	Bulls win second consecutive NBA title	Over 1000 arrests, two police officers shot, 90 others injured. 14 fires set, and two 'celebrants' seriously burned.	*Calgary Herald*, 16 June 1992
June 1990	Detroit	Pistons win NBA title	Eight people die, hundreds injured in fighting, including stabbings and gunfire. Over 100 arrests.	*Calgary Herald*, 16 June 1990
November 1986	Hamilton, Ontario	Tiger-Cats win CFL Grey Cup	Fires and vandalism resulting in $55,000 in damage, 13 arrests and one police officer hospitalized.	*Hamilton Spectator*, 1 December 1986
May 1986	Montreal	Canadiens win NHL Stanley Cup	Several thousand fans gather in downtown Montreal, 20 stores are looted, six arrests, 76 charges of mischief and breaking and entering laid and $1 million in damage.	*Globe and Mail*, 26–27 May 1986
October 1984	Detroit	Tigers win World Series	One dead, 80 injured, 41 arrested, cars overturned and burned, mass looting and $100,000 in property damage.	*Time*, 29 October 1984
November 1983	Toronto	Argonauts win CFL Grey Cup	$100,000 tab for thefts and vandalism, and 22 fans charged with criminal offences.	*Toronto Daily Star*, 29 November 1983
October 1971	Pittsburgh	Pirates win World Series	Over 100 arrests, over 100 injured, 30 shops looted, two sexual assaults, eight armed robberies and 4 vehicles overturned.	*Time*, 29 October 1984

between 1991–1993, the cumulative damage reported by Chicago police included 1,700 arrests, over 100 police cars burned or destroyed, two people shot dead and approximately $8 million in damages to property. After the defeat of the Vancouver Canucks to the New York Rangers in the 1994 Stanley Cup Final (following a game played in New York), up to 70,000 people poured into the Vancouver downtown core. Police deployed tear gas to disperse the crowd and fired a fatal rubber bullet. Over 200 people were injured, 50 people were arrested and dozens of shops and properties were damaged. Following the LA Lakers' 2000 NBA World Championship victory, police battled rioting fans outside the Los Angeles Staples Center, trapping other fans, players and celebrities inside for several hours. Twelve people were injured and a further dozen arrested. Similar episodes occurred in Los Angeles during the NBA World Championship in 2010. And, most recently, in a replay of the 1994 riot in the same city, after the Vancouver Canucks lost to Boston in the final game of the 2011 NHL Stanley Cup Finals, a three-hour period of rioting, featuring riot squads and tear gas, led to over 100 arrests, 15 cars being burned (including two police cars), dozens of people injured and hospitalized, and at least four stabbings (Kane and Sinoski 2011: A1).

The policing and understanding of such episodes are made none the easier by the fact that many participants are known not to have attended the event in question or in fact to be sport spectators at all. For example, several post-event troubles in Chicago and Detroit in the early 1990s displayed evidence of street-gang involvement and have led to concerns with so-called 'band-wagoning' during these occasions. In the aforementioned 2011 Vancouver NHL riots, the Mayor of Vancouver explicitly blamed the incident on 'anarchists and criminals' (Kane and Sinoksi 2011: A1). At the time of writing, police investigations continue, and the validity of his claim is unlikely, but unclear.

In sum, relatively speaking, North American sports crowd disorder may not have posed as ominous, or consistent, a problem as its European counterpart, but there is more than enough evidence to suggest that the view, still tightly held onto in some quarters, that there is no 'serious' or 'patterned' fan violence in North American sport is severely, and perhaps dangerously, flawed.

Explanations and perspectives

Given the cultural resonance of sport in North American life, and abundant historical and contemporary evidence of crowd violence, remarkably little systematic sociological research has actually been conducted on the phenomenon. Many of the existing assessments are speculative rather than empirically tested, and a considerable portion of this work is journalistic and psychological rather than sociological. In general, it is fair to say that much of this work is weakly theorized, ahistorical or outdated. It is certainly true that the trenchant historical examinations and the rich ethnographies of fan violence in the UK and continental Europe have not been replicated in North America. However, at least three general explanatory strands may be identified in the research.

Social and psychological conflicts

Under this heading, a number of early attempts were made to explain crowd disorder in terms of tensions that emerged in the second half of the twentieth century between the fan, the athlete and society. They may be linked, in general terms, with Rollo May's (1972) observation that all humans require some sense of personal and group significance in their lives. They also share thematic similarities with Ian Taylor's early explanations of soccer hooliganism in the UK, which essentially focus on spectator problems as outcomes of post-war changes both in the game of British soccer itself and, more importantly, in changes in the relationship of fans to the game (Taylor 1971). Fimrite (1976), for example, argued that workplace and family pressures in American society cause widespread social frustration that becomes vented by crowd members at sports events. Similarly, Fontana (1978) proposed that violent conduct in a sports crowd could be explained in terms of a loss of individuality in an increasingly competitive, fractured and impersonal society. From these vantage points, disorder is seen as an attempt to reassert individualism and personal distinctness in a culturally resonant setting.

Based on these and similar assumptions, a so-called 're-integration' thesis emerged in the 1960s and 1970s focusing on spectators' needs to re-establish forms of group identification (Beisser 1967; Petryszak 1977). In the words of Irving Goldaber, founder of the now defunct Centre for the Study of Crowd and Spectator Behavior in Miami: 'There are increasing numbers of people who are deeply frustrated because they feel they have very little power over their lives. They come to sporting events to experience, vicariously, a sense of power' (cited in Gilbert and Twyman 1983: 71). More recently, Wann and colleagues (Branscombe and Wann 1992; Wann 1993; Wann et al. 1999) have also emphasized the notion of spectators' needs for (social and psychological sources of) identification by suggesting that certain aspects of crowd violence emerge in a process where fans 'over-identify' with a particular team.

Also under the aegis of broad 'social conflicts taking place in society' fall approaches that account for crowd violence by looking at other ways that society is stratified, such as religion, race and ethnicity. For example, numerous race-related riots at US high school and college football and basketball games in the 1960s and 1970s support Edwards' (1973) early claim that crowd violence may develop out of racial tensions. In Canada, Levitt and Shaffir (1987) have shown how the Christie Pits softball riots in Toronto in 1933 resulted from a series of anti-Semitic acts perpetrated by English Canadians. The Montreal 'Rocket Richard Riots' of March 1955 have also been interpreted in terms of ethnic hostilities between anglophone and francophone Canadians (Katz 1955; Duperrault 1981; Bélanger 1999). More recently, a spate of mass fighting at Toronto high school basketball games and numerous post-event riots show clear evidence of an interface between crowd violence, youth gangs, social class and race, and legal sources linked to post-event riot episodes in Detroit and Chicago have drawn similar conclusions (Nelson 1994). Further, as has been shown with soccer hooliganism in the UK (Dunning et al.

1988; Murphy et al. 1990; Dunning 1999), it is quite clear that crowd violence in North America, as with sports violence more broadly, is a largely male domain. In this sense, it seems imperative to understand crowd violence as a practice that intersects with wider codes of gender expression and ordering.

The celebratory nature of sport

A second set of explanations for crowd violence in North American sport is based on the notion that the structural organization and culture of sport encourages expressive, and often aggressive, behaviour by players and fans alike, normally under carnival-like conditions. Because many sports spectators have an informed knowledge of their game, they can immediately identify the significance of an event either in terms of seasonal goals (e.g. making the play-offs, winning championships etc.) or in terms of the relations and rivalries that have developed historically between the contestants or, in some cases, the fans. Unlike crowds in other social contexts, the result is that sports crowds show a vested interest – a 'fanaticism' – in the outcome of the event at hand. Combined with factors caused by aggregation (such as physical closeness, milling, tension and noise), sporting contests are thus characterized by emotionally charged behaviour on the part of participants and spectators alike where proceedings can, under the appropriate conditions, 'get out of hand.'

Adopting this approach, Listiak (1981) and Manning (1983) demonstrate how sports events are settings for organized public celebrations. Listiak, for example, used the context of the CFL's 'Grey Cup' celebrations to show how widespread public revelry, and in some cases disorder, are often excused by authorities, as well as local business people such as bar owners. In a study of the macro and micro aspects of North American sports crowd disorder, Young (1988) showed that stadium vandalism and the now infamous post-event riot are consistent forms of such excessive behaviour that have been rationalized by those responsible for organizing sport and, at times, both under- and over-policed by the authorities.

Precipitating factors at sports events

A third explanatory theme zones in on aspects of the sports event itself as likely precursors to crowd disturbances. For example, early work by Smith (1976) examined crowd violence at a number of soccer games using Smelser's (1962) 'value-added' theory of collective behaviour. Focusing on Smelser's notion of 'structural conduciveness,' Smith found one of the most common causes of crowd hostility to be player violence and unpopular decisions by officials. Careful also to emphasize the social causes of violence, these findings led Smith to suggest that crowd violence grows out of both situational and broader social tensions: 'Sport probably often exacerbates the very strains that initially give rise to collective hostility' (p. 205). Following Edwards and Rackages (1977), White (1970) and Lewis (1982), Smith (1983) went on to validate the 'violence-precipitates-violence' hypothesis using examples of crowd disturbances from several sports including ice hockey, baseball and basketball.

Although some research into North American crowd violence (Smith's in particular) has attempted to couch the phenomenon in social, historical and cultural antecedents, in general, this third strand of the literature has tended to view disorder as a response to aspects of the sports event itself. Dewar's (1979) attempt to link spectator fights at baseball with such factors as the day of the week, starting time, seat location, inning of the game and even temperature, and Geen and O'Neal's (1976) account of how crowd size affects fan violence are classic examples of game-specific (i.e. situational) explanations that are clearly limited in their explanatory scope and potential; they provide next to no insight into the *sociological* dimensions of crowd violence. Consequently, other than some isolated examples, surprisingly little is known about the social causes of crowd violence or about the demographics, lifestyles and motives of disorderly North American sports fans.

In sum, while modest efforts have been made to explain the causes of North American sports crowd disorder, far more detailed research is required. In particular, while violent crowd dynamics and other situational factors are clearly important in this endeavour, understanding the phenomena sociologically means attending to the broad social context in which they occur. Coakley (1998: 204) captures this sociological approach incisively:

> Sport events do not occur in social vacuums. When spectators attend events, they bring with them the histories, issues, controversies and ideologies of the communities and societies in which they live. They may be racists who want to harass those they identify as targets for discrimination. They may come from ethnic neighbourhoods and want to express and reaffirm their ethnicity. They may resent negative circumstances in their lives and want to express their bitterness. They may be members of groups or gangs in which status is gained partly through fighting. They may be powerless and alienated and looking for ways to be noticed and defined as socially important. They may be young men who believe that manhood is achieved through violence and domination over others. Or they may be living lives so devoid of significance and excitement that they want to create a memorable occasion they can boastfully discuss with friend for weeks and years to come. In other words, when thousands of spectators attend a sports event, their behaviours are grounded in factors far beyond the event and the stadium.

Of course, given the apparent absence in North America to date of organized 'hooligan' groups, the aforementioned absence of in-depth ethnographic work in the British sense (which might produce the sorts of insights Coakley hints at) is hardly surprising. However, this is not to discount the possibility of producing ethnographies of North American fan groups known for their hostile behaviour, or of stadiums infamous for aggression and intimidation (the NFL alone could provide several examples of both), or the possibility of systematic historical examinations of trends in North American disorder. Such work would surely enhance our existing knowledge of the phenomenon.

Is crowd violence a global problem?

In the spirit of Dunning et al.'s (2002b) claim noted in the introduction to this chapter, and notwithstanding context variance in form and frequency, the short answer to the question 'Does crowd violence cross the globe?' appears to be 'yes.' Janet Lever's (1983) work on fan violence associated with Brazilian soccer set an early marker for the international research. Using a structural functionalist approach, Lever sought to show how sport in South America can represent both unifying and divisive properties – unifying in the sense that it may enhance community awareness and loyalty, but divisive because it underlines social class distinctions. Fan violence, she argued, is but one side effect of failed attempts by the Brazilian authorities to deal with poverty and such class distinctions. Soccer stadiums have often been used as a venue for the expression of class conflict such as missile throwing from the 'poorer' stadium sections into the 'richer' sections. Arguably, Lever's functionalist approach cannot easily account for these tensions and her study is now outdated, but it nevertheless represents groundbreaking sociological work on fan violence in South America. A more contemporary account of fan violence in this context may be found in Archetti and Romero (1994).

By now, most serious students of sports violence recognize that the argument that soccer hooliganism is a British, or English, 'disease' is a myth. In their early figurational studies, Williams et al. (1984) uncovered numerous media reports between 1904 and 1983 documenting crowd violence at European soccer games in 30 different countries in which English fans were not involved. Slightly later, Williams and Goldberg (1989: 7) identified several cases of hooliganism where English fans were, in fact, the 'victims of foreign hooliganism' rather than the assailants. Today, cases of fan violence in diverse international contexts are routinely reported in the popular media and over the Internet, and organized hooliganism has become a problem for the authorities in many countries. Indeed, Dunning et al.'s (2002b) collection of essays on hooliganism as a 'world phenomenon' contains evidence of sports crowd problems in the Czech Republic, France, Hungary, Italy, Portugal, Argentina, Peru, West Africa, South Africa, Japan and Australia.

The research indicates that soccer hooliganism expanded throughout the 1980s in a number of European countries, and that a considerable continental European literature also emerged at this time. Greece, France, Spain, Belgium, Austria, Sweden, the Netherlands, Germany and Italy are among countries known to have experienced significant problems with soccer hooliganism and their own versions of hard-core fans (Young 2000: 389; Guschwan 2006; Spaaij 2006). In many of these locations, fan violence has been shown to intersect with far-right-wing politics and racist ideologies (see cells 13 and 14 in Figure 4.1 in the following chapter), demonstrating again a clear sociological link between problems in sport and those in the wider society (Müller et al. 2007).

While care must always be taken to differentiate between injuries caused by intentional crowd violence and those caused by 'accidental' crowd surges or stampedes prompted by such things as over-ticketing, negligent policing or stadium collapses, in terms of total numbers of injuries and fatalities, some of the most serious cases of injurious and fatal fan episodes have occurred in South and Central American and African locations. For example, a riot broke out at the National Stadium in Lima, Peru in May 1964, resulting in over 300 deaths and, in another notorious case of soccer-related violence, a so-called 'Soccer War' lasting several days was waged between Honduras and El Salvador in the summer of 1969 following a game played between the two countries. In 1996, 83 people were killed and over 150 others injured in a stampede linked to the distribution of forged tickets at a World Cup qualifying game held in Guatemala City (Young 2000: 389). In other words, while it may not, as yet, have been assembled in a rigorous scientific manner, evidence of the footprint left by crowd violence in almost all places sport is taken seriously is not hard to find.

Conclusion

Sports crowd violence has initiated a significant body of research. As an expansive literature on hooliganism attests, soccer-related disorder has prompted solicitous reactions from politicians, police, sports authorities and the media in numerous settings. For instance, it has precipitated the introduction of new laws, expensive and expansive community programmes aimed at education, respect and cooperation, and massive policing operations and security preparations for events. The research on soccer hooliganism also demonstrates clear evidence of both continuity and change in the phenomena (Spaaij 2006; Redhead 1996, 2008).

However, the research on crowd violence also shows serious imbalances. For example, while there seems little doubt that the most substantial and rigorously theorized body of work in this area has examined forms and causes of British and European soccer hooliganism (here, central themes highlight interactions between social class, gender, jingoism and race), relatively little is known about crowd violence in other parts of the world. Although expanding slowly, the international research remains slim, and there are no clear ways of categorizing this work into thematic 'schools' or coherent bodies of theory that accurately represent ongoing research.

This is true of North America. Despite the volume and frequency of outbursts during the twentieth century and already into the twenty-first century that range from simple streaking to murder, North American crowd violence has been, and remains, *relatively* immune to serious debate and sustained official attention, including scholarship. Simply put, the stigma (Goffman 1963), stereotypes (Hall 1978) and moral panic (Murphy et al. 1988; Young 1986, 1988) now long-associated with soccer and its fans in the UK and elsewhere have been eluded in North America. While this may be justified in terms of the *relative* scale of disorderly incidents, North American sport has shown a stubborn, if perhaps faltering, resilience in maintaining its 'squeaky clean,' family-centered and essentially safe image despite the fact that crowd disorder is well-known to the authorities, shows patterned dimensions and has clearly changed the configuration of stadia and game-day experiences in a number of sports.

Because unhelpful and, indeed, invidious comparisons persist (e.g. Wann et al. 2001: 148–151), it seems important to emphasize that soccer hooliganism and the miscellaneous North American fan disorders neither represent social problems of the same magnitude nor are one and the same thing. While there are some common sociological threads in crowd disorders on both sides of the Atlantic (especially gender – crowd violence is predominantly a male domain in all locations), and while the problem may reflect similar social causes in those contexts (such as socio-economic status, the cultural significance of sport and its related celebratory conventions, social and psychological conflicts occurring in the wider society, pride in local community and xenophobic or racist attitudes towards 'outsiders'), it is also clear that many aspects of sports crowd disorder are culturally specific. This certainly seems true of the North American case where, to date, the problem is less institutionalized than in Europe, where there has been no major at-stadium crowd tragedy, no travelling 'super crews' or 'firms' of hooligan supporters, no paramilitary policing operations punctuating the sporting calendar (inflated policing at North American championship games are more related to the perception of terrorist threats in a post-'9/11' world) and no judicial reviews prompting sweeping organizational changes. But comparing the North American scenario, where there is clear evidence of crowd disorder, to its counterpart in other parts of the world is less than helpful if we want to understand the phenomenon objectively and, more importantly, be prepared to tackle it.

4

FORMATIONS OF SPORTS-RELATED VIOLENCE

Widening the focus

Introduction

In the Preface and in Chapter 1, it was argued that it is not only sociologically useful, but indeed sociologically *necessary*, to approach the full range of the subject matter as SRV rather than as 'sports violence' per se. As such, and having reviewed the research related to the two principal ways in which sports violence has traditionally been conceived of in Chapters 2 and 3, Chapter 4 now considers the scope of SRV in a much wider focus. To accomplish this, it adopts a two-pronged approach. First, it suggests that SRV is comprised of at least 16 further behavioural components. Each of these is referred to as a 'cell' in a broader matrix of formations. Beginning with cell 3 (since cells 1 and 2 are showcased in the preceding chapters), each cell is described and illustrated, and the existing knowledge on the behaviour is discussed. Following this sequence, a more dynamic and processual way of thinking about SRV is offered. Once again, the main purpose of this chapter is to move beyond the limiting and de-contextualizing inclination of existing research that tends to focus on players and crowds in a quite rigid sense and view types of sports violence as separate episodes of social action, unrelated to other types or to broader social structures and processes. In contrast, this chapter demonstrates how forms of SRV link and are interconnected.

The SRV matrix: a linear typology of SRV

Table 4.1 represents one way that we might imagine the broad landscape of SRV. With such a fluid and changing phenomenon as SRV, there is clearly no fixed, definitive or exhaustive 'magic number' of behavioural components, but the table identifies the central ways in which violence related to sport is acted out and experienced by persons and groups involved. These are now discussed individually.

TABLE 4.1 Formations of sports-related violence

1.	Player violence	2.	Crowd violence
3.	Individualized fan–player violence	4.	Player violence away from the game
5.	Street crimes	6.	Violence against the self
7.	Athlete initiation/hazing	8.	Harassment, stalking and threat
9.	Sexual assault	10.	Partner abuse/domestic violence
11.	Offences by coaches/ administrators/medical staff	12.	Parental abuse
13.	Sexism/racism	14.	Other identity violence
15.	Animal abuse	16.	Political violence/terrorism
17.	Offences against workers and the public	18.	Offences against the environment

Cell 3: individualized fan–player violence

With some justification, crowd violence has typically been approached in terms of collective episodes of action. For example, soccer hooliganism in Europe and post-event riots in North America have been shown to be enacted, for the most part, by large and/or rival groups of fans behaving in a disorderly, threatening or violent manner. As noted in Chapter 3, much of the early literature on sports violence explained fan violence as a form of 'collective behaviour' using principles of group dynamics such as 'emergent norm' theory, 'value-added' theory and 'contagion' theory (Lewis 1982; Smith 1983), and the bulk of sociological research on fan violence seems to suggest that the phenomenon is expressed only in group form. However, not all fan violence is perpetrated by organized or identifiable groups (the precise ratio of individualized vs. collective fan violence is difficult to measure, varies within events and across sport cultures and is rarely recorded as such), and not all fan violence involves other fans. Athletes themselves may also be targets of attack.

The following are examples of incidents of individualized fan–player violence:

- April 1993: 19-year-old American female professional tennis player, Monica Seles, was stabbed in the back by a 39-year-old unemployed lathe operator (Gunter Parche) obsessed with seeing Germany's Steffi Graf regain the world no.1 ranking. The attack took place in full view of a Hamburg crowd during a break in her match against Bulgarian Maggie Maleeva. Parche was subsequently given a two-year suspended sentence (*Sports Illustrated*, 17 July 1995: 18–26).
- September 1999: Houston Astros right fielder, Bill Spiers, a former player for the Milwaukee Brewers, was attacked on the field by a disgruntled 23-year-old Brewers fan, resulting in a bloodied face and whiplash (http://sportsillustrated. cnn.com/baseball/news/2002/09/19/fan_violence).
- August 2004: With only four miles to go, Brazilian runner Vanderlei de Lima was leading the men's marathon at the Athens Olympics when Irish protester and former priest, Cornelius 'Neil' Horan, accosted him. De Lima was able to

fend off the assault and return to the race, winning the bronze medal. For his efforts and demonstration of Olympic 'spirit,' he was awarded the Pierre de Coubertin Medal at the closing ceremonies (Owens 2004: A1).

- March 2007: Frank Lampard of Chelsea FC was attacked on the field of play while celebrating with his team after their FA Cup victory over Tottenham Hotspur FC. 'Spurs' fan, Tim Smith, ran on to the field and barraged Lampard with a series of missed punches (http://www.mirror.co.uk/sport/tm_ headline=lampard--never-again&method=full&objectid=18784809&siteid= 89520-name_page.html).

- March 2011: During a gymnastics meet at the Minnesota Sports Pavilion, the team mascot of the University of Minnesota-Twin Cities, Goldy, was punched by a 60-year-old fan after being taunted by the mascot throughout the event (Zimmerman 2011).

Cell 4: player violence away from the game

It is also the case that the bulk of the existing research has restricted its examination of player violence to incidents occurring within the context of the game itself. Despite the fact that Smith's (1983) widely used early sports violence typology (see Chapter 2) underlined the possibility of player violence occurring away from the field of play or outside the arena in its fourth and final category ('criminal violence'), most researchers have limited their examination of player violence to conduct taking place during the game and inside the stadium. From one point of view, this is understandable – statistically speaking, this is clearly the locus of most player violence 'action.' However, episodes of participant involvement in violence occurring away from the game have taken place.

The following are examples of incidents of player violence away from the game:

- January 1994: One of the most shocking episodes in this category comes from an unlikely source – figure skating. It involved a planned attack upon American skater, and favourite to win the women's US Championship, Nancy Kerrigan, by acquaintances of her direct rival, Tonya Harding, in the build-up to the Lillehammer Winter Olympics (*Time*, 24 January 1994: 34–38). The off-ice assault on Kerrigan following a practice session held in Detroit, and perpetrated with a lead pipe striking her right knee, resulted in criminal charges being laid against the assailant. Harding avoided a likely jail sentence by pleading guilty to conspiring to hinder prosecution of the attackers. She received three years probation, 500 hours of community service and a $160,000 fine. Concluding that she was involved in the attack and displayed 'a clear disregard for fairness, good sportsmanship and ethical behavior,' the governing body of the sport, the United States Figure Skating Association, levied a lengthy suspension on Harding, who has been *persona non grata* in the skating world ever since.

- February 2010: After a heated minor hockey game between the Cumberland County Bombers and the Brookfield Elks (Nova Scotia, Canada), the members of both teams met in the parking lot to continue hostilities initiated on the ice. In the ensuing mêlée, three players were sent to the hospital with injuries including a broken nose (CBC News, 5 February 2010).

Cell 5: street crimes

There is abundant evidence from a number of countries of athletes and other sports personnel behaving badly, including criminally, in their 'regular' lives away from the stadium. Although the evidence is not restricted to any one setting, certain sports have repeatedly been the source of concern, as the title of Benedict and Yaeger's provocative study suggests – *Pros and Cons: The Criminals Who Play in the NFL* (1998) (see also Benedict and Keteyian (2011) on crimes by US college football players). Further, there is also concern that athletes involved in street crimes have, until recently, been given preferential treatment by sport and legal authorities, and that 'dodging convictions [is] too often a slam dunk for athletes' (Bianchi 2005). Critical questions, almost always surrounding the behaviours of men, have been asked regarding the cultural significance of sport, which seems to provide (especially elite and high profile) male athletes in trouble with sports bodies and the law a certain amount of leniency to what, for others, may be serious charges, as well as regarding the collective hubris that allows some athletes to believe that they live outside the boundaries of the general community (Coakley and Donnelly 2009: 205). McCallum's (2003: 44) list of US athletes behaving unlawfully includes high profile players involved in, for example, sodomy, manslaughter, aggravated battery, sexual assault, homicide, sexual battery and aggravated battery.

The following are examples of incidents of street crimes involving athletes:

- December 1998: Along with his younger brother Jesse, US Junior Wheelchair racer, Ted Ernst, was charged with the felony murder of Larry Streeter, a Bigfork, Montana builder and entrepreneur. The Ernst brothers were found guilty of committing a homicide during the process of carrying out a burglary at a Bigfork, Montana residence where Streeter was staying (Nack 2000: 72–82).
- January 2000: Baltimore Ravens linebacker, Ray Lewis, and two friends were indicted for murder and aggravated assault, in connection to the murders of 21-year-old Jacinth Baker and 24-year old Richard Lollar. Testifying against his two friends, Lewis pleaded guilty to the misdemeanour charge of obstructing justice, and was sentenced to one year probation and fined $250,000 by the NFL (http://sportsillustrated.cnn.com/football/nfl/news/19/06/04/lewis_agreement/).
- January 2001: Former Carolina Panthers wide receiver, Rae Carruth, was charged in connection to the murder of his pregnant girlfriend, Cherica Adams. Adams, who was pregnant with Carruth's twin babies at the time, was shot repeatedly in a drive-by shooting in November 1999. Only one

of the babies survived the attack. Carruth was found guilty of conspiring to commit murder, illegally discharging a firearm and using an instrument to kill an unborn child. He was sentenced to 18 years in jail (http://archives.cnn.com/2000/LAW/10/columns/cossack.carruth.10.23/).

- April 2004: NHL player, Mike Danton, was arrested and charged with conspiracy to murder his agent, David Frost, using a hitman who was actually a police dispatcher. Sentenced to seven-and-a-half years in a US federal prison, Danton subsequently reported that his intended target was Steve Jefferson, his estranged father (http://www.cbc.ca/sports/indepth/danton/).

- January 2008: Former NHL defenceman with the LA Kings, Jere Karalahti, was charged in connection with his involvement in the smuggling of 4 kilograms of amphetamine drugs into his native Finland. In 2001, Karalahti was suspended from the NHL for violating the league's policy on substance abuse. At the time of his arrest, Karalahti was playing in the Finnish Elite Hockey League (*Sports Illustrated*, 11 February 2008: 108).

Cell 6: violence against the self

It has rarely been viewed as such, but the range of forms of 'violence' that occur in sport involves types of harm perpetrated against the self, especially visible in behaviours such as sports-related eating disorders and chronic drug use, which can reach serious and occasionally life-threatening proportions. For instance, American journalist Joan Ryan (1995) and Canadian social scientist Caroline Davis (1999) have written compellingly on the dangers of anorexia nervosa and bulimia, especially in the so-called 'appearance' sports such as gymnastics and figure skating where so much emphasis is placed (particularly on young females) on weight control. This may also be problematic for male competitors in a range of other sports and physical cultures including horse-racing (where jockeys must conform to strict weight expectations), boxing, wrestling and dance (Kirkland and Lawrence 1986; McEwen and Young 2011).

Conversely, it is equally clear that many popular sports encourage, and even require, in their current format at least, huge body mass and musculature. Sports such as gridiron football, rugby, ice hockey, throwing and sprint events in track and field, and bodybuilding, with their ever-increasing emphasis on size and strength, have had long and persistent problems with anabolic steroids (cf. Courson 1991; Young 1993; Waddington 2000) and other performance-enhancing drugs. Augmenting the body unnaturally may also be found in a cluster of other sports, such as those requiring excessive endurance, for which the body is not naturally suited (Young et al. 1994; Atkinson 2005; Atkinson and Young 2008). The possible outcomes of forms of violence against the self may include addictions (e.g. to performance-enhancers, alcohol, painkillers and other drugs), body pathologies (e.g. anorexia, bulimia, 'bigorexia'), mental and psychological disturbances (e.g. self-confidence and self-esteem issues) and threats to physical wellbeing (e.g. chronic injuries, concussions, suicide or death).

The link between the expectations of sport and forms of risk and violence done to the self seems clear. As American sociologist Michael Messner (1990) has argued, the injured athlete (including the *self*-injured athlete) represents the ultimate paradox of sport – the use of the body as a weapon against others, or as a vehicle to exceed physical and athletic 'frontiers' (Young 1993: 376) seems, almost inevitably, to result in violence *against* one's body. Once again, burgeoning literatures on risk, pain and injury in sport, and on health and sport (see Chapter 5), emphasize this point austerely (cf. Waddington 2000; Young 2004a; Roderick 2006a, 2006b).

The following are examples of incidents of violence against the self:

- February 1982: Reacting to being constantly tormented by thoughts about food that her sport involvement prevented her from enjoying, former distance runner for the University of Georgetown, Mary Wazeter, attempted to commit suicide by jumping off a bridge, leaving her paralyzed (Noden 1994).
- July 1994: US Olympic gymnast, Christy Henrich, died from heart complications resulting from years of battling anorexia nervosa. As she entered hospital for the last time, Henrich did so with a suitcase concealing laxatives and other drugs. This high profile tragedy resulting from a widely recognized problem in gymnastics prompted the International Olympic Committee (IOC) to form a task force to deal with the prevalence of eating disorders among elite male and female athletes (Noden 1994). Henrich's story is captured in the video, 'Dying to Win' (*Dateline NBC* 1995).
- 2005: Retired athlete, Jose Canseco, released an autobiography on his life as a professional baseball player and avid steroid user. The book detailed Canseco's experiences using steroids to 'gain a competitive edge,' and explains how he introduced steroids to many other players, including such baseball luminaries as Mark McGwire and Sammy Sosa, both of whom subsequently vehemently denied using performance-enhancing drugs (Canseco 2005).
- A substantial academic, biographical and journalistic literature continues to record the risks of extreme sports, such as climbing the world's highest and most dangerous mountains. Poignant book titles such as *Into Thin Air* (Krakauer 1997), *Deep Survival: Who Lives, Who Dies, and Why* (Gonzales 2003) and *High Crimes: The Fate of Everest in an Age of Greed* (Kodas 2008) hint not only at the excessive chances athletes take regarding their own lives, but how their risks cannot be separated from cultures of greed and selfishness in extreme sports, which often result in tragedy and enduring losses to families and loved ones.

Cell 7: athlete initiation/hazing

Hazing, or the required performance by neophyte athletes of often traumatic initiation rituals in the pursuit of a new group identity and induction into a new team setting, is one of the worst kept secrets in all of sport. It has been traced back centuries and identified in a number of social institutions, notably education and the military (Bryshun and Young 1999, 2007). Not all athletes are 'hazed,' but many are at many levels of sport in many countries, and almost every athlete knows another who has been hazed. In North American, British or Australian sport, for instance, initiation is simply part of the lexicon and experience of sport, although a growing trend towards policing and anti-hazing policy, such as on school and college and campuses, has changed its manifestation somewhat, as well as consolidated codes of silence around the practice. There is clear evidence on both sides of the Atlantic that neophyte athletes may be coerced into embarrassing, degrading and often high-risk initiation practices (Bryshun and Young 1999, 2007; King 2000; Johnson and Holman 2004), and there is increasing concern with the complicity of coaches, administrators, parents and social institutions (including colleges and universities) in condoning, or facilitating, hazing. With the frequency of troubling episodes reported in the popular media, with concern over matters such as the hazing of child athletes, and with questions of institutional complicity being raised more and more, it is likely that hazing research will continue to expand.

The following are examples of incidents of initiation/hazing:

• 1994: Four members of a male ice-hockey team in Chatham, Ontario, reported that they were forced to masturbate publicly. Thirteen people were charged with over 100 sexual offences in the case (*Maclean's*, 30 January 1995: 17).
• 1996: Three University of Guelph students were dropped from the men's Gryphons ice-hockey team for refusing to participate in an initiation party in the team dressing room. The event involved drinking volumes of alcohol through funnels, and games that included nude players eating faeces-contaminated marshmallows (CBC, *The Fifth Estate*, 29 October 1997; *Toronto Sun*, 28 February 1996: 5).
• October 1997: Former soccer player with the University of Oklahoma Women's Soccer team, Kathleen Peay, filed a federal lawsuit against her former coach, Bettina Fletcher (Cook and Mravic 1999: 32). The lawsuit claimed that Fletcher and two other defendants committed physical and emotional abuse during an initiation event in which Peay and other rookie players were forced to wear adult diapers and to imitate fellatio using bananas (*Sports Illustrated*, 1 November 1999: 91–107).
• 1999: During the New Orleans Saints' training camp, rookie players (including defensive tackle Jeff Danish), were subjected to a rookie hazing that resulted in three players needing medical attention for injuries sustained while being forced to run blind-folded through a 'gauntlet of punches, pushes, and wallops with coin-filled socks' (Wahl and Wertheim 2003: 70). After being thrown through a window and requiring 13 stitches, Danish was dropped from the team in 1999. He later filed a lawsuit against the Saints, in which he received an undisclosed settlement (*Sports Illustrated*, 22 December 2003: 99).
• August 2003: One senior tackle and one junior linebacker from the WC Mepham High School football team in Long Island, New York, were charged with sexually assaulting three rookie players with broomsticks, golf balls and pine cones, during a rookie hazing while attending their pre-season

training camp. Public complaints, criminal charges and lawsuits prompted the school district's decision to cancel the team's season and to not renew the contracts of the coaches for the following season (*Sports Illustrated*, 22 December 2003: 99).

• 2005: The head coach of the Windsor Spitfires of the Ontario Hockey League was suspended for 40 games and his team was fined $35,000 (the league maximum) following a hazing incident held on a team bus in which rookie players were stripped and crowded into the bathroom for up to ten minutes at a time (*Calgary Herald*, 19 October 2005: E1). This widely used and familiar ritual in Canadian ice hockey is referred to as 'The Holocaust' or 'The Hotbox' (Bryshun and Young 2007: 311).

Cell 8: harassment, stalking and threat

Although its full scope is not known and it is difficult to measure, there is compelling evidence to suggest that sport is replete with a range of unwelcome conventions and behaviours that represent, at best, a 'chilly climate' for many participants and, at worst, a locus of exploitation and vulnerability for others (Kirby et al. 2000). These behaviours range from persons in positions of authority and power (often, but not always, males), taking advantage of young, impressionable athletes (often, but not always, females), to 'superstar' athletes and outspoken coaches being followed or threatened by fans. Work conducted in England (Brackenridge 2001; Hartill 2010), Norway (Fasting et al. 2000), and Canada (Kirby and Greaves 1996; Robinson 1998; Donnelly 1999, 2007; Kirby et al. 2000) has examined the causes, manifestations and outcomes of sexual harassment. Such work adds scientific weight to the already considerable information produced by investigative journalists who have uncovered deep harassment and abuse scandals in British and Canadian sport (see BBC's 'Secrets of the Coach,' 1993, and CBC's 'Crossing the Line: The Sexual Harassment of Athletes,' 1993). However, sociologists have, in general, been very slow in acknowledging the need for research on forms of stalking and threat, despite their known existence as sports–related practices. For instance, widespread cases of stalking and threat throughout the world of sport have spawned a thriving muscle-for-hire security industry for both male and female athletes.

The following are examples of incidents of harassment, stalking and threat:

• July 1992: Among a long list of recognized male and female athletes from a range of sports in many countries who report being stalked, harassed or threatened is figure skater Katarina Witt. In 1992, an obsessed fan was charged on seven counts of sending obscene and threatening mail, and was sentenced to three years in a US psychiatric centre. In the case it was revealed that Harry Veltman II had followed Witt around the world attempting to distract her as she skated in competition (*USA Today*, 14 July 1995: 3C).

• September 2002: 34-year-old Frankfurt-native, Albrecht Stromeyer, was charged with two counts of stalking female tennis player Serena Williams.

Police reported that Stromeyer had been harassing Williams since 2001, including travelling around the world to follow her progress (*Sports Illustrated*, 9 September 2002: 97).

• May 2005: Malcolm Glazer, owner of the Tampa Bay Buccaneers NFL football team, along with his family, received several death threats from outraged fans in response to his $1.47 billion purchase of 75 per cent interest in Manchester United FC (*Sports Illustrated*, 30 May 2005: 102–122). A year earlier, John Magnier, the then multi-millionaire owner of the same soccer club, was forced to hire a group of bodyguards following similar threats from fans (Syal 2004: 5).

• Winter 2005/2006: US Olympic Skeleton Coach, Tim Nardiello, was accused on two separate occasions of sexual harassment by former US Olympic skeleton competitors Felicia Canfield and Tristan Gale. Nardiello was placed on leave with pay pending a federation decision to reinstate him in time to coach at the competition in Turin, Italy (*Sports Illustrated*, 9 January 2006: 104).

• May 2011: A woman who repeatedly showed up at the house of English Premier League soccer player, Rio Ferdinand, was charged and convicted of harassment. In the case, it was found that 38-year-old Susanne Ibru stalked Ferdinand and his family for several years. The Crewe Magistrates' Court sentenced Ibru to 10 weeks in jail and a 10-year restraining order (http://www.independent.co.uk/news/uk/crime/rio-ferdinand-stalker-jailed-2281475.html).

Cell 9: sexual assault

The extent to which athletes and other sports personnel are involved in forms of sexual assault against adults and children is not known precisely but, again, that behaviours such as sexual assault and rape occur in the world of sport, and at every level of sport from high school to professional, cannot be denied. Sadly, news of them in the local media is routine, certainly in North America. Some research is available (Curry 1991; Crosset et al. 1995; Benedict and Klein 1997; Benedict and Yaeger 1998) but, while researchers have, on the whole, been appropriately cautious with respect to matters such as root causes and generalizability, it is difficult to assess whether the involvement of (almost always) male athletes in cases of sexual assault is similar or disproportional to the general population (cf. Coakley and Donnelly 2004). Most researchers (e.g. Curry 1991; Young 1993; Messner and Sabo 1994) agree, however, that sexual assault by male athletes is bound up with wider social structures of gender and power and, in particular, with the acting out of codes of hegemonic masculinity, sexism and misogyny – which, again, are far from rare in the often hyper-macho world of sport (see Chapter 8). Far less frequently, female athletes and coaches offend in episodes of sexual assault, and incidents of same sex (particularly male–male) abuse also occur, which suggests that power relations per se are at least as important as gender dynamics in explaining the practice.

The following are examples of incidents of sexual assault:

- February 1992: Former heavyweight boxer, Mike Tyson, was sentenced to 10 years in jail after being found guilty in a 1991 charge of sexual assault against former Miss Black America pageant contestant, Desiree Washington. Tyson eventually served three years in prison, but was permitted by boxing authorities to return to his sport upon his release (Cashmore 2005: 108–130).

- February 1997: Veteran NBC sports announcer, Marv Albert, was charged with assaulting and forcibly sodomizing a 42-year-old woman, with whom he acknowledged a long-standing sexual relationship. Albert was charged with assault and battery and received a 12-month suspended sentence (Kennedy and O'Brien 1997: 20).

- 1997: Where sexual assault against youth athletes is concerned, Canadian sport has been 'in the news' for some time. Specifically, there have been scandals throughout many levels of Canadian ice hockey regarding the sexual abuse of young boys, some of whom, now adults, have 'gone public' with their histories of victimization. In early 1997, NHL player, Sheldon Kennedy, claimed that his junior coach had sexually abused him on over 300 occasions. After a short trial, in which the complicity of others, including some high profile names within the hockey community, was revealed or implied, hockey coach Graham James pleaded guilty to 350 sexual assaults and was sentenced to three-and-a-half years in jail. He was paroled in 2001 (Vine and Challen 2002; Donnelly 2007; *Maclean's* 26 October 2009: 64). In 2009, former Calgary Flames player, Theoren Fleury, released a lengthy autobiography detailing how he had also been molested for years as a junior player by James (Fleury 2009). Other former players are also known to have filed complaints against the same coach. Another man laid sexual abuse charges against two employees of the Maple Leaf Gardens (former home of the NHL's Toronto Maple Leafs) relating to his time as a teenage employee in the stadium. In the inquiry that followed, it was acknowledged that the Maple Leaf Gardens had earlier reached an out-of-court settlement with the man in return for not bringing criminal charges against them. Before the inquiry concluded, the Canadian police received a flood of telephone calls from male players across the country alleging similarly abusive experiences at the hands of coaching 'predators' (Donnelly 2007).

- May 1998: Former Little League Baseball coach, 54-year-old Norman Watson of Highland, CA, was found guilty of 39 counts of lewd acts with children between 1990 and 1996, and sentenced to 84 years in jail. Watson had previous convictions of child molestation in the 1980s, and had spent five years in two state mental hospitals to receive intensive counselling before being released and subsequently hired as a Little League Baseball coach (*Sports Illustrated*, 13 September 1999: 91).

- June 2003: LA Lakers player Kobe Bryant was charged with sexually assaulting 19-year-old hotel employee, Katelyn Faber, in his Colorado hotel room. Before the case went to trial, Faber filed a civil lawsuit against Bryant over the incident. The two parties agreed on a settlement, but its specific terms were not made public. The sexual assault charge was later dismissed, as Faber was unwilling to testify (McCallum 2003; Muraskin and Domash 2007: 71–78).

• April–May 2006: Three members of the Duke University men's lacrosse team were charged with forcible rape, sexual offence and kidnapping, resulting from the allegations brought forward by a 19-year-old exotic dancer hired to provide entertainment at a team house party (Kwak 2006: 78–79).

• January 2008: Former Charlottetown girls' soccer coach, 23-year-old Jillian Anderson, was sentenced to ten months in prison, two years probation and a 20-year mandatory listing on the sexual-offenders registry, after being found guilty of two counts of sexual exploitation. The charges stemmed from an inappropriate relationship that was formed by Anderson with a 15-year-old former female player (http://cbc.ca/canada/prince-edward-island/story/2008/01/18/anderson-sentence.html).

• April 2011: Police charged Calgary ringette coach, 22-year-old Kelsea Joy Hepburn, with sexual assault and sexual exploitation following allegations from a 13-year-old female player (Zickefoose 2011).

Cell 10: partner abuse/domestic violence

Since publicized cases of female athletes assaulting their partners or being involved in sexual assault, gang rape or other such crimes of violence are extremely rare, and since most offending athletes appear, in most of the evidence that we have available, to be men, the values and behaviours reported in cells 5 and 9 intersect with the subject in focus here. The involvement of many male athletes in partner abuse, or what, almost 20 years ago, *Sports Illustrated* provocatively called 'sport's dirty little secret' (Nack and Munson 1995b), is highly controversial because no-one really knows, to invoke the oldest of criminological quandaries, whether the information we receive through such means as media coverage is an outcome of actual incidence or of reporting and perception. Here again, while the general literature on domestic violence is substantial and sophisticated, the sociological research on the possible link between sport and partner abuse/domestic violence is negligible, and much of our existing knowledge comes from other disciplines (e.g. Rees and Schnepel 2009; Card and Dahl 2009).

However, even just a glance at, for instance, the British, Australian or North American media suggests a problem with partner abuse among male athletes, and the list of known athletes in trouble with the law for assaulting their female partners is depressingly long, but media reportage is hardly scientific fact, and far more research is needed. Some of the most rigorous sociological work conducted on this topic may again be found in the now-dated US-based studies of Messner and Sabo (1994), Crosset (1999) and Benedict and Yaeger (1998), all of which suggest that the problem with male athletes and partner abuse is real, significant and patterned. More recent US research on college male athletes and dating aggression is supportive (Forbes et al. 2006; Kreager 2007 – see Chapter 8).

The following are examples of incidents of partner abuse/domestic violence:

- July 1995: Former NFL quarterback, Warren Moon, was charged with misdemeanour assault in connection with an altercation involving his wife, Felicia. Subsequently, Felicia refused to testify and take further legal action against her husband, and Moon was acquitted (Nack and Munson 1995b).
- March 2002: Retired NFL player and renowned tough-guy, 66-year-old Jim Brown, was sentenced to 180 days in prison, after being found guilty of misdemeanour vandalism with domestic-violence conditions, stemming from an altercation with his 25-year-old wife. Brown was given the jail term after he refused to enter domestic violence counselling (Yaeger and Brown 2002).
- July 2002: NBA player Allen Iverson was charged with four felonies and ten misdemeanours stemming from altercations with his wife and allegations of death threats and the brandishing of a firearm. The charges were later dropped due to conflicting testimonies (*Sports Illustrated*, 29 July 2002: 97).
- May 2003: Former Tampa Bay Buccaneers running back, Michael Pittman, was arrested and charged with two counts of felony assault against his wife, Melissa. At the time of his arrest, Pittman was on probation for two previous misdemeanour charges also stemming from altercations with his wife (Munson et al. 2003: 22).
- June 2007: In a case made doubly controversial because most wrestling insiders preferred to view the incident as an episode of 'roid rage' rather than one of domestic violence, Montreal-born WWF wrestler, Chris Benoit, known as the 'Canadian Crippler,' murdered his wife and seven-year-old son, subsequently hanging himself (Bonnell 2007: A8). Four years earlier, Benoit's wife had applied for a restraining order and divorce following other physical disputes and threats.
- August 2010: Finnish ski-jumper, Matti Nykanen, was found guilty of aggravated assault on his wife and sentenced to 16 months in jail. The former Olympic champion attacked his wife with a knife on Christmas Day 2009, in their home in Finland (Tanner 2010: C1).

Cell 11: offences by coaches/administrators/medical staff

Coaches and persons holding administrative or medical responsibilities occupy important and trusted positions in the lives of athletes, especially child athletes. In the same way that they may positively shape a player's athletic experience so, too, may the responsibility entrusted in, for example, the coach be taken advantage of, often in the context of an athlete–coach power relationship, some of which is acted out in private (and, thus, invisibly to the rest of the community). Coaches are also central in the legitimation of aggression and the teaching of violent practices. From a social leaning point of view, they represent one principal means of learning how to 'do' violence and how to rationalize it (Bowker 1998).

For instance, through instruction and positive reinforcement, ice-hockey 'enforcers' do not only learn how to ply their trade and conform to the expectations of what is known in ice-hockey circles as 'the code' (Atkinson and Young 2011); they are also rewarded financially, subculturally, reputationally and occupationally for their particular brand of brutality. Some of the most venerated coaches in history have become revered precisely because of their commitment to a belligerent style of play and demanding an excessive 'win-at-all-costs' ethos from players (Young 1993; Gillett et al. 1996). In these ways, the pro-violence norms and conventions of sport are reproduced over time. Coaches also learn from, and imitate, other coaches, many of whom have achieved fame and respect through their reputations for intimidation and aggression. Anyone familiar with elite sport can recall incidents of players being verbally mauled by angry or tyrannical coaches. This cell also contains the values and actions of administrators, medical staff and others who practise or facilitate versions of SRV, including accepting bribes, behaving corruptly or participate in perjury, to achieve illicit goals.

The following are examples of offences by coaches/administrators/medical staff:

- 1989: In the inquiry that followed Canadian sprinter Ben Johnson being stripped of his 100m gold medal at the 1988 Seoul Summer Olympics for failing a drug test, Johnson's long-time coach, Charlie Francis, admitted introducing the runner to steroids (Dubin 1990; Francis 1991).
- December 1998: In the build-up to the 2002 Salt Lake City Winter Games, it was discovered that several IOC members had accepted bribes. In exchange for supporting the Salt Lake bid, members were given unorthodox perks ranging from all-expenses-paid ski trips, to real estate, to jobs for their family members. Following a complicated set of investigations, ten members of the IOC were expelled and a further ten were sanctioned (McLaughlin 1999).
- September 2006: 29-year-old American Little League T-Ball coach, Mark Downs Jr, was found guilty of 'criminal conspiracy to commit simple assault and corruption of minors' (Bechtel and Cannella 2006: 26). The charges stemmed from an incident involving Downs offering one of his players $25 'to knock a mildly retarded teammate out of a game by hitting him with a baseball.'
- March 2008: Patrick Roy, former NHL goalie and head coach of his son Jonathan's Quebec Major Hockey League team, the Quebec Ramparts, was suspended for five games and the team was fined $4,000 for his part in one of Junior Hockey's worst ever fights. The senior Roy was cited for encouraging the bench-clearing brawl, along with goading his goal-tending son to challenge, and then attack, his opposing goalie, who remained unwilling to fight even as the junior Roy punched him repeatedly (see Table 2.1). Jonathan Roy was suspended for seven games and fined $500 for his role in the brawl (http://www.cbc.ca/sports/hockey/story/2008/03/25/roy-suspension.html).

Cell 12: parental abuse

There are many disturbing practices that occur in the world of sport that even casual observers know something about and regular participants know all too well, but on which there is scant sociological research (e.g. Engh 1999; Baron 2007; Hennessy and Schwartz 2007; Hyman 2009; Thompson 2010). Parental abuse is one such topic. Not all parents offend, and not all fathers or mothers leave 'wounds' (Connell 1992; Young and White 2000), but all parents who coach, volunteer, administer or simply stand on the sidelines of their kids' games are aware of 'problem parents.' Every parent knows an angry 'hockey Dad' or 'soccer Mom,' and most parents have witnessed other parents participate in 'verbal dueling' (Hennessy and Schwartz 2007: 206). Many child athletes have been embarrassed by it. Even more troublingly, abusive parental behaviours are often hidden from public view and, not surprisingly, tend to revolve around the *powerlessness* of children, many of whom simply do not want to play. As Crisfield (1996: 14) notes, children often feel powerless to oppose an overbearing parent who insists that they play, or play in a certain way. Outcomes may range from decreased enjoyment and motivation for children, to self-esteem problems and 'drop-out' (Hyman 2009).

The local sports media routinely contain news of ugly incidents involving parents berating players or criticizing officials. SRV in this area manifests itself in a variety of forms, including the following examples: coercing children into demanding or dangerous training regimens at extremely young ages; the harassment of coaches (both verbal and physical), many of whom are children or teenagers themselves; sideline confrontations among parents; the encouragement of inappropriate behaviours in child athletes by parents who, in turn, aim discouraging, disparaging, threatening or otherwise inappropriate comments at players and coaches; and, the encouragement of high-risk or combative play that leads almost inevitably to injuries in child athletes. Many of these behaviours are connected to unrealistic expectations parents have for their children in sport. As one of the only in-depth studies in this area, journalist Mark Hyman's (2009) recent book, *Until it Hurts*, is a troubling review of adult abuse in youth sports, and a thoughtful examination of how child athletes are placed under high-stress by over-achieving parents and adults.

The following are examples of incidents of parental abuse:

- 1993: In some of my early work on risk, pain and injury in sport, I spoke to dozens of Canadian varsity athletes, both male and female, who feared parental reaction to their play, not wanting to play or even to getting hurt and being injured (e.g. Young et al. 1994).
- April 1999: Former Cincinnati Reds third baseman and manager, Ray Knight, was charged with battery, disorderly conduct and affray following an altercation at a girls' softball game in Albany, GA (Nack and Munson 1995a: 88). Knight, who was watching his 12-year-old daughter play, and the father of a girl on the opposing team, engaged in a heated argument, which ultimately led to Knight punching the other man in the head (Nack and Munson 1995a).

- January 2000: Matteo Picca, a carpenter from Staten Island, NY, was charged with assault and criminal possession of a weapon following an altercation involving his 12-year-old son's hockey coach, Lou Aiani. Picca 'had been heard complaining angrily during the game that his son had not improved all season' (Nack and Munson 1995a: 88). An argument between Picca and Aiani resulted in Aiani being struck in the face by hockey sticks wielded by Picca.
- January 2002: A Massachusetts judge sentenced Thomas Junta to six–ten years in prison for the beating death of another father, 40-year-old Michael Costin, in a fight after a youth hockey practice in which the sons of both men participated. Junta, a 44-year-old truck driver weighing 270lbs, struck Costin, who was 100lbs lighter, repeatedly and slammed his head into the ground until he became unconscious (*Maclean's*, 21 January 2002: 11).
- January 2005: A 47-year-old Toronto man was criminally charged after choking the coach of his nine-year-old son's minor ice-hockey team and was banned from attending arenas for five years – the harshest penalty ever levied by the Greater Toronto Hockey League (http://www.ctv.ca/servlet/Article-News/story/CTVNews/1106308011832_81/?hub=TopStories).
- January 2007: Jim Gahan, father of former US Junior National in-line speed skating champion Corey Gahan, was found guilty of conspiracy to distribute steroids to a minor, and sentenced to six years in prison. Gahan is 'believed to be the first *parent* convicted of providing steroids to his own child' (Llosa and Wertheim 2008: 31). The charges stem from Jim Gahan's placing his rising-star son on regimens of anabolic steroids and human growth hormone, beginning when Corey was 12 years old and continuing until he was disqualified from competition at age 17 (Llosa and Wertheim 2008).
- March 2009: Hockey Calgary's Vice President of Operations reported 'an alarming escalation' of incidents involving parents verbally or physically abusing referees (Ferguson 2009: B1). Speaking on the behaviour of parents in minor hockey four years earlier, NHL legend Bobby Orr noted: 'Anyone who thinks we don't have problems, get your head out of the sand. Because we do' (*Calgary Herald*, 5 November 2005: E2).

Cell 13: sexism/racism

Likely representing the most common forms of identity violence, examples of sexism and racism can be found almost anywhere in sport and are expansive enough to warrant their own 'cells.'

Where sexism (or gender discrimination) is concerned, the world of sport is replete with structural, ideological and experiential barriers for females that, cumulatively, add up to patterned and systemic forms of oppression (Birrell 2000; Messner 2002). This is not the only form of 'sexism' (stereotypical and trivializing attitudes can also affect men), but it is a central manifestation. A range of possibilities are involved, including prohibiting females from competing or restricting involvement, to diminishing their participation, to commodifying ('sexploiting') their participation to promote sales.

The following are examples of incidents of sexism:

*   February 2007: After years of holding out against equal prize money for the winners of the men's and women's tennis competitions, the Wimbledon All England Club agreed to fall in line with other Grand Slam events (such as the US Open) and award men and women equal prize money (http://www.independent. co.uk/sport/tennis/wimbledon-officials-relent-on-equal-pay-437390.html).
*   January 2011: Former soccer player and Sky Sports commentator, Andy Gray, was initially suspended, and then fired, following controversial comments aimed at a female assistant referee, and lewd comments directed towards a female fellow TV presenter (Gibson 2011). (He was, however, later compensated by Sky for being sacked: http://www.guardian. co.uk/football/2011/feb/06/andy-gray-sky-settlement.)
*   March 2011: Adding to the long-standing tradition of female cheerleaders and girls and women being used as 'props' performing in some peripheral way at all-male sports (such as scantily-clad 'ice girls' shoveling excess ice during NHL intermissions, and equally scantily-clad 'tub girls' selling beer at CFL and NFL games), the Lingerie Football League, featuring female players wearing only helmets and underwear, announced that it was expanding from US cities into Canadian cities in the summer of 2011 (http://www.calgaryherald.com/ sports/Lingerie+Football+coming+Canada/4610463/story.html).
*   April 2011: Following years of struggle, including legal action and human rights complaints, the IOC finally agreed to include women's ski jumping as an Olympic event at the 2014 Winter Games in Sochi, Russia (Hall 2011: F2). As Coakley and Donnelly (2009) show, many Olympic events continue to be closed to females.

Research shows that racism, or the expression of systems of racially or ethnically motivated intolerance, intersects with the world of sport in a number of disturbing ways. These include, but are not restricted to, the following examples: fans of soccer teams, sometimes associated with far-right political parties, using racist chants, songs and threats against players of colour in a number of countries (e.g. many black English players claim to have been harassed both at home and abroad over the years, and Caucasian current Celtic FC manager, Neil Lennon, has been the victim of numerous sectarian attacks and threats – see below); hooligan fan groups, again sometimes linked with organized right-wing politics, abusing immigrants and ethnic minorities in the context of soccer games (e.g. Murphy et al. 1990); and media personnel making flagrantly racist claims and slurs during sports events (e.g. in North American sports television, this has led to the instant removal of numerous high profile commentators such as CBS reporter Jimmy 'The Greek' Snyder, fired in 1988 after publicly stating that African Americans were naturally superior athletes because they had been 'bred' to produce stronger offspring during slavery).

In response to sports-related racism, many groups have 'fought back,' as may be witnessed in the anti-racist initiatives of British soccer clubs (e.g. Leicester City's 'Foxes Against Racism'), and in the efforts of FIFA (Fédération Internationale de Football Association) to emblazon the centre of World Cup soccer pitches on match-days with huge banners appealing to the public to 'Say No to Racism.'

The following are examples of incidents of racism:

- February 2001: Jason Williams, a white forward with the NBA's Sacramento Kings, made racist comments during a heated exchange with an Asian American spectator, while Williams was sitting on the bench during a game. The comments resulted in a $15,000 fine from the NBA, a public apology and a suspended Nike ad-campaign (Wertheim 2001: 26).
- September 2001: During the 2001 US Open, white Australian tennis player, Lleyton Hewitt, made headlines for uttering racist remarks aimed towards both his African American opponent, James Blake, and Marion Johnson, an African American official. After being called for a costly foot-foul by Johnson, Hewitt allegedly remarked to the umpire, 'Look at him. Look at him. Look at him, mate. Look at him, and you tell me what the similarity is' (*Sports Illustrated*, 10 September 2001: 74). Hewitt denied that his comments were in any way 'racial.'
- September 2003: Former ESPN 'Sunday NFL Countdown' host and outspoken Conservative, Rush Limbaugh, caused controversy with his on-air comment, in the context of the success of black NFL quarterback Donovan McNabb, that '[t]he media has been very desirous that a black quarterback do well. There is a little hope invested in McNabb, and he got a lot of credit for the performance of this team that he didn't deserve' (Kennedy and Bechtel 2003: 22). Limbaugh's comments sparked national outrage; he resigned three days later. McNabb continues to play in the NFL.
- May 2011: Former player and current manager of Celtic FC, Neil Lennon, has repeatedly been the target of sectarian abuse over the years. Lennon stopped playing international soccer following death threats in 2002. Two men were sent to prison for attacking him in the street in 2008. In 2011, bullets were sent to his home in the mail and, most recently, he was attacked on the sidelines by an enraged fan in full view of a crowded stadium (http://www.bbc.co.uk/news/uk-scotland-13368945).

Cell 14: other identity violence

They may be among the most common articulations of identity violence, but sexism and racism are not the only ways that persons and groups are treated prejudicially, even abusively, because of an 'achieved' characteristic they display, or an identity ascribed to them. Sport is replete with insensitive and victimizing ideologies that compromise, or block, sports experience for participants, but three other forms of identity violence are worthy of note:

- Homophobia is a fear or intolerance of lesbian, gay, bi-sexual or trans-gendered (LGBT) persons (Pronger 1990; Anderson 2000, 2005; Cauldwell 2007). As Coakley and Donnelly (2009: 229) write: 'It is based on the notion that homosexuality is "deviant" or immoral, and it supports prejudice, discrimination, harassment, and violence toward those identified.' Homophobia at all levels of North American sport, where very few athletes have spoken in support of gay rights, is common. At the professional level and in the NBA specifically, widely reported recent incidents include former Miami Heat guard Tim Hardaway stating on a radio programme that he 'hates' gay people, and Los Angeles Lakers star Kobe Bryant being fined $100,000 by the league for shouting homophobic slurs at an opponent (*Calgary Herald*, 14 April 2011: F2).

- Ableism refers to the privileging of able-bodied activity and participants, and to assigning inferior value or worth to persons who face developmental, physical or emotional challenges (Nixon 2000). It may be seen in sport in the way in which sport has, until relatively recently, been a context of cultural exclusion for people who are visually- or hearing-impaired, or physically or mentally challenged in some way. Howe (2004), Joukowsky and Rothstein (2002) and Hoyle and White (1999) have all demonstrated how sport privileges conventional notions of the 'athletic' body, rejecting or diminishing bodies perceived to be 'deviant.' The creation of events such as the Paralympics in 1960, the Special Olympics in 1962 and amateur athletic bodies such as Disabled Sports USA and the English Federation of Disability Sport rejects binary notions of the normal/deviant body, and provides hope for challenged athletes (Howe 2008; Brittain 2009).

- Jingoism refers to an excessive sense of nationalism, while xenophobia refers to a fear, or hatred, of strangers. Both are, again, depressingly visible in sport. Almost all of the extensive literature on European soccer hooliganism makes note of how rival fan chants, fights and other rituals at international matches are driven, at least in part, by excessive notions of nationhood and national identity (e.g. Williams et al. 1984; Bairner 2001). In Canada, Gillett et al. (1996) have shown how ice hockey is enmeshed in xenophobic codes that systematically disrespect and disparage Russian and Scandinavian players, among others.

Cell 15: animal abuse

Although animal sports go back to antiquity (animal–human contests were popular in ancient Greece and Rome – Cashmore 2000), relatively little sociological work has been carried out. Perhaps the best known early scholarly research on animal sports was produced by the anthropologist Clifford Geertz (1972) whose study of the cultural meanings of Balinese cockfighting is well known and widely cited, as is Eric Dunning's figurational work on the social class origins of fox hunting in the UK (Elias and Dunning 1986; Dunning 1999). Information in varying degrees of detail is also available on other animal sports involving horses (Yates et al. 2001;

Herzog and Golden 2009; Gerber and Young 2011), dogs (Baker 1996; Atkinson and Young 2005a), hares, stags and deer (Windeatt 1982) and other animals (Wade 1990, 1996). But, in general, this strand of research is slight.

The focus of 'speciesism' and animal exploitation research (e.g. Atkinson and Young 2005a) takes two forms. The first approach considers the explicit nature of the activity itself and how animals are used, while the second zones in on less obvious, accidental or hidden dimensions. In this respect, animal sports may be understood in terms of what Goffman (1959) would call the 'front' and 'back' regions of social settings. Examples of the 'front' regions might include the graphically bloody way that a fox or a hare is literally torn to pieces by mauling hounds, or the slow, torturous violence imposed upon a bull by repeated bull ring 'performers' culminating, depending on the setting in which it takes place, in its public suffering and killing. Meanwhile, the 'back' regions of such pursuits would include practices related, for instance, to the preparation of the event, or the manner in which the participants are treated. Here, the focus shifts to the lesser known, and often hidden, aspects of these activities, such as the ways in which a bull is 'prepared' for its fight (for instance, by being antagonized behind the scenes, by having petroleum jelly rubbed in its eyes, and other cruelty aimed at 'taking the fight' out of the animal), how horses used in bullfights may be drugged to dull the pain of goring, how rodeo horses sustain injuries that necessitate their euthanization (Gerber and Young 2011), and how racehorses are given drug cocktails to 'produce winners' or the ways in which racing dogs are sometimes kept, housed and/or discarded under inhumane circumstances (Atkinson and Young 2005a).

The following are examples of incidents of animal abuse:

- Accidents, injuries and fatalities are a routine feature of rodeo events such as the chuckwagon races at the annual Calgary Stampede. In 2005, nine horses died while being herded to Stampede Park. In 2006, two horses died in the races and, in 2007, three died. One horse died in 2008, two in 2009 and, in 2010, six horses died – four in chuckwagon racing competitions and the other two in other rodeo events (Gerber and Young 2011).
- One of Britain's best known steeple-chases, known as the 'Grand National,' is held annually at Aintree, close to Liverpool. Since just 2000, at least 30 horses have died during, or related to, competition or in training (Davies 2011). In North America, the Equine Injury Database reports that there are two horse deaths per 1,000 starts in thoroughbred racing (The Jockey Club 2010), and PETA claim that US tracks are the 'world's deadliest' (Mullins 2010).
- December 2007: Former Atlanta Falcons quarterback, Michael Vick, was sentenced to 23 months in a federal prison after being found guilty of animal cruelty and conspiracy to operate a dog fighting enterprise. Despite an initial ban from the League, Vick continues to play and prosper in the NFL, now with the Philadelphia Eagles (Hack 2007).
- April 2010: Following the Vancouver Winter Olympic Games, an employee of Howling Dog Tours, Whistler, British Columbia, killed 100 sled dogs by

shooting and stabbing them and dumping their bodies into a mass grave. The justification provided was that this was the cheapest way of disposing of the dogs following a slow winter season interrupted by the Olympics (Pemberton 2011). Tougher animal cruelty laws, including jail time, are currently under consideration in the province of British Columbia.

• February 2011: San Diego authorities stumbled across a cockfighting ring with more than 400 birds. Authorities charged two men with possession of gamecocks with intent to fight. In San Diego, this represents a misdemeanour charge only, and the leniency of the punishment is thought to be a contributing factor to the prevalence of cockfighting in the area (Lowrey 2011).

• May 2011: Due to widespread doping problems throughout the world of thoroughbred horse racing, federal regulations are currently under review in the US. Discussion includes the drug furosemide, which keeps the animal's lungs and airways from bleeding while it runs (horses that have this problem are known as 'bleeders') (http://www.drf.com/news/federal-regulation-could-cripple-horse-racing).

Cell 16: political violence/terrorism

This cell embodies aspects of violence threatened or perpetrated at sports events in the pursuit of political or ideological goals. Even before the 11 September 2001 attacks on the US, preparations for international sports events such as the FIFA World Cup, the Commonwealth Games and the Olympic Games had long involved the international exchange of policing and security information on possible problems and probable offenders. But it is unlikely that any single sport event has been plagued for as long with international political tensions as the Olympics. Atkinson and Young (2003, 2005b) provide a detailed summary of such tensions, such as those occurring at: the 1908 Summer Games in London, where tensions bubbled between English Protestants and Irish Catholics; the 1936 so-called 'Nazi Games,' held in Berlin, and used by Hitler to showcase German military might to the world; the 1968 Mexico City Games, remembered more for the 'Black Power' salute of two African American sprinters than for the deaths of hundreds of young protesters at the hands of a government seeking to quell student protests; the 1972 Munich Games, where members of the Palestinian 'Black September' group killed 11 members of the Israeli team; the 'Cold War' Games in Moscow and Los Angeles in 1980 and 1984, remembered for their boycotts; and the Atlanta Games in 1996 where a pipe bomb hidden in a knapsack exploded, ripping screws and nails through a huge crowd, killing one woman and injuring over 100 others. The sharing of international criminal intelligence in advance of large-scale sports events is clearly not new, but since the events of '9/11,' security preparations guarding against the threat of political violence and terrorism have been significantly stepped up, and the mere suggestion that a host city may be politically or militarily vulnerable to an attack is now enough to squash a bid. Consequently, many of the world's sports mega-events (the Olympics, FIFA's World Cup, the Commonwealth Games etc.) now assume more of the appearance of an armed military camp (replete with fighter jets, armed guards, machine guns, razor wire, electronic scanners and the like) than a festive public spectacle. The cost of 'securing the (Olympic) Games' currently sits at approximately one quarter of the overall budget (Atkinson and Young 2008).

Cell 17: offences against workers and the public

Offences against workers and the public include harmful (mental, physical and sexual) forms of human rights violations of often under-age workers in sports-related 'sweat-shop' industries located in the poorer countries and regions of the world, such as Malaysia, Indonesia, Pakistan and China. Recently, there has been a growth in international campaigns against the use of exploitative, coercive and high-pressure labour in settings where sport merchandise (such as running shoes and outdoor recreation equipment) is produced very cheaply by workers who are often young, poor, under-paid, and employed in problematic labour environments (Wazir 2001: 12). As Donnelly (2003, 2007) indicates, such workers may suffer further forms of abuse at the hands of powerful bosses, whom they may fear. A modest but growing body of research has been produced on the ways in which the production of sport, sport equipment and sport paraphernalia, interfaces with the violation of human justices for workers and the public (cf. Sage 1999; Kidd and Donnelly 2000). Notable also are human rights movements that have sprung up in opposition to these sorts of abuses, such as the US anti-Nike movement (Eitzen and Sage 2003: 201). Offences against workers and the public may also occur in more affluent settings, which are not usually viewed as sites of sports-related exploitation.

The following are examples of offences against workers and the public:

- April 1998: Mark Kasky, an anti-globalization activist, launched a lawsuit against Nike alleging that the company was in violation of California's Unfair Competition and False Advertising laws, citing that the company was making false claims in their advertisements about ensuring safe working conditions in their factories overseas. In 2002, the California Supreme Court ruled in favour of Kasky, finding that Nike was in fact making 'Commercial Speech,' which is subject to government regulation, and therefore Kasky could successfully sue Nike. In 2003, the case was settled out of court with Nike paying $1.5 million to the 'Washington, DC-based Fair Labor Association (FLA) for program operations and worker development programs focused on education and economic opportunity' (http://cbc.ca/news/story/2003/04/24/Nike_030424. html).
- February 2003: Martha Burk and the National Council of Women's Organizations endorsed the Women's National Basketball Association's Players Association (WNBAPA) in their goal of seeking more equitable working conditions. As Kennedy and McEntegart (2003) reported: 'According to the WNBAPA,

players earned less than 15% of revenue generated by the still unprofitable league, compared with 55% or more earned by athletes in other sports.'

- March 2004: A 75-page report commissioned by Oxfam, the Trade Union Congress and Labour Behind the Label, was released focusing on working conditions in Bulgaria, Cambodia, Thailand, China, Indonesia and Turkey. The report claimed that companies including Nike, Adidas, Puma and Umbro were forcing employees to work longer and harder for less money, in order to prepare their product for the Summer Olympic Games in Athens (http://www.cbc.ca/sports/story/2004/03/04/olympicgear0303.html).

- August 2007: In the build-up to the 2008 Beijing Olympic Games, and citing 'abuse behind the rings' (Yardley 2007: 4), human rights groups pressured the Chinese government to release journalists and dissidents who had critiqued the organization of the Games and its impositions on ordinary Chinese people. Groups such as Amnesty International and the Committee to Protect Journalists (*USA Today*, 8 August 2007) expressed concern on several fronts: that China would fall short on Olympic commitments to the environment and press freedoms; that widespread 'civility training' for locals was coercive; that human rights violations were routine; and, that worksites had been dangerous and caused worker fatalities and injuries ('Olympic Stadium deaths covered up,' *Calgary Herald*, 30 January 2008: A12).

- January 2010: In the long-standing and well-documented tradition of community 'cleansing' and image-enhancement by Olympic cities, in preparation for the 2010 Vancouver Winter Olympics, up to two dozen homeless men and women were forced by city officials to relocate from Whistler (the site of alpine skiing) to emergency shelters in Squamish, out of town (CBC News, 8 January 2010).

Cell 18: offences against the environment

While traditional sport is played, and modern sports tourism (e.g. skiing, golf, trekking, cycling, fishing, hunting, paddling, surfing, diving, sailing etc.) is undertaken, by people throughout the world in varying ways, one factor unites all versions of sport and exercise everywhere – it requires space, equipment and resources. Concerns that sports events, venues and patterns may have harmful ecological and environmental effects have recently prompted research in the sociology of sport. For example, Bale (1994) and Lenskyj (2000) have investigated the negative impact on the environment of hosting large-scale sports events, such as the Olympic Games, that require the development of huge areas of land and may produce 'degraded environments' (Lenskyj 2000: 155), habitat loss and expedite wildlife extinction. Similarly, critics have decried the development of golf courses and ski resorts, both of which again require massive parcels of land, often in untouched and pristine wilderness where wildlife and natural habitat may be damaged or lost altogether. Yet others have drawn attention to the 'oiling' of rivers, lakes and waterways used for boating and waterskiing. Consistent political pressure to respect 'sustainability,' and growing threats from interest groups (opposed to land loss, noise pollution, damage to vegetation and wildlife and the generation of waste) to invoke environmental laws have led to an increasingly 'green' fitness and 'eco-exercise' movements in many countries (Benidickson 1997; Weiss et al. 1998; Collins et al. 2007; Mansfield 2009) and increasingly politicized sport subcultures, such as 'Surfers Against Sewage' (Wheaton 2008).

Social and political opposition to sport venue development is such that proposed plans for modestly-sized sports facilities (such as gyms, shooting ranges, or volleyball domes), medium-sized venues (such as soccer stadiums or ice-hockey arenas) and certainly so-called 'mega' sports events (such as FIFA World Cup venues or Olympic Games sites), now require compelling evidence that construction will not unduly compromise the environment or living conditions in the community. Detailed environmental statements have become a required staple of all Olympic bids, though not all such 'footprint' promises are genuine or kept. On a global scale, such is the push for a 'greener' sport that the United Nations Environment Programme began actively promoting the integration of environmental considerations into sports development and the growth of responsible sport manufacturing in 1994 (www.unep.org).

As an example of how traditional sport can 'offend' the environment, consider the following figures from two of the most popular sports in the US: The average capacity of an MLB stadium is approximately 40,000 (football stadia tend to be far larger). Aside from the energy it takes to fuel these stadia and the greenhouse gas emissions produced by and at them, the volume of garbage produced is enormous. At one LA Dodgers game in 2010 there was 3.11 tons of garbage produced (Blair 2009). Each MLB team plays 81 home games per year, resulting in an aggregate seasonal garbage volume in the thousands of tons. Clearly, this has to be disposed of. The new Dallas Cowboys stadium cost over $1 billion dollars to build and approximately $200,000 in monthly utility bills (Blair 2009).

In light of such patterned 'norms,' it is unsurprising that the world of sport finds itself under increasing scrutiny from critics who demand not only more respect for diminishing environments, flora and fauna, but also more transparency and responsibility in the operationalization of new sports initiatives. Once again, examples of the sheer span of this cell across the globe are not hard to find, and asking questions about 'how green is sport?' (Maguire et al. 2002) seems increasingly relevant and responsible.

The following are examples of offences against the environment:

*   November 1993: International concerns were raised when Sir Edmund Hillary, the first person to successfully climb Mt Everest, criticized the huge amount of garbage and debris that has been left behind at several of the mountain's camps. The accumulation of debris, human waste and human corpses (referred to throughout the climbing literature – e.g. Krakauer 1997) comes from hundreds of expeditions to the mountain over the past half a century. Even 20 years ago, environmentalists estimated at the time that over 50

tonnes of garbage had been scattered across Everest (O'Brien and McCallum 1993). Since that time, there have been several 'Eco Everest Expeditions' aimed solely at ridding the mountain of refuse. For instance, the 2011 Expedition aims to clean up over 5,000 kilograms of garbage (http://www.theuiaa.org/news_300_Eco-Everest-Expedition-2011-underway).

• June 1999: In what is believed to be the largest act of vandalism to a major golf championship venue in US history, Rich Jones allegedly destroyed 12 greens and three tee boxes at the Southern Hills Country Club in Tulsa Oklahoma, site of the 2001 US Open, by spraying acid on them. The total damage from one night of vandalism cost approximately $2.9 million (Maisel et al. 2001).

• February 2006: The Italian and European Alpine chapters of the World Wildlife Fund raised concerns about environmental issues surrounding the preparations being made in the months leading up to the 2006 Winter Olympics in Turin, Italy. As Llanos observed, these concerns included:

> New ski jumps and a bobsled run that required clearing forests when existing courses in neighboring France could have been used; reliance on artificial snow which, the report said, weighs as much as five times more than real snow and damages the ground, in addition to requiring millions of gallons of water; and exceptions being made with respect to environmental, landscape and urban planning laws.
>
> (*Llanos 2006*)

• September 2007: In an attempt to counter some of the environmental damage that has taken place in increasingly popular tourist and climbing destinations of Patagonia, including the Fitz Roy and Cerro Torre Massif in the northern part of Los Glaciares National Park, officials passed new regulations prohibiting the use of horses to transport food and equipment to the various climbing and trekking destinations, and the building of permanent structures, or 'climber's huts,' is no longer permitted (Duprez 2006).

• September 2009: Despite claims that the 2010 Vancouver Winter Olympic Games would be the 'greenest' ever, and related cavalier claims from organizers that 'the environment is the third pillar of the Olympics' (after sport and culture), respected Canadian naturalist, David Suzuki, concluded: 'We've seen very little evidence that the environment is really a high priority' (http://news.bbc.co.uk/2/hi/americas/8176865.stm).

Thinking sociologically about formations of SRV

Not all of the practices encapsulated in the SRV matrix of cells are normally thought of as 'sports violence,' but they are all clearly potentially harmful or intentionally abusive acts that cannot easily be separated from the sports process and that only begin to 'make sense' when the social significance of sport is closely examined. That is to say, they all fall within the jurisdiction of the definition of SRV offered in Chapter 1. On a scale of social legitimacy, and echoing Smith's (1983: 9) earlier typology, some of the cells (e.g. 1, 7, 11) represent behaviours that are *relatively* legitimate and, while considered 'deviant' in the eyes of some observers, occur frequently and may be widely acknowledged and accepted within the world and culture of sport. On the other hand, other cells (e.g. 8, 9, 16) represent behaviours that are entirely less acceptable on a number of levels including the official rules of a given sport, the informal norms and values of players, the general public, as well as the law of the land. Needless to say, in both cases, what is considered as 'legitimate' and 'illegitimate' depends on who is doing the defining, and it is on this exact matter – the matter of how we understand violence in sport and what we propose to do about it – that people and groups disagree, and where violence in sport intersects with questions of culture, power and ideology (Coakley and Donnelly 2009; Donnelly and Young 2004). As with sport more generally, what is considered as *sports violence* is certainly 'contested terrain' (Donnelly and Young 1985: 20) and means different things to different groups of people (Bourdieu 1978: 826).

All of the cells, including those examined in Chapters 2 and 3, are dynamic. They have not remained static over time, and many have significantly changed in their form. For instance, as most British researchers have acknowledged, soccer hooliganism grew far more organized and 'global' between the period of the 1970s and the new millennium, and its local and domestic manifestations also changed considerably in concert with widely implemented policing modifications in the 1970s and 1980s. Specifically, at this time, one unintended effect of increases in policing mechanisms *inside* soccer stadia was to displace the problem to *outside* stadia, and to also affect the timing of hooligan encounters (Dunning et al. 1988; Murphy et al. 1990). In this way, it is important to note the *changing* character and expression of SRV.

Some behaviours are deeply grounded in culture, tradition and ritual and, despite facing robust opposition, show no signs of disappearing any time soon. Boxing, bullfighting, fox hunting, dog and horse racing, ice hockey and golf are all sports which have been forced to counter resistance to their 'violent' outcomes – whether the injured parties are human, animal or environmental. Fox hunting in Britain represents an exceptional recent case as a 'blood' sport that has been both prohibited at the level of government and marginalized at the level of popular reputation, though such is the strength of its place in British society that it persists, according to the League of Cruel Sports (http://www.league.org.uk/uploads/media/28/7382. pdf) despite an outright ban. Further, other types of SRV, though hardly new, have taken on entirely more sinister trappings in a changed and changing global community, as Atkinson and Young demonstrate in their study of political violence and terrorism at the Olympic Games (2005b). In this particular case, the threat of political violence has now significantly altered the way that sport is played, funded, policed and insured. The ripple effects on what a 'secure' Olympic Games both costs and 'looks like' are enormous (Atkinson and Young 2012).

Each of the behaviours represented by the respective cells has received a certain amount of scholarly attention, though some (soccer hooliganism (cell 3) and fist-fighting in ice hockey (cell 2) in particular) have been far more comprehensively studied than others, and some have been curiously under-studied (such as cruelty in animal sports (cell 15), parental abuse (cell 12), political violence related to sport (cell 16) and environmental offences (cell 18)). Taken individually, the cells have certainly been approached as forms of aggression, violence or abuse that may threaten, hurt or victimize, but scholars have fallen short of interpreting them as dimensions of 'sports violence' per se. Very little is known about the links that they may share. In this sense, a sociological assessment is important because it acknowledges differences at the same time as underscoring common threads and overlaps.

A number of points can be made in this regard. First, and perhaps most importantly, the cells demonstrate one critical feature in common: they all unite violent, harmful or victimizing practices *through* sport – that is to say, *sport* (rather than, for instance, other social institutions such as the workplace, the family, the church or education etc.) is the context of, and common denominator for, these activities. In order to both understand SRV phenomena and to react responsibly to them, acknowledging that they are centrally connected to the sports process is critical. Second, all of the cells represent the attempt by a group or individual to exert *control* over others. In this respect, all dimensions of SRV may be understood in terms of themes of power, dominance and control, or what Donnelly and Young (borrowing from sociologist David Garland) call 'cultures of control' (2004). Third, in terms of who 'does' the behaviour, who supports and funds the behaviour and who consumes and watches it, most, if not all, of the cells display strongly *gendered* underpinnings (see Chapter 8). Unsurprisingly, given the male preserve that sport has traditionally represented, men and masculinity feature centrally, and rarely flatteringly. However, as the preceding review of the cells shows, and Chapter 8 goes on to discuss, the involvement of females is certainly increasing as opportunities for female involvement in sport have opened up. This raises important questions as to whether aggressive and violent sports behaviour is best understood as part of socialization into *gendered* roles and identities in sport, or socialization into sport per se.

Crucially, it is when one delves into the question of such commonalities and interconnections between the various dimensions of SRV that its sociological essence becomes clear. While genes and impulses and individualized pathologies likely play some role in violence in sport (see Figure 4.1 on page 97) – these also remain to be adequately researched and demonstrated – the fundamentally *sociological* causes and character of SRV are obvious.

The cells are meant to be understood as interactive rather than exclusive or isolated components of SRV. Indeed, around particular behaviours, and in certain cases, many of them coalesce and overlap. For instance, using real cases of SRV (described earlier) as examples:

- A college hazing incident involving male wrestlers in lewd and harassing acts in a public bar links cells 4 ('player violence away from the game'), 5 ('street crimes'), 7 ('athlete initiation/hazing'), 9 ('sexual assault'), 17 ('offences against workers and the public') and, since coaches may be complicit in the act, cell 11 ('offences by coaches/administrators/medical staff').
- A young female gymnast starving herself due to repeated criticism from coaches and judges for being 'too fat,' and eventually dying from anorexia, links cells 6 ('violence against the self'), 11 ('offences by coaches/administrators/medical staff') and, since it seems unreasonable to accept that parents who see their daughter every day might not 'notice' her losing 50lbs of body weight (*Dateline NBC* 1995), cell 12 ('parental abuse').
- A bomb intentionally deployed to cause harm at an Olympic event may bring together cells 3 ('crowd violence'), 5 ('street crimes'), 16 ('political violence/terrorism'), 17 ('offences against workers and the public') and even 18 ('offences against the environment').
- A post-event riot following an NBA World Championship or NHL Stanley Cup links cells 3 ('crowd violence'), 5 ('street crimes' – because behaviours such as looting, trespassing and arson are involved), 17 ('offences against workers and the public' – because public property is destroyed and civil servants such as the police and others are threatened or hurt) and 9 ('sexual assault' – because sexual assaults may occur in the context of the riot).

Further, each individual cell should be examined for its sociological underpinnings, and its association with factors such as age, gender, social class, regionality, race and ethnicity, on its own accord, as well as for the links it may share with other cells along these axes. For instance: soccer hooliganism (cell 3) and fox hunting (cell 15) clearly demonstrate strong social class attachments (on the lower and upper ends respectively); predominantly Caucasian (Young 1988) North American sports crowd disorder (cell 3) and fan assaults on non-white soccer players (cells 2 and 13) demonstrate strong racial underpinnings (they are both manifested mostly by white offenders); and, once again, gender is a common thread throughout most, if not all, of the cells in the matrix. As Coakley and Donnelly (2009) have emphasized in this connection, it is important to understand that all aspects of violence in sport are related to wider historical and cultural factors, and to questions of power.

Finally, there is a clear and important *clustering* effect taking place in the world of SRV. As suggested by Bronfenbrenner's (1979) human ecology model, the breadth of any social process, such as the SRV process, moves from the inter- (and even intra-) personal level (as Brackenridge (2001) has shown in her work on sexual harassment), all the way through to the global level of action and impact (as Maguire (1999) has shown in his work on 'global sport'). In this way, some of the SRV behaviours operate at the level of the individual (e.g. a trainer treats her horse cruelly; a bodybuilder pumps himself full of steroids), some operate at the level of the community (e.g. coaches in an entire hockey league require their players to bodycheck dangerously; managers in a factory making running shoes underpay and overwork their employees) and some operate at far wider, even global, levels (e.g. the governing body of an entire sport requires its young, female competitors to suppress natural body and weight standards to an unhealthy extent; a powerful international sports association stipulates that its female athletes must wear clothing that amounts to what critics have called 'sexploitation'). In these ways, and as with other established social processes, the SRV process should be understood in terms of organizational clustering effects that span the individual *and* society.

The SRV wheel

To avoid separating SRV from the causes that give rise to it in the first place, it is critical to think about SRV as a *dynamic* process. The SRV wheel (see Figure 4.1)[1] thus reconfigures the previous, and clearly too static, matrix of cells (Table 4.1) in a way that allows us to understand the interaction between macro and

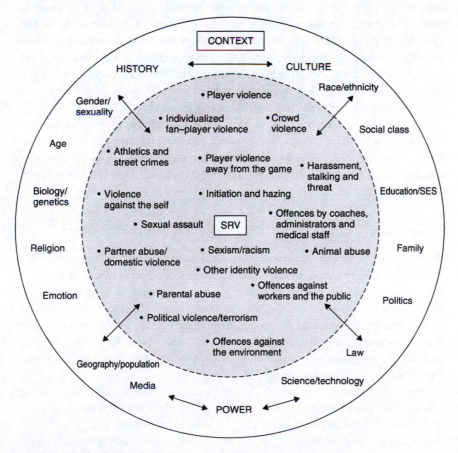

FIGURE 4.1 The SRV wheel

micro elements of the sports violence process. The outer circle, or 'contextual zone,' represents macro factors. These are mostly sociological and institutional (e.g. social class, gender, age, race etc.), although other factors that represent possible contextual causes for, or facilitators of, SRV also appear here (e.g. biology/genetics, science/technology, media). Of utmost importance in the contextual zone are the roles played by history, culture and power in shaping SRV, as well as shaping responses to SRV. Some of the contextual factors are more impacting than others, but their respective impact may change and shift over time. Meanwhile, the inner circle, or 'action zone,' contains the formations (i.e. the expressions and manifestations) of SRV. These are the 'shapes' that SRV typically assumes; the replicated patterns and forms that group together sub-strands of social behaviour into one larger cluster. Again, far from mutually exclusive, these SRV forms may overlap and bleed together, as may be seen in the cases of a harassing coach (linking cells 8, 9 and 11 – the Canadian ice-hockey case involving Graham James discussed earlier is an obvious, real-life illustration), or in the case of a violently xenophobic soccer crowd (linking cells 3 and 14). There is more than enough evidence to suggest that each of the forms ('cells') in the action zone should be viewed as an autonomous entity, comprised of numerous sub-strands of behaviour. The dotted lining of the inner circle represents the permeability and flow between contextual structures and SRV formations. Similarly, because it is not a unidirectional relationship, the multidimensional arrows signify how the contextual factors and formations of SRV are interactive and have effects on each other, as is evident from so many of the concrete SRV examples provided earlier in this chapter.

It is not easy to visually depict an SRV schema that fully captures every movement and action that is taking place, at both contextual (macro) and action (micro) levels. However, the SRV wheel represents a useful, and sociological way, of thinking about the fluid relationship between these levels, as well as between the SRV cells themselves.

Conclusion

Whether one prefers to adhere to traditional lines of thinking and conceive of 'sports violence' primarily in terms of crowd violence and player violence, or to accept the broader notion of SRV, it is clear that violence in sport assumes a far wider variety of forms and expressions than the research suggests so far. This chapter has attempted to expand the way that we think about violence *related to* sport. The initial matrix of cells representing varied formations of SRV offers one way that we might usefully expand our understanding of behaviours that threaten, harm and victimize *in and through* sport.

Arguably, this sort of approach to a more inclusive notion of SRV is needed because, far from existing in a vacuum, violent practices related to sport grow out of, and exist relationally with, other aspects of the social process, such as relations of power, as well as social stratifiers such as social class, gender/sexuality, race/ethnicity, religion, age etc. In this respect, and illustrated using the more dynamic image of the SRV wheel, this SRV approach contains a number of potential strengths. It provides, for example, a useful tool and a fresh lens through which we may consider the subject matter in a broader social and sociological light, and a model in which the dynamic connections between SRV and other social issues can be identified and analysed. Additionally, rather than seeing the formations of SRV as mutually exclusive, the cells can be used in conjunction with one another to account for the genesis, manifestation and ramification of sport cultures in many settings and, as noted, at different levels.

The vast majority of existing sociological studies of SRV are limited to the behaviour of fans and players in quite specific contexts. Of course, this is both understandable and useful. However, if the sociological and, indeed, social purpose of sports violence research is to better understand not only direct acts of physical violence that may result in personal injury, but also harmful acts perpetrated in the context of sport that threaten or produce injury, or in some other way compromise human justice and civil liberty (i.e. to stay true to the definition of SRV offered in Chapter 1), then we need to widen the focus of what we consider 'violence' and to change the type of sociological lens we are using.

Arguably, with very few exceptions (cf. Dunning 1999), conventional approaches to sports violence have produced sociologically and socially isolated snapshots of violence. The empirical moments they represent are, of course, important enough. We need them, and they provide the crucial 'lived experiences' that empirically minded sociologists and anthropologists cherish. But what matters most is that these snapshots are placed in the context of broader *formations* of sports–related and social violence; what matters most is the tracing, in Elias's (cited in Rojek 1985: 159) terms, of the interdependencies among the many and varied individuals and groups involved.

An excellent final empirical example of Elias's suggestion comes from someone with no scholarly interest in sport at all. Writing on formations of political violence in Northern Ireland, Allen Feldman (1991: 1) talks about the importance of seeing violent practices as 'relational sequences of action.' What Feldman means by this is that ostensibly unrelated practices are likely deeply connected and interlaced, and that it is important to uncover these links to truly understand patterns and trends, as well as to enable predictions about future violent phenomena to be made (which may be of practical benefit to policy makers and the authorities). Whether the focus is on practitioners of political terror or acts and actors of SRV, the important socio-logical point is to trace back the behaviour under investigation to the communities that forge it in the first place, and to look for parallels in other, apparently disparate, social behaviours and settings. To do this with respect to violence in sport, we need to consider the landscape of the phenomenon in its *widest* and *fullest* form.

5

RISK, PAIN AND INJURY IN SPORT

A cause or effect of violence?

Introduction

In contrast to other disciplines such as medicine, biomechanics, exercise physiology or psychology, sociological research on sports-related risk, pain and injury remains in its infancy. A partial explanation may be found in the fact that sociological attention to risk, pain and injury has consistently been subsumed under the umbrella classification of 'sports violence' rather than viewed as an area of study unto itself. In Canada, for instance, initial sociological enquiry was pioneered in the 1980s and 1990s by Michael Smith (1983, 1987, 1991) who posed preliminary questions about the social, physical and legal dimensions of risk. While recognizing the significance of injury research and laying the foundation for future work, Smith mainly approached injury as the 'downside' to aggressive sport and sport played aggressively, rather than as an autonomous field of research per se.

Beginning in the 1980s, and likely in-step with a broader turn to 'body' studies in the parent discipline over the past quarter of a century (cf. Featherstone et al. 1991; Frank 1991, 1995; Freund 1991; Shilling 1993; Lupton 1995), a number of sociologists of sport (mainly based in Britain and North America, but also increasingly from continental European and Australasian countries), examined elements of the subject matter more closely. Indeed, the literature on pain, injury and physicality in sport has expanded rapidly. Aspects of injury which have been examined so far by sociologists include contextual factors, injury rates and explanations of how injury is directly 'lived' and reflected upon by athletes themselves, as well as social responses to injury such as how media, medical and legal organizations have responded to it, and the implications of injury for health and social policy.

As the following list demonstrates, the sociological injury literature is already impressively diverse:

- Nixon (1992, 1993, 1994a, 1994b, 1996) has placed pain and injury in the context of 'cultures of risk' that characterize sport, as well as the socially stratified 'sportsnets' (or networks of social relationships) that athletes belong to;
- Sabo (1986, 1994) has examined the gendered underpinnings of sports injury and the philosophical codes many athletes adopt to approach pain;
- Hughes and Coakley (1991) have drawn from deviancy theory to explain violence and injury in sport as outcomes of over-conformity to a 'sport ethic' (see Chapter 1) that pervades much of modern sport and that prioritizes risk over wellbeing;
- Curry (1993), Donnelly and Young (1988) and Holmes and Frey (1990) have shown how athletes who shy away from pain are seldom attributed status as 'real athletes' in sport groups;
- Roderick and colleagues (Roderick 1998, 2006a, 2006b; Roderick et al. 2000), Safai (2001), Howe (2001), Malcolm (2009) and Walk (1997) have explored the complicity of the medical industry in sports injury;
- Theberge (1997), Pike (2000), Charlesworth (2004) and Cove (2006) are among the first sociologists examining the experience of pain and injury in the lives of female athletes; and
- I have, accompanied by colleagues and singly, investigated (1) how risk has social, subcultural and economic/occupational dimensions (Young 1993); (2) the various sense-making strategies male and female athletes use to play through pain that allow them to return to play even when at risk of further injury (Young et al. 1994; Young and White 1995; Young 1997), as well as (3) how consent and liability issues are interpreted by the courts when sports injury has been litigated (Young 1993; Young and Wamsley 1996).

But, for all its richness and diversity, this is only a partial picture of the variety of work on the subject that is currently being undertaken and compiled by sociologists.

This chapter takes stock of what sociologists have to say regarding the central dimensions and implications of risky athletic 'pain zones.' It examines the existing research, what themes are being pursued and how, what problems are emerging and, finally, what gaps exist and how they might be filled.

The social basis of risk, pain and injury

Among the most important sociological questions any student of sport must ask when examining sports-related pain and injury are 'what causes it?' and 'where does it come from?' There is a range of appropriate answers and, unsurprisingly, these answers are splintered along disciplinary lines.

Physiologically, one can point to a number of causal factors such as the basic technical requirements of sport and the various stresses and strains placed on bones, joints and muscles. For example, in Britain, the Football Association's Head of Sports Medicine, Alan Hodson, has remarked that '58% of injuries in football [soccer] are non-contact, arising from things like turning, landing, slowing down and sprinting . . . that is the nature of the game' (*The Independent*, 26 January 2001: 28). Some subdisciplines within the sport sciences, such as sports medicine and exercise physiology, have produced copious volumes of epidemiological research (cf. Vinger and Hoerner 1981; Adams et al. 1987; Caine et al. 1996; Harries et al. 1996; Mueller et al. 1996; Tator 2008) on the link between specific athletic pursuits and, for instance, acute, chronic or catastrophic injuries to particular body parts of general athlete populations, as well as more narrowly defined groups such as 'growing' (paediatric) athletes (Hyndman 1996), ageing athletes (Menard 1996) and athletes with disabilities (Booth 1996). Similarly extensive literatures on injury are available for athletes in most sports (Tator 2008).

Although obviously significant in and of themselves, sociologists are less concerned with these 'nature-of-the-game' sorts of factors than they are with the kinds of macro and micro contexts (sport-related cultures, structures, processes and mores) that represent the settings and circumstances in which sports injury occurs. In this respect, and once again, sports injury can indeed be seen to result from the nature of sport itself, but also from the way it is played, administered and managed.

Several sociologists such as Frey (1991), Hughes and Coakley (1991) and Nixon (1992) have suggested that sport occurs in a cultural context that normalizes and glorifies risk, pain and injury, and amid an institutional network of social relationships ('sportsnets') that pressures athletes to play with pain. This is the context for the creation of the so-called 'sport ethic' – as we saw in Chapter 1, a value embodied in many sport subcultures that encourages athletes to strive for distinction, make sacrifices, play through pain and accept few limits in their quest for success, team spirit and status. Nixon calls this overall setting a 'culture of risk' – here athletes accept the probability of minor injury and the possibility of major injury. For Hughes and Coakley and Nixon, it is 'over-conformity' to the norms of the sport ethic that produces, in athletes, a willingness to play through pain, return hastily from injury and disrespect and even vilify other athletes who refuse to conform to the same set of expectations.

A focus on how pain and injury are routinely normalized in sport can also be found in other work. In their study of elite amateur wrestling, Curry and Strauss (1994) show that the social organization of college sport in the US widely accepts injury as an expected feature of sport, so much so that athletes 'who demonstrate the least amount of reaction to pain and injury are then glorified as good examples' (p. 197). Alone and with colleagues, Roderick (1998, 2006a, 2006b; Roderick et al. 2000) found similar justification techniques and institutional pressures in studies of professional soccer players in England. Importantly, Roderick et al. (2000: 71) demonstrate how pain normalization emerges out of both externally imposed institutional settings, as well as self-imposed values athletes learn to accept as participants early on. In their words:

> Playing with pain or when injured is a central aspect of the culture of professional football. Young players quickly learn that one of the characteristics

which football club managers look for in a player is that he should have what, in professional football, is regarded as a 'good attitude.' One way in which players can demonstrate to their manager that they have such an attitude is by being prepared to play with pain or when injured.

Such normalization processes and value systems, which make themselves known to many recreational and amateur athletes as *choices*, become systematized as *prerequisites* at the elite, and certainly the professional, level. As I argued in an earlier paper assessing injury in some professional sports as a form of workplace victimization and organizational neglect:

> By any measure, professional sport is a violent and hazardous workplace, replete with its own unique forms of 'industrial disease.' No other single milieu, including the risky and labour-intensive settings of miners, oil drillers or construction site workers can compare with the routine injuries of team sports such as football, ice hockey, soccer, rugby and the like . . . Athletic injury results from the nature of forceful sports work itself but also . . . from its organization (ownership, management) and supervision (coaching) in a venal occupational culture designed to produce profit. Over-training, playing while injured, and improper coaching or tackling/hitting techniques, all of which are usually avoidable, represent examples of the conventional hazards of sports workplaces.
>
> (*Young 1993: 373, 377*)

At the professional level at least, injury may thus be understood as the outcome of intricate relationships which involve levels of both player consent and compliance, as well as employee exploitation, victimization and abuse.

Socialization into sports realms with specific traditions and cultures is thus seen as a key to understanding sports-related pain and injury and, as we shall see in Chapter 8, the sociological literature also underscores the primacy of *gendered* roles and identities in athletic settings. For instance, much of the literature that has tackled the experience of male athletes in North America and Britain has linked the acceptance of pain and the tolerance of risk to dominant notions of masculinity pervading sport in those societies (cf. Sabo 1986; Messner 1990, 1992; Young 1993). Sport thus becomes viewed as a context for the expression and reproduction of hegemonic forms of masculinity where violence, pain and injury are legitimate and, indeed, 'make sense.' Male athletes unwilling to conform to such standards of 'manliness' may become mocked, ostracized or even drop out altogether (Young et al. 1994).

In this connection, where injury in athletes is concerned, there is a striking parallel between male athletes and male military personnel – that is, in their ordinary pursuits, they become injured, maimed or sometimes killed and go on to receive commendations, such as awards and special tributes, for their dedication and sacrifice. Recognition of this kind serves not just to honour the hurt individual, but also to rationalize any doubts one might have as to the merits of the act, and consolidate it as admirable and 'manly.' In this sense, male tolerance of risk and injury becomes reframed as masculinizing and meaningful. In turn, this message then pervades sport at many levels and in many forms, and becomes a kind of standard for young and aspiring athletes to try to replicate and model.

Adding together what the victimology and the gender literatures have to say about professional male athletes, we can begin to grasp how many male athletes feel that they are locked into an occupational trap. While acknowledging that playing at risk and with injuries can lead to permanent physical damage, most athletes are aware that their work setting is largely intolerant to injury. Under further pressure to display a particular brand of tough masculinity and not to complain about being hurt, the professional athlete falls prey to both legally binding professional obligations ('play or don't get paid') *and* to the revered values of his own work culture ('play hurt and show that you can take the pain like a man'). Unsurprisingly, this 'double-jeopardy' is especially true of heavy contact team sports such as 'gridiron' football, rugby and ice hockey, where styles of speaking about injury are often telling. For instance, in the ultra-macho culture of North American football, the phrase 'you play unless the bone sticks through meat' has become so pervasive that I found the very same rationales and discourses being used at far lower levels of the game in Western Canadian universities (Young et al. 1994).

But what do such masculinist value systems tell us about female participants, if anything? Very recently, there has been a growth in the number of studies of risk, physicality, pain and injury in the lives of females (Snyder 1990; Rail 1992; Young and White 1995; Halbert 1997; Theberge 1997; Young 1997; Johns 1998; Pike 2000; Charlesworth 2004; Cove 2006). While this literature has clearly indicated that female athletes may also accept risk-tolerant sports cultures in the pursuit of sports commitment and athletic identity, the degree to which they 'over-conform' to the conventions of the so-called sport ethic and cultures of risk relative to their male counterparts is less clear.

A review of the literature on gender differences in sport injury in Young and White (2000: 117–122) shows that there is some persuasive evidence from a number of countries that female athletes in certain sports are injured far less than their male counterparts. This is true, for instance, for some US high school sports, for serious and catastrophic sport injuries in winter sports (such as ice hockey), water sports (such as swimming, diving and boating), and motor sports (such as snowmobiling) in Canada, as well as for young Finnish athletes in sports such as soccer, volleyball and basketball. It is apparent, then, that gender is *some sort of determinant* of sport injury, though we are uncertain as to the exact nature of this relationship. What is also unclear from the data is why males tend to incur more severe injuries than do females, but the weight of the evidence seems to point, once again, to the way that sport is played, and to the already well-studied link between sports-related aggression and risk-taking in the process of masculinization.

Undoubtedly, the causes of sports-related pain and injury are neither homogeneous nor unidimensional. In addition to value systems that represent the playing and subcultural sides of sport, as well as 'nature of the game' issues discussed above, pain and injury may be linked to a constellation of factors such as: the positional requirements of a given sport; over-training; playing while unfit; improper coaching or tackling/hitting techniques; reckless styles of play; outdated, faulty or dangerous equipment or facilities; the violent conduct or intentions of opponents; irresponsible medical advice; poor or negligent officiating; the taking of expected risks and the taking of risks that cannot reasonably be expected; and, numerous other factors, all of which are, again, usually avoidable. Indeed, one of the only factors that injured athletes and the groups that assemble and administer them cannot fully control is bad luck, though even this can be anticipated responsibly. For the most part, however, sociologists have been concerned with placing injury in the sport settings that encourage, facilitate and champion pain and injury in the first instance. As such, the literature suggests that the two major sociological *causes* of sport injury are (1) socialization into specific sport cultures where risk is widely tolerated, and (2) socialization into gendered identities strongly linked to these cultures.

Rate-and-extent approaches

As noted, we have extensive knowledge about the different types, rates and levels of injury in the varied micro settings of sport. While this information has not always been brought together or made publicly accessible as systematically as it might have been, many teams, leagues and sports organizations have collected data on injuries in their respective settings. To date, and again, far more of this collation work has been completed by sports administrators, medically oriented sport scientists, physiologists and psychologists (e.g. Sports Council 1991; Larson et al. 1996; Mueller et al. 1996; Tator 2008; Tucker Center 2011) than by sociologists. McCutcheon et al. (1997) is an exception to this rule. While usually descriptive and seldom theoretically driven, rate-and-extent work is important; we simply need to know this basic kind of information before proceeding to explanatory and interpretational levels of analysis.

As one small example, it seems reasonable to assert that it would be difficult to find a sport setting more routinely injurious than North American football. Here, we have an injury culture that casts the sport in an unambiguously negative light, and where there is growing concern with long-term disability and post-retirement problems, such as dementia, as well as premature death.[1] In an earlier study, I collated data from diverse disciplinary sources, as well as media commentaries, to report that 'football injuries may include arthritis, concussion, fractures, and, most catastrophically, blindness, paralysis and even death' (Young 1993: 377). Larson et al. (1996), Mueller et al. (1996) and many others have shown similar evidence of disturbingly severe injury records in football, a sport scattered with many 'forgotten warriors' (Hall 2009: B1). More recently, risks related to the weight and size requirements, training protocols and other subcultural norms of the game have been brought into sharp relief by the collapse or deaths of several top-flight players. This includes the case of 27-year-old Minnesota Vikings 'All-Pro' lineman Korey Stringer, who died in 2001 from heat stroke following practice on what was described as one of the hottest days of the year in Makato, Minnesota (*Time*, 13 August 2001: 54).[2] But football is not the only sport where catastrophic injury and untimely deaths occur, as Table 5.1 shows.

Using such rate-and-extent data as are available, however varied in their derivation, nature and scope, it now becomes possible to probe sports for factors such as the conventions, common practices and subcultural value systems – that is, dimensions of more interest to sociologists. The fact of the matter is that rate-and-extent data *are* available for most sports, including non-contact and non-team sports, and it seems reasonable to argue that better use of them could be made by sociologists.

Breathing life into injury: personal accounts

Learning to live with pain and injury is a requirement of many sports. The message is plain enough – pain and injury simply 'come with the territory.' It is expected in the very fabric of almost all sport settings. It is almost impossible to play sport without experiencing pain; every athlete has a story to tell about injury, and every athlete has to learn how to cope with it. Consider, for instance, the injury-normalization strategies in the following 'painful reminders' offered by four former professional athletes:

> As a boxer, you build up tolerance to pain. In fact, your immune system learns how to deal with it . . . disguising pain is imperative. It becomes instinctive. Boxing *is* the acceptance of pain.
>
> (*Barry McGuigan, professional boxer* – Independent on Sunday, *15 February 2004: 16*)

> After my retirement in 1998, it had taken around 18 months until my body started to feel good again. During my playing days, I didn't realize how accustomed my body became to the constant abuse we put ourselves through each season.
>
> (*Kelly Hrudey, NHL* – Hrudey 2005: D2)

> I've never had any serious injuries. I've broken a collar bone, a forearm, a bunch of fingers. Other than that, I'm fine.
>
> (*Jason Taylor, NFL*)[3]

> I've had 10 separate surgeries on both knees . . . Over the years, wreck after wreck . . . The first one (bull riding), I hit the ground, twisted and tore off every ligament in my knee . . . I came back and just keep adding up the surgeries I guess.
>
> (*Tyler Thomson, professional rodeo bull rider* – Calgary Herald, *10 July 2010: E5*)

TABLE 5.1 Risk-sport participant deaths, 1992–2011

Date	Sport	Athlete and age	Incident	Source
May 2011	Cycling	Wouter Weylandt (26)	Taking a steep descent during the Giro d'Italia race, the Belgian cyclist lost control and crashed, resulting in severe bleeding and head trauma. Italian Fabio Casartelli had previously died in the 1995 Tour de France.	The Guardian, 9 May 2011; Calgary Herald, 10 May 2011
February 2010	Luge	Nodar Kumaritashvili (21)	During a trial run at the 2010 Winter Olympics, the Georgian athlete failed to complete the most challenging corner, and flew into a steel pole at 90 mph.	CBC News, 12 February 2010
April 2009	Extreme skiing	Shane McConkey (39)	During a base jump off a cliff while skiing in the Dolomite mountains in Italy, the Canadian-born athlete failed to release his skis in time, preventing him from using his glider suit or his reserve chute.	Sports Illustrated, 2 April 2009
December 2009	Ice climbing	Guy Lacelle (54)	While free climbing a gully in Hyalite Canyon, Montana, the world-class climber was swept off his holding by an avalanche triggered by the climber above.	The Guardian, 11 December 2009
May 2008	Lacrosse	Jamieson Kuhlmann (15)	Colliding with a player at midfield during a midget game, Toronto athlete Kuhlmann was knocked unconscious and never recovered. He was taken off life support several days later.	CBC, 22 May 2008
December 2007	Boxing	Yo-Sam Choi (35)	During a boxing match, the Korean WBC flyweight butted heads repeatedly with his Indonesian opponent. In the twelfth round he received a punch to the skull resulting in brain trauma, which, days later, led to him being pronounced 'brain dead.'	Yahoo! Sports, 10 January 2008
March 2006	Gymnastics (trampoline)	Chris Fordham (23)	During a routine dismount from the trampoline at a training session, the Welsh trampolinist fell, fracturing his skull. He was taken off life support several days later.	WalesOnline, 2 March 2006
September 2005	Longboarding	Jamie McBryan (20)	While attempting a routine practice run, the Canadian collided with a truck that rolled over his torso. He died later from massive head injuries.	Calgary Herald, 9 September 2005
September 2004	Canadian football	Tyler Zeer (16)	While performing a drill at a high school practice, the linesman from Calgary butted heads with a team-mate causing him to collapse. He fell into a coma and was taken off life support less than a week later.	CBC News, 9 September 2004; Calgary Herald, 20 November 2005

TABLE 5.1 *Continued*

Date	Sport	Athlete and age	Incident	Source
October 2001	Stock car racing	Blaise Alexander (25)	Battling for position with Kerry Earnhardt, the NASCAR racer was pushed out of control, hitting a retaining wall head-on and causing massive head trauma.	NASCAR News, 7 October 2001
July 1998	Skydiving	Nadia Kanji (18)	While free falling, the novice's parachute and her back-up failed to open. Questions of possible negligence on the part of the instructor were raised at a subsequent inquiry.	CBC News, 30 March 2005
January 1992	Ice hockey	Miran Schrott (19)	During an Italian Division 'B' game, Jimi Boni, a Canadian, slashed Miran Schrott across the chest with his stick while jockeying for position in front of the net. Schrott died of cardiac arrest shortly afterwards.	*Sports Illustrated*, 6 December 1993

Sources:

(May 2011 incident) Fotheringham, W. Belgian cyclist Wouter Weylandt killed in Giro D'Italia crash. *The Guardian*, 9 May 2011. http://www.guardian. co.uk/sport/2011/may/09/wouter-weylandt-giro-ditalia.

(February 2010 incident) Georgian luger dies in crash. CBC Sports, 12 February 2010. http://www.cbc.ca/olympics/luge/story/2010/02/12/spo-luge-georgian-alert.html.

(April 2009 incident) Murphy, A. Death of Shane McConkey rocks extreme skiing community. *Sports Illustrated*, 2 April 2009. http://sportsillustrated.cnn.com/2009/writers/austin_murphy/04/02/shane-mcconkey/index.html.

(December 2009 incident) Pilkington, E. 'Free solo' ice climber killed in Montana avalanche. *The Guardian*, 11 December 2009. http://www.guardian. co.uk/world/2009/dec/11/guy-lacelle-ice-climber-dies.

(May 2008 incident) Teen dies after lacrosse game in Newmarket. CBC News, 22 May 2008. http://www.cbc.ca/news/canada/toronto/story/2008/05/22/lacrosse-death. html.

(December 2007 incident) Conway, B. Looking at Yo Sam Choi. Yahoo! Sports, 10 January 2008. http://sports.yahoo.com/box/news?slug=ys-maxboxchoi011008.

(March 2006 incident) Brindley, M. Champion gymnast dies in freak fall. WalesOnline, 2 March 2006. http://www.walesonline.co.uk/news/wales-news/tm_objectid=167 61889&method=full&siteid=50082&headline=champion-gymnast-dies-in--freak-fall--name_page.html.

(September 2005 incident) *Calgary Herald*, 9 September 2005.

(September 2004 incident) Students mourn high-school football player's death. CBC News, 9 September 2004. http://www.cbc.ca/news/canada/story/2004/09/09/football_death040909.html.

(October 2001 incident) Packman, T. Blaise Alexander dies in ARCA crash. NASCAR News, 7 October 2001. http://www.nascar.com/2001/NEWS/10/05/alexander_crash/index.html.

(July 1998 incident) Parachute packed properly before death, inquiry told. CBC News, 30 March 2005. http://www.cbc.ca/news/canada/story/2005/03/29/skydive-050329.html.

(January 1992 incident) *Sports Illustrated*, 6 December 1993.

Representing the broadest strand of sociological research on pain and injury so far available, and reflecting wider sociological calls to tap 'wounded storytellers' (Frank 1991, 1995), a number of interpretive qualitative studies undertaken on a range of sports participants, and from a range of theoretical points of view, have uncovered the varied ways in which risk, pain and injury are directly experienced. This body of work includes studies of pain 'lived' by participants in a wide spectrum of sports, such as rowers (Pike 2000), cyclists (Albert 1999), wrestlers (Curry 1993), soccer players (Roderick 2006a, 2006b), bodybuilders (Smith 1989), runners (Ewald and Jiobu 1985), wreck divers (Hunt 1996), rugby players (Howe 2001; Malcolm and Sheard 2002), female boxers (Cove 2006) and rodeo participants and football players (Frey et al, 1997), as well as studies of injury experiences from miscellaneous clusters of sports (Young and White 1995; Young 1997; Charlesworth 2004).

In a study of the role that physicality plays in the construction of masculinity and men's health, and using data from Canadian university athletes, Young et al. (1994) discovered that male athletes use a range of interpretive strategies to make sense of pain which amount to what classic American sociologist C. Wright Mills (1959) would call 'vocabularies of motive' and mid-twentieth century American criminologists Sykes and Matza would call 'techniques of neutralization' (1957) (see Chapter 1). These include: going out of one's way to ignore pain (*hidden pain*); adopting an attitude of irreverence to it and prioritizing certain kinds of pain over others (*disrespected pain*); understanding that pain may be poorly received by team-mates, coaches, and others and that acknowledging it may lead to sanctions or Garfinkel-esque 'degradation ceremonies' (1967) (*unwelcomed pain*); and, adopting a particular way of thinking and speaking about pain that allows one's sense on invulnerability to persist (*depersonalized pain*). The same Young et al. (1994) study also uncovered common techniques used by athletes to 'reframe' injury in positive ways in order to allow them to return to play, even while at risk of prolonging, or even exacerbating, pain and suffering.

Similar investigations into the meanings and narratives of embodied pain in diverse athletic settings have been undertaken by Kotarba (1983), Theberge (1997), Thomas and Rintala (1989), Snyder (1990), Roderick et al. (2000), Pike (2000), Charlesworth (2004) and, more recently in the context of the physical entertainment professions such as dance and ballet, by Aalten (2007), Wainwright and Turner (2006) and McEwen and Young (2011). Importantly, such work has started to uncover close parallels in the ways in which male and female athletes understand pain and injury, in the ways they rationalize it, and use its symptoms and its effects to judge character and status in sports groups. Indeed, so strikingly similar have been the results of their interview-based studies conducted with Canadian male and female athletes, that Young and White (1995: 55–56) have contended:

> Both female and male discourses of sport were replete with the language of conquest (performance orientations and achievement principles). Female

athletes were as willing as men to expose themselves to physical risk, and women *and* men were relatively unreflexive on matters such as being pressured to perform aggressively [and] to play with injury.

While their data led Young and White to argue that '[i]f there is a difference between the way male and female athletes in our projects appear to understand pain and injury, it is only a matter of degree' (p. 51), they also cautiously recommend more research on the ways that female athletes appear to be colonizing traditionally male-exclusive spaces in sport, before conclusions regarding the implications of that colonization, including approaches to pain and injury within it, can be made with confidence. It certainly seems likely that as female sport expands, and as sport opportunity for girls and women increases, female experiences of sport injury will also amplify. Understanding the full ramifications of these experiences will require more consistent research efforts by sociologists of sport.

Finally, the interpretive sociological literature on anticipating and living with pain and recovering from injury features a growing collection of biographical and 'self-reflexive' studies. Apparently compelled by Millsian (Mills 1959) notions of the importance of biography in sociological ventures, and by Frank's claim that 'the beginning of theorizing about the body . . . lies in our own embodiment as theorists' (1996: 57), several sport researchers have explained pain in their own athletic lives using techniques of 'narrative reconstruction' (Frank 1991). These studies include Sparkes' (1996, 1999) 'auto-ethnographical' explorations of encounters with pain and body 'disruptions,' Smith's (2008a, 2008b) investigations into spinal cord injury and other disabilities, Collinson's (2005) 'temporal' account of the frustrations of both running-related injuries and often unreliable and unsympathetic medical practitioners, and Charlesworth's (2004) examination of the physical and emotional dimensions of female athlete pain interpreted from the perspective of an author with chronic illness.

What does injury 'cost'?

Defined economically, the costs of sports injury are startling. Injury represents a massive imposition for national, regional and local governments, as well as sports and health organizations every year in many countries.

Collating the existing research on health care costs from a number of national contexts, Young and White (2000) found the literature to be dated but nevertheless revealing. Their review cites evidence that

[i]n the United Kingdom . . . 7% of sports injuries resulted in participants taking time off work, resulting in a total of 11.5 million working days lost annually in England and Wales, at a cost of £575 million in production value . . . In Denmark . . . the annual cost of treating 'acute sports injuries' was £2.3 million. A Swiss study . . . estimated that the total direct and indirect

costs of sport accidents in 1976 [was] £400 million . . . [and] From New
Zealand . . . [it was] reported that 15% of the treatments received at the
Dunedin Hospital Emergency Department were for sports injuries and that
sport accounted for 17% of all injuries compensated by the Accident Compensation Corporation.

(*Young and White 2000: 122*)

A 1990 report on sports injuries to the Australian National Better Health Programme
noted that the medical treatment of sport injury in Australia cost an estimated
$330–400 million in 1987–1988, and a further $400 million lost through worker
absenteeism (Centre for Health Promotion and Research 1990). Kirkby (1995)
reports that sport injuries cost Germany more than $2,500 million per year, and
that, in the US, 'the yearly cost to the economy of roller skating accidents alone was
[in 1983] $100 million' (p. 456). More recently, research in New Zealand shows
that, unsurprisingly, rugby has a 'high incidence of injury, estimated at 900 hospi-
talizations per 100,000 participants per year and incurs a high cost' (Simpson et al.
1999: 86), and Yang et al. (2007) estimate the hospital Emergency Department costs
of treating sport injuries incurred by American youth to be $1.8 billion, and the
annual cost of hospitalization for sports-related injuries in the US to be over $100
million. Similarly astounding figures can be provided for most countries where
sports participation is common. In Western societies, at least, the proliferation of
sports injuries has given rise to enormously successful treatment industries such as
sports medicine, sports massage, physiotherapy and chiropractic medicine, whose
success, ironically, depends on there being a cost to heal sport injury in the first
place.

In addition to the toll that injury takes on states and governments, the financial
cost of injuries is also a critical factor in the everyday business of professional sport
where injury 'losses' can be huge. One illustration comes from England, where
player injuries – that is to say, the number of athletes unavailable to train and play
each week due to injury – have been reported to cost English soccer clubs £40
million every year (*The Independent*, 26 January 2001: 28). Clearly, this example
underscores the capitalist dimensions of elite sport, where athlete labour is but one
aspect of any given club's business plan (Young 1993).

Needless to say, the 'costs' associated with sport injury go well beyond matters
of finance. As Mueller et al. (1996: 99) have remarked with respect to catastrophic
sport injury in young athletes: 'injury is devastating not only to the injured athlete,
but also the athlete's family, school and community.' While it may be true that
sociologists have not played a central role in examining the economic impact of
injury, there is certainly work available on the human costs. This work comes in a
variety of forms, which includes examinations of how injuries may leave athletes
with a compromised or destroyed sense of self-worth, or even suicidal (Young et
al. 1994; Pike 2000; Charlesworth 2004). Touching on each of these dimensions
of the phenomena, White (2004) adds significantly to what we know about the
assorted 'costs' of sport injury.

Taking advantage of pain

Though most people know from first-hand experience what sports-related pain and injury *feel like* in a sensory or tactile way, it is nevertheless the case that sports injury reaches most people indirectly through media images. In many ways, the contemporary emphasis placed on competition and winning-at-all-costs and the omnipresence of the sports media means that professional and elite sport have become mediated, and often celebrated, worlds of hurt and disability. As Chapter 7 shows, the roaming television lens captures and replays the writhing athletic body in 'super slo-mo,' while commentators and recognized media personalities respond using discourses of approval and rationalization (Young 1991b; Gillett et al. 1996). Meanwhile, the carefully selected and edited tabloid photograph freezes the injurious moment, as humorous and 'punny' captions belie the actual agony behind the contact in focus. Combined, visual and verbal media messages serve to marginalize pain, and to re-present the now commodified sports moment not as hurt per se, but as a routine – Morse (1983) argues *artistic* and even *scopophilic* – sign of athletic commitment. In the process, injured athletes become lionized as heroes exposing themselves to danger, and showing willingness, in the vernacular of North American televised football and ice hockey, to 'pay the price' (Young, S. 1990; Young 1990, 1991b; Nixon 1993). Numerous examples could be provided, but perhaps two of the most recognizable in recent memory are the cases of American gymnast Kerri Strug and alpine skier Lindsey Vonn, both of whom completed their respective Olympic events (at the 1996 Atlanta Summer Games and the 2010 Vancouver Winter Games respectively) experiencing serious leg damage and 'excrutiating pain' and subsequently became internationally lauded for their courage and character (*Sports Illustrated*, 5 August 1996: 58–65).[4]

A further aspect of sport injury as 'spectacle' that has so far received scant sociological attention may be found in sport advertising. Here, too, pain and injury are both trivialized and made to appear normal and unthreatening. Complementing wider ideologies throughout North American sport (witness, for example, sport stadia known to local fans as the 'House of Pain,' or the seemingly ubiquitous attitude/rationale 'No Pain, No Gain' in gyms across the continent), the sport magazine industry is replete with examples of well-known sports companies using snappy (but often literally untrue) catch-phrases to sell their products: 'Just Do It' (Nike); 'Own the Pain and You Will Own the Game' (Adidas); 'Pain is Weakness Leaving the Body' (Adidas); 'Rubber, Chains and Pain. You'll Love It!' (Carrera); 'Good Pain to Keep in the Game' (Lululemon). Needless to say, these mediated codes only add to an already pervasive culture of risk in sport lapped up by consumers, especially impressionable youngsters who care less about the vulnerability of their bodies.

Relatively few sociologists have looked at mediated pain and injury. One of the most interesting, if dated, studies can be found in Nixon (1993) who conducted research on what he calls the 'mediated cultural influences of playing hurt,' and who similarly concludes that the sports media frequently 'convey the messages of the culture of risk' (p. 190). This includes, for him, the way in which these messages encourage a 'kind of self-abusive addiction' (p. 189) in athletes. However, Nixon goes on to comment thoughtfully about the fact that media messages do not become wholly or uncritically absorbed into social practice by 'unthinking' players. He writes: 'we should not conclude . . . that athletes are so effectively socialized or strongly influenced that they cannot see behind the messages and pressures to play with pain and injuries or that they cannot make their own decisions about these matters' (p. 188). In these respects, Nixon's arguments regarding the power and influence of the culture of risk he describes so convincingly in his numerous other studies parallel the work of others, such as Young's (1993) discussion of the consent/manipulation paradox in some professional sport settings, Stebbins' (1987) study of Canadian football players, and Roderick's (2006a, 2006b) studies of professional soccer players, all of which show that athletes may be quite aware of their own subjugation and exploitation at the hands of ownership as well as the media industry, but feel relatively powerless to oppose or resist.

In brief, and anticipating arguments made in Chapter 7, the media play an active and participatory role in popular impressions of risk, pain and injury in sport, including consolidating the message that injury is inevitable, acceptable and even laudable, and that conforming to the sport ethic shows athletic integrity and social character.

Is sports injury a black eye for the whole community?

While sport is often assumed to lead to health, the relationship between the two can often be ambiguous and, in fact, participation in many sports at many levels is accompanied by common and often serious health risks (Hardman and Stensel 2003). In 1999, Hawkins and Fuller showed the risk of injury in English professional soccer players to be 1,000 times greater than the risk to labourers working in blue-collar settings such as mining. Many similar studies are available in many countries. The data on retired athletes can be even more disturbing. For example, in 2006, Hargrove reported the following figures on premature death of NFL players: 28 per cent of 'obese' NFL players died before their fiftieth birthday, one out of every 69 players born since 1955 had died before 2006 and, of them, 22 per cent died from heart disease and 19 per cent from homicides or suicides. Obviously, there are many interacting factors at play here, but these sorts of figures from the NFL are not in any way 'normal' or average; cardiological research shows that football linemen have the greatest risk of dying early (e.g. Miller et al. 2008; Selden et al. 2009).

It is not fair, realistic or, indeed, helpful to generalize about the health ramifications of all sports, or all levels of sport, and it seems reasonable on the basis of what we know so far to argue that more could be done to better understand the origins of risk, and make particular sports safer in particular ways. As such, research on the policy implications of risk, pain and injury for individual and community health is very much needed. So far, this work is in short supply, at least as it applies to sociology. Again, much of it has been undertaken in the 'epidemiological' sciences such as community medicine.

Predictably, the disruption caused by pain and injury in sport to individuals and those around them has prompted a considerable literature on the prevention of sports injuries. As Kirkby (1995: 469) has written:

> Whether it is viewed from the perspective of the financial cost of sport injuries to society, the personal and social distress and disruption caused by sport injuries at all levels of competition, or their effects on domestic and international success in elite sport, there is no doubting the importance of the prevention of sport injuries and rehabilitation to sport.

Much of this prevention work has been amassed by psychologists of sport who have focused on 'coping and social support' issues (Kirkby 1995: 468). This sort of work is important enough, though critics might raise questions regarding how sport and its participants can be made safer, and unreasonable risks removed, by simply adjusting the structure of sport itself (including equipment – see Chapter 6) when so many of the causes of injury are obviously *social*. Given the cultural resonance of sport in so many societies, this, it seems, is hard to do – witness, for instance, calls to eliminate fist-fighting in ice hockey, to ban boxing or to make headgear mandatory, to decrease the speed car racers drive at and to make their vehicles more robust, to reduce eye and facial injuries in ice hockey by requiring visors, and the like. Recommendations such as these have all been met with considerable opposition from groups who quite clearly define risk differently – or, just as likely, simply *revere* risk.

It is true, however, that player safety and individual/public health is a matter on the radar screens of many sport organizations and bodies. These 'matters' have been studied by social scientists, including sociologists: Hawkins and Fuller (1998) have studied the health regulatory practices of soccer clubs in England and Wales using a public health/socio-legal perspective; Waddington (2000) has examined the health implications of a sportsworld immersed in drug use and cheating; Fuller (1995) has looked at health and safety legislation for a cluster of professional sports in Britain; and Young (1993) has explored the need for regulatory laws to reduce the number of 'white-collar crimes' he argues take place in many of the self-policing sport bodies of North America.

Of course, this brief selection of sources and the public health interests they represent has been complemented by national survey work conducted by states and governments in a number of countries, both with adult and child participants, as well as by the controlling bodies of individual sports. However, since so many sport cultures define sport and athletic success in terms of pushing the frontiers of human performance, which renders risk praiseworthy, it remains to be seen how effective such work might be. When one adds the drive toward corporate profit in the administration of many of our most popular sports, and the health risks we know that this implies, it is difficult to remain optimistic about the impact well-meaning policy makers might have on dominant sports models.

Under-exposure in the research

That some of the central dimensions of 'pain zones' have been 'exposed,' and that our knowledge and understanding of sports-related risk, pain and injury are growing should not lead us to think that we know all there is to know. On the overall trajectory of understanding the social dimensions of sports-related risk, pain and injury, we are just beginning. Certain aspects of injury that are of clear significance both to sociology and to society have been 'under-exposed,' and our knowledge of these factors remains vague. The following points are salient, but certainly not exhaustive, in this connection:

• Most pain and injury studies have dealt with the experiences of male athletes and, despite gradual shifts in the gender focus of injury work, have neglected or under-emphasized those of females (Tucker Center 2011).

• Despite the fact that sports injury is clearly not restricted to adult participation, the physically and emotionally painful ramifications of injury for young and child athletes, and the extent to which sport might be abusive to children's bodies, has been almost entirely ignored (Donnelly 2003).

• The bulk of our knowledge of sports-related injury and pain derives from surveys and other quantitative techniques conducted in the other sports sciences and by the sport industry itself which, while useful in its own way, does not normally illuminate key matters such as how pain and injury are lived, reflected upon or resolved at various levels.

• We still have relatively little knowledge of how pain and injury are responded to by the media, though (more extensive) evidence from the sports violence literature strongly suggests that the media may choreograph and exploit sports injury in the pursuit of sales and profit.[5]

• With only a few exceptions, much of the research is limited to injured elite participants (e.g. Brock and Kleiber 1994; Young and White 1995; Howe 2001; Roderick 2006a, 2006b), despite the fact that the majority of athletes who play, or who have been injured, are not and never will be involved at the highest levels of their sport.

• Despite much conjecture, the links between injury and practices known to be common in certain sports such as eating disorders (Ryan 1995) and steroid use (Tricker and Cook 1990; Courson 1991; Goldman and Klatz 1992; Huizenga 1994; Yesalis and Cowart 1998; Monaghan 2001; Canseco 2005) remain unclear.

• We have some knowledge about the way sport injury disrupts lives and interferes with notions of self-concept in a temporary sense, but less knowledge about the long-term effects of injury for individual physical and mental health and wellbeing. This has only been touched on by a small handful of sociologists (cf. Messner 1990; Roderick et al. 2000).[6]

• Despite enormous potential given the fundamentally physical, social and emotional nature of the problem, sociologists seem reluctant to approach their work in an interdisciplinary way and to take advantage of the sophisticated clinical literatures in the 'harder' sports science disciplines such as biomechanics and physiology, as well as psychology.

• Finally, despite definitional efforts in the mainstream (Kotarba 1983; Morris 1991) and some modest efforts in the sociology of sport literature to have athletes differentiate between pain and injury using their own terms and categories (e.g. Young et al. 1994), definitional work on what constitutes and distinguishes 'risk,' 'pain' and 'injury' remains to be undertaken with the same sort of rigour with which, for instance, Lyng (1990) has defined risky 'edgework,'[7] as at least two philosophers of sport have correctly noted (McNamee 2004; Parry 2004).

As fresh and welcome as the growing body of sociological work on sports-related pain and injury is, it is equally clear that gaps in knowledge such as these exist and that more research is needed.

Conclusion

Injury in sport is so ubiquitous that it has long been viewed as an 'unthwarted epidemic' (Vinger and Hoerner 1981). As with its partner concepts, risk and pain, it is also intertwined with gender dynamics. As Sparkes and Smith (2008: 689) observe:

> Sporting men and boys, particularly in contact sports like rugby with a high risk of injury, are socialized to mask, hide and disregard pain, as well as to objectify and dissociate from their bodies and the bodies of others in order that they might both take and inflict pain. Thus, pain is normalized in specific sporting subcultures and certain ways of coping . . . and functioning . . . are valorized and legitimated as part of the social construction of gender identity.

However, since an expanding literature on females and injury is showing that girls and women also prize risk, and willingly subject themselves to pain and injury on a regular basis using the same normalizing strategies as men (Young and White 1995; Young 1997), socialization into sport per se and the sport ethic seems at least as important as gender in explaining why both male and female athletes accept risk, and live through, and return from, pain and injury in sport.

Existing at both the 'cause' *and* 'effect' ends of the sport-safety continuum, the partnership between risk, pain and injury represents a menacing alliance with real consequences for individuals, communities and nations. Where the study of the constituent elements of this partnership is concerned, sociologists of sport have made encouraging advances, despite coming to the area relatively late. These advances have taken us beyond the uncritical, and rather limiting, explanatory borders of the early epidemiological work on the subject, but more work and knowledge are needed, on all fronts, especially as the risks associated with certain sports become clearer. At the time of writing, North American sports bodies, and ice-hockey and football regulators in particular, seem to be taking head injuries and concussions more seriously than ever before, and extensive studies are underway (e.g. www. stopconcussions.com or www.cdc.gov/concussion/sports).

It is clear from what we know so far that sport can lead to injurious outcomes not only because of the inherent nature of athletic activity per se, or the equipment needed to play it, but also because of the way that sport activity is perceived, planned, practised and policed. Obviously, these multiple elements and levels point to the importance of considering the contributory roles of parents, coaches, administrators, sponsors and peer subcultures, as well as players. As our understanding of both the potential intrinsic dangers of sport and the socially constructed ways of perceiving, planning, practising and policing sport grows, and as public concern mounts regarding participant, and especially child, safety throughout the sports world, it seems likely that this 'unthwarted epidemic' will continue for some time to come.

6

SPORT IN THE PANOPTICON

The social control of SRV

Introduction

Chapter 2 offered an examination of the role of the authorities and the law in policing player violence and, in particular, the 'drift' over the course of the twentieth century to 'criminalizing' violent and injurious player behaviour. While a central feature in an increasingly panopticon-like[1] world of sport where everyone is watching, judgement is constant, and news is immediate, the surveillance and sanction of athletes is not the only manifestation of how SRV is socially controlled. Forms of internal and external control, and formal and informal control, in sport go well beyond violating participants in the popular team sports (and certainly beyond professional ice hockey), as well as beyond the field of play.

Sport is not known as an institution that is quick to change, but neither is it static. One dimension of change may be seen in the many ways sport both modifies itself from within to fit a changing social climate, as well as becomes exposed to, and affected by, external structures and expectations, including policies and laws. In principle, every sport experiences social control, and at every level but, in practice, some sports have been more socially controlled than others, while others have been ignored, treated lightly, condoned or rewarded, even when representing dangerous violations of rules and laws.

Although not always easy to measure, what is interesting is how sport, in all of its different guises, reacts to social control, especially when it comes from 'the outside' in the form of instructions, sanctions or laws. Also interesting are the *reasons* for social control. Some 'interventions' exist because there is a clear need or desire to improve relationships or apply greater safety, some are political and meant to improve the image of a sport, and some are purely tokenistic, administered as smokescreens by groups that have no real interest in changing the status quo, but who feel that they should, or must. Some social control mechanisms are seen as panaceas to solve existing problems, and others are viewed as an intrusive nuisance from the outset. And, of course, on any one of these matters, there are conflicting perspectives.

This chapter explores how forms of social control are woven into the fabric of sport. After an initial description of how sociologists conceive of *social control*, the chapter goes on to review some of the processes, structures and interventions that represent attempts to 'control' SRV with, first, sports crowds, and second, other SRV cells. It also considers the various levels on which social control operates, and considers the intended and unintended effects of social control. Finally, three theoretical approaches that help in making sense of the relationship between SRV and social control are discussed.

What is social control?

Sociologists, who have written extensively on *social control* (e.g. Durkheim 1893; Weber 1947; Becker 1963; Goffman 1963; Elias 1994; Elias and Dunning 1986), use the term to refer to the ways that persons and groups are encouraged, coerced or manipulated into behaving in a socially desirable manner. As Salomone (2001: 360) puts it:

> In one way or another . . . social control is an attempt to bring about con-
> formity in the behavior of the members of society. Needless to say, these
> efforts are never completely effective, giving rise to instances of noncon-
> formity or deviance.

Not surprisingly, standards of conduct cannot be separated from relations of power and, as such, how one group wants another to behave (in sport, as in any other social milieu) is not always unambiguous, uncontroversial or without struggle. Because social control is generally associated with illegalities, it features centrally in the study of crime, juvenile delinquency and criminal justice. But sociologists think more broadly about social control and apply it to human compliance in all social institutions, including sport.

Social control comes in many forms, but most sociologists distinguish between 'internal' and 'external' versions, and between 'formal' and 'informal' versions. Although they are socially learned, internal controls reside mostly within individuals and come in the form of personality, conscience, restraint or personal commitment to some standard of behaviour. External controls are found outside the individual, and reflect the norms and expectations of the wider culture and society. No society exists without some combination of formal and informal social controls. Formal social controls refer to systems of rules and regulations, such as those found in institutions such as prisons, schools, workplaces or sport. These are codified entities that provide the basic structure and shape for behaviour. At the level of the state, the most obvious example of such structures is the legal system. By compari-son, informal controls emerge from more interpersonal settings and face-to-face interactions (Salomone 2001: 362). In sport, the influences of coaches, peers and friends are critical to how athletes behave, and are monitored, within the small group settings of a team, a league or a subculture (Donnelly and Young 1988).

In the same way that not all societies agree on what forms crime control should take, sports (which themselves are shaped by the cultures around them) display varying norms and standards not only in how they are played but also in how they are controlled. Sport is thus replete with significant variance in social control, not only across nations, but also between sports, types of sport and levels of sport. For example, where player aggression and violence in sport are concerned, consider the following differences in how sports are socially controlled:

- While North American ice-hockey 'enforcers' playing an acknowledged pugilistic role are often given a tokenistic penalty by game officials for fist-fighting, players fighting in other rough contact sports such as lacrosse or gridiron football are removed from the game and likely incur sanctions.
- While professional soccer players exist in a culture where verbal, and often aggressively verbal, abuse of officials is the norm, other sports impose immediate penalties for such behaviour.
- While bodychecking is banned in women's ice hockey, the male version of the game is built centrally around brutal forms of bodychecking that continue to cause serious injury.
- While British and European soccer games are often played in the presence of significant numbers of armed police, police horses, attack dogs and the like, North American stadia operationalize an entirely less visible and intimidating version of 'security.'

Of course, these are all very general illustrations, and there are variations and complexities within them all. The relevant point is that when one adds tradition, subculture, level and type of sport, who plays the sport (i.e. children or adults, women or men etc.) and culture into the mix, the variance in the ways that sport is socially controlled is considerable.

Forms of social control pervade every level of human activity. In sport, whether they are intended as safety measures, value-shaping initiatives, or simply shifts in preferred behaviour, formal and informal control processes occur at the individual level, the interpersonal level, the institutional level, the community level and the social structural level. As we shall see, forms of social control also take place at the global level.

Policing SRV

The varied dimensions of SRV have elicited equally varied forms of social control. These have been applied, for instance, as rules of participation, guidelines and codes of practice and ethics, as well as forms of surveillance and discipline, and any number of in-house or external mechanisms and interventions. Following the lengthy discussion of forms of social control with violent athletes in Chapter 2, we now examine how social control has manifested itself within the broader landscape of SRV cells, beginning with crowd violence.

Crowd violence

Forms of social control with British soccer hooliganism

Unsurprisingly, across the decades, recommendations for deterring, controlling and sanctioning British soccer hooliganism have given rise to a mind-boggling constellation of initiatives and changes, many of which are emulated in other countries (Dunning et al. 2002b). There is an extensive body of research on the 'changing face of policing football' in the UK (e.g. Houlihan 1991; Garland and Rowe 2000). During the 1980s, the Conservative government of Margaret Thatcher viewed hooliganism as a national social problem requiring stiff remedial responses by the authorities. Adopting language from the then-recent Falklands War, a so-called 'War Cabinet' was established aimed, especially in the immediate post-Heysel era, at 'stamping out' the hooligan issue. In practice, however, and as numerous critics noted at the time (Williams et al. 1984; Dunning et al. 1988), a long sequence of hastily planned, and present-centred, initiatives were introduced that certainly increased the image of soccer as a 'crime culture,' but did not 'resolve' the problem of hooliganism per se.

The British government has sponsored detailed investigations into soccer hooliganism since at least the 1960s. These efforts include the Harrington Report (Harrington 1968), the Lang Report (Lang 1969), the Wheatley Report (Wheatley 1972), the Report of a Joint Sports Council/Social Science Research Council Panel (1978) and the Popplewell Report (Popplewell 1985). For the most part, documents resulting from these sorts of enquiries have been met with, at best, lukewarm responses from academics concerned with the long-term effectiveness of 'control-centred' law-and-order responses. Typical, in this respect, was the Report of *Committee of Inquiry into Crowd Safety and Control at Soccer Grounds*, supervised by Mr Justice Popplewell, following the 1985 Bradford Fire and Heysel Stadium riot discussed in Chapter 3. Taylor's (1987: 174) description of the report's content is broadly applicable to other official reports:

> The Report is . . . notable for the general support it gives to the theory, held to so fruitlessly by authority in Britain since the mid-1960s, that there is some kind of solution to the problem of soccer hooliganism in the extension of powers of search and arrest and in the general revision of criminal law.

Similar criticisms have also been made of measures taken by British soccer clubs themselves, some of which may only be described as desperate. Such was the case with Chelsea FC in 1985 when the club chairman suggested installing an electrified fence around the playing field until the Greater London Council convinced the club that the idea was irresponsible and dangerous.

The use of perimeter fencing as a crowd control procedure in British soccer has also proven to be highly controversial over the years. As described in Chapter 3, after perimeter fencing was installed at most stadia in the 1970s and 1980s, it was subsequently discovered that such fencing may, in fact, offer more of an endangerment to fans than a safety device. Notable among other incidents, the Bradford fire and the Hillsborough Stadium crush in which, cumulatively, dozens of people lost their lives trying to scale walls and fences designed originally to keep fans off the field, brought this fact into sharp and disturbing relief. Since that time, perimeter fencing has been removed from most stadia in the UK, although other countries continue to use it as an anti-field-encroachment apparatus.

Many other anti-hooligan deterrent schemes have been experimented with, if no more successfully. One of the most widely publicized initiatives throughout the 1970s and 1980s was the idea of introducing a national identity card programme aimed at removing the protection of anonymous membership in the soccer crowd normally enjoyed by hooligan fans. From its inception, the long-term effectiveness of the scheme was questionable. Critics raised concerns about the feasibility of implementing an expensive identity card programme when many of the larger clubs in Britain enjoy huge cumulative regular *and* occasional spectator followings. Additional concerns surrounded the practicality, or fairness, of introducing a widespread identity card programme when those with hooligan proclivities represent such a relatively small percentage of the total fan base.

Since the 1970s, anti-hooligan techniques for dealing with the problems posed by violent or disorderly soccer fans have been wide-ranging. They include, but are not restricted to: trained stewards and 'spotters' liaising between fans and the police; soliciting the help of the public by publishing 'wanted' photographs of hooligans in the print media; using special vehicles (including the so-called 'hoolivan,' which features hydraulic cameras designed to raise high above crowds) equipped with CCTV cameras and hi-tech computer equipment; the use of specialty hand-held devices (such as 'photo-phones' and cameras) allowing police to quickly exchange information on potential offenders (Marsh et al. 1996); and, most recently, the opening of 'hooligan hot-lines' enabling other fans, or non-attending members of the public, to report 'trouble.' Most of these sorts of controls have been imposed by policing bodies. The leagues (such as the Football Association) have also imposed controls and sanctions, including fines and requiring clubs with hooligan problems to play games away from home or behind 'closed doors.' In the latter case, the rather odd logic has been to force clubs to take a firm stance on crowd violence by threatening financial penalties (in the form of revenue losses 'at the gate').

Anti-hooligan campaigns have also spread to stadium design. Assuming that violence inside stadia is caused or exacerbated by the traditional British arrangement of standing to watch soccer games, and influenced by the perception that all-seater stadia in North America are safer and less prone to collective crowd disorder, in the 1980s many British clubs started to reconfigure their stadia to include all-seater arrangements. Since a significant amount of hooligan violence occurred then (and still today) outside of the stadium itself, and since hooligan groups have been known to vandalize newly installed seating sections, and have been captured on film using seats as missiles in aerial confrontations with police, the long-term effectiveness of changing the stadium environment was, and is, questionable. While policing procedures inside the soccer stadiums have clearly had the effect of displacing the problem to outside the grounds, there is little hard evidence to suggest that hooligan practices per se are resolved by such things as seating arrangements, or any other feature of stadia design.

In contrast to measures of this type, academics have generally been critical of looking solely to game-centred solutions for soccer hooliganism, and the implementation of short-term measures. Events over the past four decades in the UK show that the incidence of hooliganism does not necessarily decrease as more draconian policies are imposed. Sociologists argue that, since hooliganism is symptomatic of broader social factors such as social class, masculinity and race, only thoughtful and deeper *social* change is likely to seriously challenge the hooligan problem. Recognizing that such social change would not come 'overnight,' in the 1980s and 1990s research at the Sir Norman Chester Centre for Football Research at Leicester University (e.g. 1984, 1995) made, or supported, several practical recommendations for tackling hooliganism, domestically and abroad. Suggestions included more efficient and careful ticket distribution, comprehensive travel schedules enabling specially appointed 'stewards' to supervise groups of travelling fans, fan membership schemes, adequate segregation by host clubs and the establishment of stronger community links with soccer fans.

More recently, the Football Intelligence Unit linked to the National Criminal Intelligence Service became operational at the start of the 1990s, and the *UK Football Offences and Disorder Act* was introduced in 1999. A response to a prolonged period of fan-related violence in English soccer, and in the immediate post-Hillsborough context, the Act was aimed at reducing certain types of threatening and dangerous behaviour inside soccer stadia. Under the aforementioned Act, British and other international courts were empowered to impose international or domestic 'banning orders' to restrict or exclude those convicted of soccer-related offences. Understandably, these sorts of legislative changes have been criticized for violating a basic civil right; that is, the presumption of innocence until proven guilty. At the time of writing, while all of the social control ideas described here may be well-intentioned, and may even have served a deterring role, soccer hooliganism remains an issue of real significance throughout Europe, as well as other parts of the world, such as South America.

Forms of social control with North American crowd violence

As noted in Chapter 3, scholars have been slow to turn their research attention to North American crowd violence, and some have even suggested it is an issue of relatively little social significance (Wann et al. 2001: 148). The authorities, and sports clubs and leagues themselves, obviously disagree. Indeed, anyone who thinks that North American sports crowd disorder is innocuous, or unpatterned, needs to look no further than the increasingly resolute role played by law enforcers of late. While their rate of success remains vague, it is clear that North American sports and legal authorities have perceived a need to significantly improve security measures and violence prevention strategies at sports events. Having treated sports crowds more or less with 'kid gloves' until the mid-1970s, sports and security groups have begun to introduce much more stringent social control measures both in anticipation of, and in response to, crowd violence. Generally, these changes have taken the form of revisions to security procedures and efforts to anticipate and decrease abusive, profane, threatening or violent fan behaviour.

As an indication of the breadth of both informal and formal control efforts, concrete changes include, but again are not limited to, the following organizational and security trends at North American sports stadia:

- More circumspect ticketing procedures and the introduction of educational programmes aimed at improving spectator orderliness (Riseling 1994).
- Increases in fines for trespassing on the field of play and the introduction of local by-laws to protect against field encroachment.
- A heightened police presence at the end of play.
- A general reduction in security tolerance of profane, abusive and violent fan behaviour. For example, much like British 'spotters,' many stadiums now employ teams of 'guest relations' representatives to anonymously filter into, and patrol, the crowd.
- Improved security arrangements including the use of 'hi-tech' surveillance systems, screening procedures at the gate, significant increases in numbers of security personnel at games, and the construction of makeshift 'courtrooms' and jail cells inside stadia, such as in the cases of NFL teams Philadelphia Eagles and Baltimore Ravens (Gramling 2001: 143).
- Modifications in alcohol concessions, including the sale of low alcohol beer, the banning of hard liquor and the earlier termination of sales; coordinated efforts between 'stakeholders' to reduce alcohol-related behaviour linked to sports events.
- Improved record keeping processes and facilities, such as the creation of ejection reports and personal profiles of offenders, confiscation or suspension of season tickets and improved liaison between clubs and leagues and the police.
- Remodelling of (especially baseball and football) stadia to include the construction of protective tunnels and temporary and permanent canopies for players and officials to safely enter and exit the field, and the construction of specially designated 'family' enclosures. The possibility of taunting or missile throwing in baseball by abusive fans (e.g. in 'bullpens' and close to the outfield fence) has also prompted innovations in stadia design (Schwarz 2001; 'Bullpen Protection' 2001: 5).
- Temporary closure of bleacher sections known to house chronically rambunctious fans.

- Judicious security planning in anticipation of post-event revelry and the assignment of special investigation units, including riot squads.
- Improvements in criminal intelligence and anti-terrorist preparations in advance of national and international sports tournaments and festivals, such as the 1994 World Cup in the US (Van Zunderd 1994), the 1996 Summer Olympic Games in Atlanta (Kelley 1994) and the 2002 Winter Games in Salt Lake (Glendinning 2001).
- Punitive legal responses to those involved in anti-social fan behaviour, including heavy fines and jail terms.
- Team- and sport-specific initiatives have sprung up across the continent aimed at creating safer, and more respectful, fan environments (e.g. the Texas Longhorns 'Make Us Proud' and the Canadian Interuniversity Sport codes of conduct, the National Collegiate Athletic Association (NCAA) Division III 'Be Loud, Be Proud, Be Positive' programme, and Hockey Canada's 'Respect in Sport' programme).

While these examples focus on situationally controlling crowd behaviour and improving fan responsibility at sports events, questions of accountability have also been directed at athletes themselves, as well as at the police and the authorities. For example, fines and other sanctions have been imposed on players for participating in what could be perceived by fans as taunts and provocative gestures. The NFL's attempt in the 1990s to prohibit the infamous 'sack dance,' 'excessive' touchdown celebrations, and other forms of 'showboating' (that may be seen by opposing fans as provocations) are cases in point. Also, concern that police had reacted with unwarranted force in the 1994 Vancouver NHL post-event riot, and conjecture that the death of a fan shot by a police officer could have been prevented, led to widespread criticism and to the preparation of three official reports, all of which 'determined' different causes for the riot (British Columbia Police Commission 1994; City of Vancouver 1994; Vancouver Police Department 1995). Despite warnings, similar concerns that the Vancouver police were ill-prepared in dealing with the crowd in the 2011 NHL post-event riot have also been expressed (*Calgary Herald*, 16–18 June 2011). Task forces examining the role of the communities, the universities and police in responding to 'celebration riots' have sprung up across the continent, and several investigations into the latest (2011) Vancouver riot are underway.

Despite what amounts to clear evidence that the North American authorities appear to be more seriously controlling sports crowds than ever before, it is also the case that North American authorities have reacted to crowd disorder on essentially local levels. In the US, other than occasional attempts to have Congress seriously address the issue of violent sports fans – most of which seem to have been ineffective or stymied – no wide-ranging legislation has been introduced to curb the problem, and state and provincial legislators do not seem to have given the problem of sports crowd disorder much thought. But, there is some evidence to suggest that this situation is slowly changing. For example, in the US, several recent state-wide, and even national, initiatives show this, including programmes aimed at repeat offenders, and tactics for dealing with dangerous-item screening and confiscation (e.g. Center for Problem-Oriented Policing 2010). There has been no such concern shown for sports crowd disorder at the level of the state in Canada.

The role of alcohol in crowd violence

Since it is thought to be a major precipitant of crowd violence (many of the manifestations of North American sports crowd disorder described in Chapter 3, and again here, are routinely attributed to it), the perceived role of alcohol, and official reactions to that role, are noteworthy. On the one hand, concern that alcohol might be a violence-accelerator has prompted not only restrictions on sales and increased frisking and confiscation procedures at many stadia, but also extensive, continent-wide efforts to reduce alcohol-related misconduct linked to sports events. For example, TEAM (Techniques for Effective Alcohol Management), one of the largest programmes of its kind, represents coordinated efforts with many professional sports teams and leagues, especially professional baseball. Similar, but smaller-scale, programmes, often involving designated driver initiatives, also exist in particular cities. On the other hand, and partly a consequence of ownership and control issues as well as local municipal laws that permit alcohol sales (Young 1988: 209), it remains the case that the vast majority of North American stadia continue to sell beer and or hard liquor, and that sport, sport spectatorship and sport business are enmeshed in what can only be called a 'culture of alcohol.'

Although many stadia have reduced the strength and volume of alcohol they sell and frequently terminate sales prior to the conclusion of games, at least one interpretation of these practices is that they are public relations strategies used by clubs to mollify frustrated orderly fans and other concerned parties. Data from the mid-1980s showed that clubs experiencing problems with inebriated fans have at times underplayed the extent and seriousness of offences taking place (Young 1988). This may be explained by the fact that many North American clubs, as with many English soccer teams (Eaves and Phillips 2000), are either sponsored or owned by breweries or alcohol companies, or that stadia and their concessions are controlled not by the teams but by external organizations including cities themselves. In these ways, then, official reactions to the role of alcohol in sports-related disorder seem at least contradictory, and possibly hypocritical. Despite the perceived primacy of alcohol in North American fan violence, it seems premature to anticipate in the near future any facsimile of Britain's 1985 *Control of Alcohol Bill*, which initially banned the possession or consumption inside soccer stadia. Put simply, the revenue and reputational issues at stake have nudged North American sports authorities more towards 'management' strategies rather than 'prohibition' strategies. As much of the British hooliganism research has found (e.g. Marsh et al. 1996), draconian efforts to completely ban alcohol seem doomed to fail anyway since fans intent on drinking will find some innovative way to do so, either at, or away from, the stadium.

Alcohol continues to feature prominently in the varied articulations of North American SRV, with crowd behaviour, and beyond. As is demonstrated by the existing evidence on, for instance, sport-related hazing (Bryshun and Young 1999, 2007), the excessive behaviour of current or retired 'superstar' athletes, as well as the myriad of alcohol-related scandals across the continent involving (usually male) athletes (Benedict and Klein 1997), what might be called a 'sport-alcohol-masculinity-aggression complex' is a matter of concern for authorities and sports officials alike. In brief, the various well-intended efforts to deal reasonably and responsibly with – or, in other words to *socially control* – the negative impact of alcohol are positioned paradoxically against the culture of modern sport, whose corporate and gender alliances (with alcohol) seem firmly rooted.

How does social control apply to other SRV cells?

Social control in sport is not restricted to the policing of athletes on the field of play and crowds in the stadium. All of the varied dimensions of SRV experience their own versions of social control. There is insufficient space here to review how all forms of prevention, surveillance, policing and sanction are woven into the remaining 16 cells of SRV, but the following provides a series of illustrations of how SRV has been socially controlled at the six different levels mentioned earlier (individual; interpersonal; institutional; community; social structural; global).

The social control of SRV at the individual level

The domain of psychology as much as sociology, the intra-personal, or individual, level of control is manifested in areas such as personality, conscience, mental health and identity. For sociologists, this level of social control invokes social learning theory. Sport is filled with programmes and regulations that players, coaches, medical practitioners and other participants must attend, or conform to, in order to learn, incorporate and act upon codes of, for example, honour, civility, leadership, teamwork, sportsmanship and respect. For coaches and players sanctioned for behaving in a sexist or racist way (SRV cell 14 – other identity violence), or athletes involved in crimes away from the field of play (SRV cell 5 – street crimes), this might involve counselling, sensitivity training, anger-management programmes or education about problem-solving skills, all aimed at the creation of 'safer' and more respectful values and behaviours in sport.[2]

Of course, under the guise of social control of SRV at the level of the individual also fall sanctions imposed upon offending athletes, coaches and others and enforced by sports clubs, leagues, authorities, as well as by the law itself. What is interesting about individual penalties is that they are often linked to broader controls aimed at *patterned* SRV. For instance, while an individual varsity athlete may be sanctioned for sexual harassment or sexual assault, his university may institute a wider educational prevention programme, and while a kennel owner treating, or euthanizing, his dogs inhumanely might be fined for his individual behaviour, new province-wide laws might be introduced aimed at deterring future animal cruelty. In other words, even though this first 'level' appears to operate in a solely intra-personal manner, it derives from, and feeds back into, the community more broadly.

However, and as demonstrated in Chapter 2, many Western countries continue to prefer an 'individualizng' approach to policing and crime. Thus, instead of holding teams, or leagues, accountable for, say, drug, alcohol or code-of-conduct violations, or player violence, individual athletes are pathologized as 'bad apples.' As Coakley and Donnelly (2009) argue, the tendency of the world of sport to strategically avoid the broader 'rotten barrel' approach (which would embarrass the clubs and leagues and, admittedly, be more difficult to administer), may help to 'contain,' or even remove, individual offenders in the short-term, but shows no sign of working in the long-term.

The social control of SRV at the interpersonal level

On this level, the focus of social control shifts to the relationships between players and coaches, peers and parents. For instance, where SRV cell 12 (parental abuse) is concerned, Minor Hockey Calgary runs a 'Respect in Sport Program' aimed at preventing verbal abuse and intimidation from the sidelines, and warning parents who 'break the rules' that disciplinary action will be taken.[3] Meanwhile, Saskatoon Youth Soccer has introduced a Field Marshall (FM) programme, whereby each team is required to provide an FM to act as a buffer to inappropriate comments made by spectators and aimed at officials during the game. If a team fails to provide an FM, it is subjected to sanctions, such as fines.[4]

The social control of SRV at the institutional level

At the institutional level, the focus shifts to efforts to monitor and sanction the behaviour of sports personnel in schools, universities and workplaces (including professional sports 'workplaces'). Examples of SRV 'controls' at this level are common. These include innovative programmes such as the 'Mentors in Violence Prevention' (MVP) programme at Northeastern University, and the 'Men Creating Attitudes for Rape-Free Environments' initiative at the University of Southern California, both of which involve multiple departments and units on their respective campuses. Other social control initiatives at the institutional level include the following:

- In cell 6 (violence against the self), and in the wake of long-standing concerns with body pathology problems (such as anorexia and bulimia) in American college sport (e.g. during the 1997 NCAA wrestling season, three collegiate athletes died in a five week period – Oppliger et al. 2006: 963), the NCAA has instituted a series of rules with respect to athlete 'weight-cutting.'
- In cell 7 (athlete initiation/hazing), most North American colleges and universities have introduced their own anti-hazing policies, and hazing-awareness counselling of one kind or another features in athletic departments across the continent. For instance, McGill University in Montreal 'forbids hazing and

any other form of inappropriate student initiation activity on property owned or occupied by the University, or in a University context,' and any persons caught engaging in hazing-related acts are subject to discipline under the University's *Code of Student Conduct and Disciplinary Procedures*.[5]

- And, in cell 14 (other identity violence), anti-racist interest groups have lobbied for the removal of flagrantly stereotypical sports mascots that characterize native Americans as 'aggressive fighters, ignore contemporary Native American life, ignore cultural differences between different native societies, and misrepresent and trivialize aspects of Native culture' (Davis-Delano 2007: 341).

The social control of SRV at the community level

Attempts to monitor and sanction SRV relate at this level to programmes within a particular municipal setting, such as a town or city, but which may not be emulated across the country. Efforts may focus on anti-crime initiatives in particular neighbourhoods and communities, or on integrating stadium design into community life in an environmentally friendly way. Most commonly, however, social control efforts here relate to actions introduced by sport associations in a specific geographical region or district. For example:

- In cell 12 (parental abuse), in 2010 the Calgary Minor Soccer Association adopted a 'Zero Tolerance Policy' after a report suggested that referee harassment by Calgary parents was common. Under the new rules, referees (most of whom are themselves teenagers) are empowered to have any sideline spectator who is acting in a degrading or intimidating manner towards them removed. A series of further 'protective' rules pertain to possible sanctions to teams involved that range from cancelling post-season games to not assigning officials.[6]
- In cell 14 (other identity violence), 'Sport England' sets out dozens of policies aimed at standardizing respectful environments in sport, which then become incorporated into communities in a manner that 'fits' the local setting. For instance, the Equity in Sport Policy of 'Swim Halifax' ensures that factors such as race, religion, sexual orientation, gender or age do not become factors of discrimination within the club. It states:

> Sports equity is about fairness in sport, equality of access, recognizing inequalities and taking steps to address them. It is about [supervising] the culture and the structure of sport to make sure that it becomes equally accessible to everyone in society . . . [and avoiding athletes being in fear of] . . . discrimination, intimidation, harassment or abuse.[7]

The social control of SRV at the social structural level

Social control applied to sport also operates at the level of entire nation-states. Again, examples are legion:

- In cell 8 (harassment, stalking and threat), to protect against harassing circumstances, the *Australian Sports Commission* (ASC) *Code of Conduct* outlines what sexual harassment is for the employees for Australia's sports industry and cautions against the 'inappropriate exercise of power . . . and influence in the conduct of activities' (ASC *Code of Conduct*, Section 4.0).[8]
- Relevant to several cells (such as 8 – harassment, stalking and threat; 9 – sexual assault; and 11 – offences by coaches/administrators/medical staff), in 2001 the UK introduced the Child Protection in Sport Unit (CPSU) (Weber 2009: 56) and, in 2003, the CPSU adopted new national standards for safeguarding and protecting children in sport. Among other features, the CPSU website contains links to a freephone number enabling children or adults to report possible abuse situations, and coaches have to undergo criminal record disclosure before being allowed to instruct.
- In cell 17 (offences against workers and the public), and stemming from the build-up to the 2008 Beijing Olympic Games, the Chinese government mandated stricter national labour laws protecting workers from abuses such as arbitrary lay-offs and the coercion of workers into excessively long shifts (Kahn and Barboza 2007).

The social control of SRV at the global level

Finally, attempts to police and sanction aspects of SRV can be found at the international level. The existence of organizations such as WADA (World Anti-Doping Agency), FIFA, the IOC and international governing bodies of dozens of sports that monitor and control behaviour not only on the field of play, but off it too (e.g. in the form of judges and representatives, safety and equipment policies, and other structures dictating what fans and crowds can and cannot do) demonstrates that, in many situations, the surveillance and control of sport is fully global. Concrete examples include the following:

- In cell 6 (violence against the self), following a doping scandal in the 1998 Tour de France that demonstrated the extent of drug use in the sport of cycling, WADA was formed in 1999 (Hanstad et al. 2008). Of particular importance where social control is concerned, WADA underlined the ineffective role of the IOC as sole arbiter of anti-doping policy. Funded by governments related to the Olympic Movement, yet an independent body, WADA has basically replaced the IOC in dealing with issues surrounding drug use in sport.
- In cell 14 (other identity violence), and to counter what is broadly thought to be a problem throughout European soccer, Nike launched its Europe-wide *Stand Up Speak Up* campaign in 2005 to bring attention to the issue of racism in soccer. It lasted for three months and featured recognized figures, such as Thierry Henry, then of Arsenal FC, as spokespersons (Müller et al. 2008).
- In cell 17 (offences against workers and the public), a 'Clean Clothes Campaign' (CCC) was initiated in the Netherlands in 1988 involving up to 11

different European countries. Aimed at protecting workers in the world's sports merchandise industries, the CCC united over 250 non-governmental organizations, trade unions and work assistance centres in the Philippines, China and Indonesia. Its main focus is on the relationship between sport brands, retailers, consumers, governments and garment workers. Among other features, it provides a means for filing complaints on behalf of disenfranchised and disadvantaged workers, as well as recording incidents of women's sexual and physical abuse within the workplace (Sluiter 2009).

In sum, the surveillance and governance of SRV weaves throughout organized sport, and may be found at all levels, from so-called 'grass-roots' activities all the way up to the most elite-level and recognized of all sports.

How theory plays in

Many sociological theories could be used to shed light upon the social control of SRV, but three perspectives seem particularly germane in this connection: the Foucauldian perspective; figurational sociology; and the work of David Garland.

The Foucauldian panopticon

In his book, *Discipline and Punish: The Birth of the Prison*, Michel Foucault (1977) introduces three dimensions of social control that help us understand the surveillance and policing of SRV. First, he introduces the notion of the *panopticon*. Originally a type of prison designed in the late 1700s by English philosopher, Jeremy Bentham, to allow prisoners to be observed without them knowing, or being sure, that they were being observed, the social meaning of the 'panopticon' has expanded. It is now used by sociologists, often metaphorically, to refer to the ways in which groups wielding power can monitor subjects who exist in a state of permanent visibility, or *perceived* permanent visibility. In this way, to be 'in the panopticon' is to be under conditions of control. What is especially relevant about 'panopticonic' thinking for SRV is the way in which, through not knowing or ambiguity, inmates or observed groups, begin to adjust and regulate their own behaviour (Caluya 2010).

The notion of the panopticon can be used to understand any everyday human behaviour or relationship. As Sheridan (1995: 205) argues:

> [I]t is a type of location of bodies in space, a distribution of individuals in relation to one another, a hierarchical organization, a disposition of control and power, a definition of the instruments and modes of power which can [be seen] in hospitals, workshops, schools and prisons.

Johns and Johns (2000) suggest that sport should be added to this list of places where panopticon-like observation and control takes place.

While critics and cynics would quickly counter that the world of sport is filled with abusive or violent athletes, coaches and fans who do not watch their behaviour *enough*, there are many components and manifestations of SRV that can be understood using the idea of the panopticon. For instance, it seems likely that the increasing presence of hi-tech surveillance cameras and security in sports crowds, and an awareness of such security procedures, has prompted potential offenders to at least reflect on their behaviour, or be more careful when it comes to hiding it. In a similar way, athletes at the elite level understand that every aspect of their training and performances are watched, analysed and dissected by teams of coaches and assessors and may adjust accordingly, and harassing coaches may work harder to disguise their behaviour and intentions.

Linked by Foucault to his notion of the panopticon are his related ideas on 'governmentality' and 'surveillance.' Governmentality (Rose and O'Malley 2006) refers to the varying styles of governance in different communities and cultures, and may be seen in sport in the different forms, and levels, of intervention of governing bodies, from team administrators to league officials. By 'surveillance,' Foucault explains how punishment is no longer confined to the formal criminal system, but operates at an informal level where persons have a heightened self-awareness, and even paranoia, about being watched or caught (Norris 2007). Again, athletes under-performing or not conforming to the rigors of the 'sport ethic' know that they may be sanctioned, or dropped altogether.

Foucault's ideas are not fully compelling, and the myriad ways that sports fans continue to act violently despite heightened security (as we have seen in the case of sports crowd riots on both sides of the Atlantic), spectating parents continue to act abusively in the presence of other parents, and athletes cheat in full view of thousands of fans are mundane examples of how SRV endures *in spite of* panopticon-like surveillance. But sports, including aspects of SRV, are increasingly exposed to forms of Foucauldian surveillance, and there is a growing literature in the sociology of sport adopting this line of enquiry (e.g. Pringle 2001; Markula and Pringle 2006; Rail and Bridel 2007; Chase 2008; Barker-Ruchti and Tinning 2010).

Figurational sociology

As noted in Chapter 2, any time the relationship between sport and violence is examined, figurational sociology holds promise. It is especially useful in shedding light upon questions of how SRV meshes with personal restraint and social control.

According to Elias, 'civilizing' occurs over time, and involves a process whereby greater restraint is exercised by the individual over habitual and impulsive acts, such as violence (Mennell 2006: 429). Importantly, this restraint does not express itself as a complete awareness of manners and 'civility' but, rather, manifests itself in the ways in which individuals become increasingly tied to, and dependent upon, one another. This process is never exhaustive, or 'total.' Elias recognizes that civilizing occurs in phases (or 'spurts') that are governed and restricted by the ebbs and flows that occur in all societies (Dunning 1997). Civilizing trends can be seen, for example, in changes in etiquette, manners, table habits, hygiene routines and also in sport-related behaviours.

Figurationalists use the ideas of Elias to show how, for example, modern boxing is increasingly regulated by strict rules that range from weight classes to how and where participants can and cannot hit, and 'blood sports' such as fox hunting have increasingly become less directly violent for participants, though ongoingly violent 'by proxy' (Elias and Dunning 1986).

The world of sport contains many 'counter-trends,' or what Elias calls 'de-civilizing spurts.' Perhaps the most obvious of these today can be seen in the juggernaut-like popularity of MMA and particular strands such as the UFC. Although increasingly regulated and encountering its own process of 'sportization,' this still-relatively new sport began in the 1990s as extreme and bloody, no-holds-barred (no gloves, few rules, mismatched opponents etc.) contests. While it is intuitively difficult to apply terms such as 'civility' to it, in its thickening rule structure, the UFC is currently undergoing its own 'sportization' process and becoming increasingly governed and rule-bound – or *socially controlled*.

Garland's 'cultures of control'

In a manner reminiscent of Foucault, David Garland's provocative study, *The Culture of Control: Crime and Social Order in Contemporary Society* (2001) is more obviously applicable to systems of crime, justice and law than it is to sport, but it contains real potential for making sense of the sports process, and SRV within that process. Essentially, Garland's book deals with the relationship between penal systems and social control. It focuses on changes in Western penal structures over the past 30 years, and especially the trend away from rehabilitation and towards punitive sanctions. All of this is contextualized against a backdrop of conservative politics, which, Garland argues, has precipitated a return to draconian systems of police surveillance and state control, and a decline in what he calls 'penal welfarism.' Ultimately doomed to fail, argues Garland, symptoms of an over-bureaucratized criminal system in places such as the US and the UK include the increasing professionalization of police forces, the commodification of justice and a shift from looking at the *causes* of crime to the *effects* of crime. Crucially, this shift is seen by Garland to have also affected the academy, as may be witnessed in the drift to theories such as routine activity theory, situational crime prevention perspectives and versions of rational choice theory (Moffat 2002; Savelsberg 2002).

Notwithstanding the obvious problem that these sorts of changes are not reflective either of penal systems in other societies, or indeed of the *entire* penal systems of the US and the UK (where, for instance, a focus on rehabilitating offenders co-exists with harsher, more punitive models), Garlandesque 'cultures of control' are certainly visible in sport. So far, Garland's work has not been heavily used or applied by sociologists of sport, but it *could* be. For instance, by examining the ubiquitous and all-encompassing effects of what they call ideologies of 'prolympism' (visible in the increase in professionalization and commercialization in Olympic and amateur sports, the increasing emphasis on outcome rather than 'play,' and the paternalistic notion that athletes would not be as committed to 'outcome' if it were not for some version of external control), Donnelly and Young (2004) argue that sport represents an overt control climate replete with its own versions of surveillance, regulation and punishment. In many sports, training and playing is highly regimented, authority is clearly delineated and athletes are motivated by fear and punishment (e.g. of being benched, traded, demoted, ridiculed, losing pay etc.). Where SRV is concerned, many of the behaviours described in Chapter 4 underline how abusive, violent or otherwise victimizing behaviours against human athletes, animal 'athletes' or the environment are expressions of sweeping cultures of control that appear to 'make sense' to insiders, and are comfortably rationalized in sport.

Conclusion

Whether it operates as *internal* or *external* control, or *formal* or *informal* control, it is not difficult to find evidence of social control in sport. Wherever sport is played, there are rules, regulations and sanctions, and in every country the sports authorities as well as the police and the government play a role in controlling sport. With respect to SRV, social control initiatives range in their intended outcomes from standardizing procedures and behaviours, to pro-active deterrence-based programmes, to fairness-, respect- and equity-restoring campaigns, to punishments of various forms, which themselves range in scope and severity. This might include outright bans on some activities, such as the UK *Hunting Act* of 2004 outlawing hunting with dogs (particularly fox hunting, but also the hunting of deer, hares and mink). Needless to say, the effectiveness of any of these 'controls' is rarely crystal clear, and always a matter for debate. Further, as Atkinson and Young (2008) show in the final chapter of their book, sport is filled with interventionist projects aimed at addressing wider social problems such as poverty, political conflict or war. In the areas of 'sport for social development and peace,' sport is viewed as an interventionist tool *in and of* itself. Again, its success rate in this pursuit is hotly debated (e.g. Okada and Young 2011; Sugden 2006, 2010).

In many respects, the relationship between sport and social control is elusive. On the one hand, it may be that sport is one of the most heavily administered, and policed, of all social institutions. On the other, and as this book demonstrates in myriads of ways, sport represents a 'protected' social space, both on and off the field, where actions that would not be allowed in any other area of life, and that range from assertive behaviour to dangerously violent and injurious behaviour, are championed and rewarded. A perfect example of this paradox may be witnessed in the case of the NHL, which, in terms of punishments and suspensions, appears to be one of the most closely monitored of all professional sports. From in-game 'penalty boxes' to post-game suspensions and mediated criticisms of unacceptable 'goonery' by out-of-control 'enforcers,' professional ice hockey is entangled in a far-reaching language of social control. But little of it seems to matter. As Chapter 7 goes on to show, while there have been some recent changes to rules and norms in the game intended to make it less obviously brutal, as well as to some aspects of its media treatment (i.e. the days of bench-clearing brawls and prolonged TV coverage of them have diminished), professional North American ice hockey, including its media coverage, endures as a celebrated, protected and relatively *uncontrolled*, arena of violence and hurt.

That said, as we have seen, elements of social control pervade all sports. Based, as so much of it is, on conflict, competition, physical force and the notion of dominating opponents, sport could not exist without some degree of internal restraint and external control. The paradox of social control is that it is precisely the surveillance around, rules within and policing of sports such as ice hockey, rugby, boxing and MMA that allow them to persist in their flagrantly violent, but ultimately socially 'legitimate,' contemporary format. For example, despite stubborn political and public opposition, in 2011, the province of Ontario acquiesced and allowed the first UFC event to take place at the Rogers Centre in Toronto.[9] As fighters, simultaneously facilitated and restricted in the octagon by internal rule structures, pummeled each other to a bloodied pulp over hours of prime-time sports 'entertainment' and millions of pay-per-view viewers tuned in around the world, the sorts of 'de-civilizing' ambiguities that Garcia and Malcolm (2010) and Van Bottenburg and Heilbron (2006) hint at became all too clear. A better example of the contradiction of 'socially controlled' sport would be hard to find.

As noted in the Introduction of this chapter, social control efforts are rarely met with complete public approval and compliance, or practical success. Some attempts (such as certain programmes aimed at teaching child athletes respect for opponents) appear to have met their desired goals and have made sport a safer and friendlier place (Thompson 2010). Others have backfired and seem to have had counterproductive effects on matters such as safety or violence-containment. Militaristic penning and fencing arrangements in British soccer, and the ultimately displacing over-policing of fan violence inside stadia, are cases in point. Yet others continue to show contradictory outcomes, as two final examples show.

First, while a blend of firm, consistent and innovative formal intervention and policing in the UK is widely thought to have 'cured' soccer hooliganism (Garland and Rowe 2000: 154), and almost certainly has helped to reduce it, the problem has not evaporated, although it may be true that 'committed football hooligans have had to go to even greater lengths to fulfil their desire for trouble' (Garland and Rowe 2000: 155).

Second, while anti-hazing policy and education campaigns must surely have sensitized some possible offenders to the dangers and inappropriateness of humiliating, degrading and risky initiation practices, hazing shows no signs of 'going away.' Indeed, despite, in North America at least, widespread anti-hazing campaigns, athletes at all levels not only continue to 'haze,' but do so either brazenly or 'in secret.' As Bryshun and Young (2007) found in their study of Canadian varsity hazing, male and female athletes intent on initiating their rookies but fearing sanctions from their coaches or schools now hold events 'behind closed doors,' often with codes of secrecy attached. The net result is a subterranean, but still active, Canadian hazing culture. In this case, the outcomes of social control have been both *intended* and *unintended*.

Finally, as we now lead into Chapter 7, it seems appropriate to mention the changing, and expanding, role of the media in social control. Since, for example, no harassing coach, animal-abusing trainer or mouthy 'soccer Mom' wants to read about himself or herself in the news, the media likely act, for some people, as a deterrent, or at least a signal of what can happen if they 'get caught.' Whether news accounts come in the form of individual whistle-blowing or collective shaming, the media may thus also serve as an informal agent of social control. At the time of writing, municipal and provincial authorities in British Columbia have established interactive Facebook accounts and other social media sites in an attempt to apprehend persons involved in offences during the 2011 Vancouver NHL riot. Call-ins to fan radio, emails sent to TV and print media sources, Internet interactions and 'tweets' and posts on social networking and micro-blogging sites are all ways in which SRV, and the control of SRV, becomes played out in popular discourse. While they may not be as formal or coercive as laws and policies, these strategies all address public opinion regarding what should be done about SRV, and indicate the extent to which SRV prevails in the panopticon of contemporary sport.

7

AN EYE ON SRV

The role of the media

Introduction

It is possible, indeed probable, that the vast majority of people with an interest in sport have never participated directly in player or crowd violence. They have never thrown a punch during a hockey game or a missile from the bleachers, or been knocked unconscious by an opponent in the octagon. Yet these behaviours are known to them. Their perceptions are far more likely to have developed *indirectly* with help from the mass media including, increasingly, images and messages of sport constantly updated on Internet sites, in blogs or in some other form of 'new media' (Wilson 2007). Answers to questions such as 'who *does* sports violence?,' 'when, where and how does it take place?' and 'what are its effects?' are routinely available in the sports media, sometimes implicitly, sometimes explicitly, but rarely innocently. In this sense, our understanding of sports violence is likely *mediated* – refracted to us through the camera lens, the printed sports report or some version of web coverage in a process where some behaviours are emphasized and others downplayed or left out altogether. This chapter examines how aspects of SRV have been portrayed in the media, as well as exploring the role of journalists in covering aggressive and injury-producing aspects of sport. As a case study, the chapter uses data gleaned from content analyses and one-on-one interviews with Canadian journalists to assess the roles and assumptions of members of the sports media, which guide the production of television and newspaper reports. The effects of mass media portrayals of violence on violence itself have, for decades, generated public debate and extensive published research. While the latter has not resulted in the conclusive establishment of a direct cause-and-effect relationship between media coverage and real life violence, evidence suggests a symbiotic co-existence. The chapter summarizes this literature and reviews the thorny question of 'media effects.' Finally, recent changes in the relationship between the media and the public, and the possibility of moving towards a more responsible sports media are considered.

The legitimation perspective

One of the most common sociological approaches to understanding the relationship between sports violence and the media – the so-called 'legitimation' perspective – focuses not so much on violence as such, but on the messages that accompany violence; messages often serving to condone, or legitimize, the behaviour of violence-doers. Nowhere do these messages seem to be more blatant and pervasive than in media presentations of sports. Precisely how much sports violence is given a positive slant is not known but, unquestionably, the media frequently convey the idea that violence is acceptable, even desirable, behaviour and that violence-doers are to be admired. This is done in a myriad of ways – some crude, some artful, some (as we will see) probably a reflection of the acceptance of pro-violence values and norms by media personnel themselves. Examples may be found in an expansive literature representing research in a variety of settings (Hall 1978; Whannel 1979; Smith 1983; Walvin 1986; Young 1986; Murphy et al. 1988; Young and Smith 1988/1989; Young 1990, 1991b, 1993; Gillett et al. 1996; Stead 2003; Cottle 2006).

Notwithstanding variance in the conventions and approaches of media outlets, Hall's (1978: 26) early description of the treatment of soccer hooliganism in the British popular press is generally indicative of the manner in which many aspects of sports violence have been, and continue to be, reported in the press in a number of countries: '[G]raphic headlines, bold type-faces, warlike imagery and epithets, vivid photographs cropped to the edges to create a strong impression of physical menace, and . . . stories [that] have been decorated with black lines and exclamation marks.' Hall speaks of 'editing for impact,' a process in which disorderly behaviour comes to be marketed by a media industry geared towards profit maximization. A cluster of issues including lurid news values, cynical production motives, dramatic and distorting reporting techniques and conservative world views combine to 'excite' the phenomena. This effect can be witnessed, in the case of crowd disorder, in the heightening of public and official sensitization to the problem (such as public overestimation of threat, increases in policing procedures etc.). More recently, Cottle (2006) uses the notion of 'mediatized rituals' to describe how the media encode, and the public decode, 'resonant [news] symbols.'

That the media may have played an active, rather than a passive, role in aspects of collective violence in European soccer including, at times, amplifying and, at other times, de-amplifying roles, has long been a view advanced in research on the British (Whannel 1979; Vulliamy 1985; Keen 1986; Taylor 1982, 1987; Walvin 1986; Young 1986; Murphy et al. 1988) and the continental European context (Pietersen and Kristensen 1988; Van Limbergen and Walgrave 1988; Stollenwerk and Sagurski 1989; Williams and Goldberg 1989). Throughout Europe, media treatment of soccer hooliganism has been associated with the creation of 'folk devils' and 'moral panics' (Young 1986). Indeed, for several decades the European, and certainly the British, media have had what can only be termed a 'love–hate' relationship with fan violence. On the one hand, its perpetrators have served as convenient targets for moral degradation and disrepute while, on the other, amplified views of their violent proclivities have fuelled market profitability in a perverse relationship where 'bad news' becomes, from a sales point of view, 'good news.'

In North America, numerous studies of media coverage have explored ways in which the electronic and print media also distort and/or exploit aspects of sports crowd and player violence (Bryant and Zillmann 1983; Morse 1983; Coakley 1988/1989; Young and Smith 1988/1989; Theberge 1989; Young, S. 1990; Young 1990, 1991b, 1993; Gillet et al. 1996), as well as other forms of SRV, such as sexual harassment (Kirby and Fusco 1998). For example, emphasizing common trends in sports commentary found especially in the daily and tabloid newspapers (such as the use of melodramatic and eye-catching headlines, commendations of violent athletes and their bellicose styles of play, and a reliance on graphically violent photographs), Smith (1983) and Young and Smith (1988/1989) concentrate on the messages that accompany acts of sports violence in the Canadian press. The result of these common coverage techniques, they contend, is at least to condone violent play and, at worst, to reproduce it. Morse (1983) and Gillett et al. (1996) have also shown how television coverage manipulates sport by stressing its rougher and often injurious elements, and how potentially health–compromising norms are reinforced by many well-known and respected sports figures who promote and defend violent play as a relatively harmless feature of sport. Finally, the active role played by the North American media in their treatment of violence has also been shown to include the dissemination of myths, such as the notion that fist-fighting in ice hockey is non-injurious (Young 1990), and that soccer hooliganism is an indigenously 'British disease' (Young 1988).

Making violence news: the treatment of CFL football and NHL ice hockey in the Canadian media

Given that the conclusion reached in much of the research is that the media play an active role in the production of sports violence, and may indeed serve to 'excite' or amplify the phenomena, very little hard evidence is provided for claims made with respect to the nature, extent and effect of media treatment. In fact, the empirical evidence seems skimpy and often taken-for-granted. Derived from aggregate studies of professional ice-hockey and football coverage in the Canadian electronic and print media, the following data[1] demonstrate how certain images are privileged over others. The data show that, for two sports whose structures and traditions carry potential for far more than aggression, violence and pain, there is nevertheless a disproportionate emphasis on these aspects in television treatment and newspaper reports.

Television

Lead-ins and intermissions (CFL football and NHL hockey)

In addition to the routine discussion of contextual items such as club standings, team rivalries, attendance and crowd factors, all channels made thematic reference to anticipated roughness, often using footage of rough play in previous games:

- Never before has the battle of Alberta reached such a peak.
- This one's not going to be pretty. We can expect some rough stuff here tonight.
- Time for the Ti-Cats to seek revenge.
- Don't expect N_____ to be a shrinking violet tonight.
- Get ready for a 'beaut.' This one's likely to be a good old fashioned scrap.

Confirming findings from earlier studies of media coverage of sport (e.g. Hall 1978), the adoption of military symbolism and imagery is common:

- It's the Lions' top secret offensive weapons against the arsenal of the Saskatchewan Rough Riders.
- Tonight the top guns go head-to-head.
- It's gonna be trenchwork all the way.
- We'll see if the Argos can withstand an all-out assault by the Stampeders.

Game commentary (CFL football)

Televised football commentary is peppered with forms of violence approval. In what is said and what is implied, it is clear that the game's rougher qualities are revered and emphasized. Given the available choices and opportunities to do so, rough play is rarely overlooked or underplayed. On the contrary, much more may be made of combative game elements than incidents appear to warrant. A common case of this occurs in football in the way potentially injurious contacts are highlighted, often using instant replays, 'super slo-mos' and extreme close-ups (ECUs), even though, relative to 'clean' tackles made within the rules of the game, such incidents tend to represent a minor portion of overall play:

- It looks like another Ivor Wynne slugfest. It'll be a dandy!
- I'm impressed. You can hear the hitting from up here. The plastic-on-plastic. And no-one's given up at this point. Look at that! Bang!

Further, the 'positive attributes' of brutal body contact and potentially injurious play are often praised in a manner intended to be humourous:

- The force of that hit actually took his feet right off the ground. You know that's gotta hurt. Not only does it kill the play but it does shake your confidence, not to mention your teeth [*laughing*].

- Boy, are they having a good fight up front. We are going to show you J_____ up there [*goes to ECU*]. Now he is fighting with everyone. First of all the centre takes him on. Now you got the head slaps goin'. Now a little double team for good measure. A pin; jump on 'em; kick 'em; punch 'em [*laughing*].

Such attempts to trivialize violence are common. One striking instance of this occurred when a so-called '6 foot 1 inch, 235 lb human projectile' left an opponent momentarily concussed and the commentator went on to describe the hit as 'just a little love bump.' On another occasion, as a player's head literally bounced off the hard AstroTurf and he had to be examined by a team physician, a commentator ad libbed lightheartedly: 'He possibly got his bell rung just enough to clear the cobwebs!'

In keeping with the well-documented tradition of image reification in the sports media (Bryant and Zillman 1983; Coakley and Donnelly 2009), an adoption of military symbolism, or what, elsewhere, I have called 'war talk' (Young 1986), represents an equally pervasive trend in football commentary:

- This man is the ideal weapon. All the ammunition you need in his position he possesses.
- A definite case of search and destroy today. He keeps hammering people as he rolls downfield like a tank.
- It's really a war out there. There's really nothing else to say.

Forms of championing bodily sacrifice and injury come together as a further commentary convention. Arguably, these tie into the manner in which football and many other all-male settings may be understood as sites of masculinity verification (Dubbert 1979: 164). As Chapter 5 has shown, a subculturally prized perspective on the game, revered by coaches, players and commentators alike, is that respect may be earned through the acceptance of risk, in both the giving out, and acceptance of, pain:

- Took a pretty good headslap there, but paid the price.
- Broken wrist and all and still gets an interception. What an athlete!
- Just trying to earn a little respect down there.
- He's gonna have to be the sacrificial lamb for the last 5 minutes and 45 seconds.

The appreciation for, indeed insistence on, bodily sacrifice underscores not only how the media legitimize violence, but also how they do so in a potentially insidious manner given the often injury-producing character of professional football (Young 1993).

This can easily be demonstrated in the use of instant replays. In one game, an ECU of a player knocked to the ground and injured ran three times as a 'colour man' bellowed: 'He drilled S_____. A reckless hard hitter. Just the kind of player you want at linebacker.' In another game, as a player writhed on the turf in obvious pain (viewers were subsequently informed that he had broken ribs), a commentator laughed his way through the following remarks about the offending player: 'It's his first start at the safety spot. If he keeps knockin' people down like that, I think he might find himself a job.'

Game commentary (NHL hockey)

If such themes represent preferred emphases within CFL football broadcasts, an even clearer case of privileging player brutality occurs in the case of televised NHL hockey. While hockey commentaries are also replete with military rhetoric ('He rifled the puck outside the zone'; 'He's a great sniper around the net') and with references to the role of sacrifice and injury ('This is a game which requires you to take those kinds of hits, regardless of outcome'), a more frequent trend is to favourably emphasize physical toughness, hitting and fighting.

Again, rationalized within masculinist sport subcultures as an indicator of commitment, brutal hitting is often explained by commentary teams as evidence of appropriate hockey *character*. As with football, although hitting/checking exists within the rules, excessive and dangerous body contact, disallowed by the rules and often penalized by officials, also receives favourable attention. The following examples demonstrate how commentators particularly emphasize so-called 'grinder hockey,' a rough style of play celebrated by many within the hockey community:

- E____ throws his weight into the corner, hits him hard and that's a good sign of what's to come. Throwing his weight like that, you can see why they're effective players.
- It's heating up at last. It's been pretty medium hot until now and now it's beginning to warm up. The penalty boxes are well populated.
- Oh, S____'s DECKED by S____ and he's hurt. S____ was run over by S____ and is ever so slow to get up. Man, WHAT A HIT!

Although condemned by media critics and sport scholars for some time, these kinds of exchanges remain standard features of Canadian ice-hockey commentary.

Almost without exception, fist-fights occurring during hockey games are not only shown but are dissected analytically, some numerous times using ECUs to zone in on players as they wrestle and punch. The general attitude appears to be, in the words of one commentary team, 'Let's see the blow-by-blow.' Underlining the usefulness of the figurational approach summarized in Chapter 1, fights (including bare-knuckle assaults, eye gouging, head-butting and the like) clearly represent 'exciting significance' (Elias and Dunning 1986) for media personnel. For instance, one sports channel colour man's voice moved from calm to frenzy as he remarked:

> It's a great physical game now. And now there's a penalty and now there's a fight. Now there's a WAR! They're standing up and going at it. Two former Western Hockey League tough guys. And what a war this is!

And, again, on Canada's publicly-funded network, CBC:

> You're going to see one of the best right hands. BINGO! Right in the eye. Down he goes! That's beautiful!

The dialogue during or following hockey fights often involves an attempt to depict violence humourously, again demonstrating how seriously commentators perceive this aspect of the sport, which is not sanctioned within the rules and has been shown to be injury-causing:

- The two heavyweights are going at it. I wonder if they'll be exchanging Christmas cards!
- Some heavy slugging behind the net there. I don't know if this is exactly peace on earth and good will towards men!

Further, attempts to deflect or rationalize the possible serious consequences of fights by underplaying any actual risk to physical safety are also common:

- This is much more of a wrestling match than any actual boxing!
- A little pushing and shoving. Nothing serious at all.

It is rare that hockey fighting is covered in a manner suggesting a serious problem medically, legally or ethically. Despite violating the rules of the sport, its association with injury including concussions, and its possible modelling effects for youngsters, it seems clear that much television coverage contributes to the normalization of fist-fighting in ice hockey.

Instant replays (CFL football and NHL hockey)

Instant replays tell us not only what one might expect in televised sports coverage, but also indicate how announcers may select and focus on game features that are assumed to carry high audience appeal. It is equally clear that whenever actual or potentially injurious contact occurs, particularly again in ice hockey, producers will run instant replays and highlight it as an important component of game coverage. At these points, and as a further indicator of how participant violence is glamorized by television, 'slo-mos,' 'super slo-mos' and ECUs depicting often graphic violence are used. This allows the viewer at home to intimately re-live the violent moment via facial and bodily expressions of anger, pain or injury, and to lip-read or, indeed, hear the often abusive and profane language of players occurring during such violent exchanges through the use of carefully placed ice-level microphones.

Newspapers

Generally speaking, themes discussed so far as trends in Canadian television coverage of CFL football and NHL ice-hockey games may also be found in Canadian

newspaper coverage. Emphases on military imagery, toughness, violence glorifica-
tion and bodily risk are all routine, with only marginal variance by type or genre of
newspaper. A brief review of newspaper headlines and photographs is illustrative.

Headlines (CFL football and NHL hockey)

The headlines of sports stories, both in the quality and popular press, frequently
reflect a very standard format. Using rhetoric laid out with large, capitalized letters,
isolated on the page for extra visual effect and replete with splatterings of emphatic
punctuation, such headlines not only signify the violent sports act, but do so in a
way that appears accurate and unquestionable:

- PASSION FOR PUNISHMENT
- TICATS MAUL ARGOS
- BRUINS OUTMUSCLE HABS
- HAWKS SOCK IT TO EDMONTON
- FLAMES WIN A SLUGFEST WITH THE OILERS
- BATTLE OF THE SHINERS

Representing common trends in the use of headlines, this list demonstrates the
manner in which the press do not simply objectively report on given sports events,
but are able to manipulate them by stressing their potentially rougher elements
(even in cases of games played within the rules and without controversy) in a
way that piques readers' curiosity and enhances entertainment value and audience
appeal. The sports headline is, then, fundamentally a strategic eye-catcher used to
entice readers towards the story to follow.

Photographs (CFL football and NHL hockey)

Students of the news process have shown how photographs constitute 'part of
the diet of news' and an 'apparently unarguable rendition of the world' (Hartley
1982: 181). In the words of the semiotician Roland Barthes (1972: 110), 'pictures
are more imperative than writing; they impose a meaning at one stroke, without
analyzing or disturbing it.'

In the case of North American sport, it is not hard to see how the press exploit
aspects of professional football and ice hockey that are potentially harmful and,
again, in the case of hockey fist-fighting, run counter to the rules of the game.
Rather than showing higher numbers of pictures of, say, touchdowns or goals
being scored, passes, skating action, poses of celebration or dejection, the press
disproportionately privilege aggressive and violent photographic material.

With respect to the enduring use of 'contact' and 'fight' pictures, where the
intended meaning of the photograph remains ambiguous to the reader, captions
serve to render it unambiguous:

- Blasting a bomber!
- Take that!
- Paying the price!
- That's gotta hurt!

Moreover, captions and 'cut lines' such as 'Nosy fellow!' (as a player had his nose crushed by a hockey stick), 'Face smack!' (as a player's head collided with an opponent's helmet) and 'Getting right (and left) to it!' (as a hockey player used both fists to assault another player) demonstrate again how the press frequently deal with illegal and potentially harmful behaviour in a non-serious way.

NHL photographs in six Canadian newspapers

In order to empirically examine ice-hockey photographic content in the Canadian media, I compared the use of photographs across two NHL seasons, ten years apart (2000/2001 and 2010/2011) in six Canadian newspapers. For reasons of manageability and access, the comparison was restricted to the first three months of the season (October–December). Newspapers selected included Canada's national 'quality' daily newspaper (*Globe and Mail*), four daily 'broadsheets' (*Calgary Herald*, *Montreal Gazette*, *Vancouver Sun* and *Toronto Star*) and one daily 'tabloid' (*Calgary Sun*). The newspapers represented four major Canadian cities, all of which have NHL teams. Only photographs of 'action' or 'game' content were included in the sample. In other words, photos that showed images such as press conferences, coaches on-or-off the ice or training sessions etc. were excluded. Photographs were coded into three categories: 'fight' (i.e. explicit images of players fighting, about to fight or having fought), 'contact' (i.e. direct physical contact between players such as body-checks or collisions, but not celebratory 'contact') and 'other' (i.e. players shooting, skating, celebrating goals etc.). The results are shown in Table 7.1.

Among the numerous conclusions that could be drawn from the study, four points seem particularly relevant for this chapter:

1   With respect to raw scores, for all newspapers except one (*Globe and Mail*), the use of 'fight' and/or 'contact' photographs increased from 2000/2001 to 2010/2011.
2   The proportion of fight images also increased. Expressed in percentage terms, the *Calgary Herald* went from 2.3 per cent to 4.0 per cent, the *Calgary Sun* went from 5.5 per cent to 8.8 per cent, the *Montreal Gazette* went from 1.9 per cent to 3.1 per cent, the *Toronto Star* went from 3.7 per cent to 5.6 per cent and the *Vancouver Sun* went from 4.1 per cent to 6.0 per cent. The *Globe and Mail* was the only newspaper to show a decrease over the two seasons (from 5.0 per cent to 4.1 per cent). Thus, while the national 'quality' newspaper showed a slight decrease, all other sources displayed noteworthy increases in fight – or violence – content.

TABLE 7.1 NHL photographs in six Canadian newspapers, 2000–2010

Newspaper		2000/2001 Season (4 Oct.–31 Dec. 2000)				2010/2011 (7 Oct.–31 Dec. 2010)			
		Fight	Contact	Other	Total	Fight	Contact	Other	Total
Calgary Herald	Raw score	5	92	122	219	11	110	156	277
	Proportion of total (%)	0.023 (2.3%)	0.420 (42.0%)	0.557 (55.7%)	1.000 (100%)	0.040 (4.0%)	0.397 (39.7%)	0.563 (56.3%)	1.000 (100%)
Calgary Sun	Raw score	12	114	92	218	30	118	194	342
	Proportion of total (%)	0.055 (5.5%)	0.523 (52.3%)	0.422 (42.2%)	1.000 (100%)	0.088 (8.8%)	0.345 (34.5%)	0.567 (56.7%)	1.000 (100%)
Globe and Mail	Raw score	5	51	44	100	4	45	48	97
	Proportion of total (%)	0.050 (5.0%)	0.510 (51.0%)	0.440 (44.0%)	1.000 (100%)	0.041 (4.1%)	0.464 (46.4%)	0.495 (49.5%)	1.000 (100%)
Montreal Gazette	Raw score	3	68	86	157	10	122	193	325
	Proportion of total (%)	0.019 (1.9%)	0.433 (43.3%)	0.548 (54.8%)	1.000 (100%)	0.031 (3.1%)	0.375 (37.5%)	0.594 (59.4%)	1.000 (100%)
Toronto Star	Raw score	6	71	87	164	8	39	97	144
	Proportion of total (%)	0.037 (3.7%)	0.433 (43.3%)	0.530 (53.0%)	1.000 (100%)	0.056 (5.6%)	0.271 (27.1%)	0.674 (67.4%)	1.000 (100%)
Vancouver Sun	Raw score	5	55	62	122	11	53	120	184
	Proportion of total (%)	0.041 (4.1%)	0.451 (45.1%)	0.508 (50.8%)	1.000 (100%)	0.060 (6.0%)	0.288 (28.8%)	0.652 (65.2%)	1.000 (100%)

3   While fight images saw a general increase in proportionality, they still represented a reasonably small percentage of the total images, with the highest percentage of any newspaper being the tabloid *Calgary Sun* at 8.8 per cent in the 2010/2011 season.
4   While photos of 'other' images were generally the most frequent, by combining the scores for the other two categories, it is clear that all sources placed significant emphasis on representing the NHL using 'fight' or 'contact' photographs, during both periods.

Cumulatively, this small study of media treatment once again demonstrates the manner in which the press do not report *neutrally* on sports events, but are able to manipulate them by stressing their potentially rougher elements in a way that is assumed to enhance entertainment value. Despite years of attention to, and criticism of, violence in the NHL, including by the media themselves, aggressive and violent play continue to hold a significant place in how the game is represented. Perhaps most revealing about cynical and exploitative sports media techniques is that photographs and headlines connoting violence, usually placed by persons who did *not* attend the game, may not necessarily be accompanied by any in-depth reports on actual violence at all, and typically represent mere seconds of action in an event that lasts up to three hours.

Journalistic rules of relevance: justifying sports violence coverage

One of the critical questions asked of semiotic and content analysis work is 'how do you know that your deconstruction of the material is accurate, or intended?' It thus becomes important to ask those responsible for creating sports messages to explain how sports news comes to take shape using their own terms and categories. Prompted by a substantial and persuasive literature indicating media exploitation, I interviewed journalists in several Canadian cities, representing a range of professional roles including sports editors and assistant editors, columnists, reporters, 'beat' writers, television play-by-play persons, colour commentators and sports talk show hosts. Many had been responsible for producing the broadcasts and reports of CFL and NHL games excerpted above. Essentially, I asked the journalists to comment on aspects of sport that they considered 'newsworthy.' Although the responses suggested some variation in approach towards and treatment of sports coverage, as a general rule what can only be described as pro-violent attitudes were expressed in rather matter-of-fact ways. Indeed, as the interviews proceeded, and normative strategies for sports reporting emerged, the kinds of coverage styles reviewed earlier became less and less surprising.

'Actuality news' and the rules of relevance

Writing on 'insider' accounts of crime news, Chibnall (1981: 87) found that journalists commonly rationalize report content and technique in terms of readership requirements: 'The rules of relevancy become associated with audience expectations and are legitimated in terms of audience desires.' As compelling evidence of this occupationally revered, but often untested, assumption, every journalist I spoke to alluded in some way to the importance of pursuing 'news' according to such 'rules of relevance.'

In general, the occupational emphasis on what a sports editor called 'actuality news' and a (hockey) beat writer called 'giving the public what it wants' is extremely popular. For example, the following views on hockey fist-fights came from a beat writer and a cameraman:

> Listen, you can criticize these fight shots 'till you're blue in the face, but hockey fights sell papers. The more violent the focus of the story, the more readers will be interested. I'm not advocating it *should* be that way, but it is. The public know what they want and we try and give it to them.

> Let's say if [a hockey superstar] does twirls and fancy things and then finally puts the puck in the net and we run the picture of him putting the puck in the net, it doesn't tell the story. You know, you usually see him going by with his arms in the air and so what! You need a story and a photo with punch. Excuse the pun! [*laughing*] I am a professional journalist. I have to get the best, most effective picture, which really means the most dramatic or the most exciting. With hockey, fight pictures are frequently the best. They're certainly the ones with the most impact and sell the best.

Unsurprisingly, and as suggested by the cameraman, such assumptions of audience desires tend to result in the roughest aspects of sport being emphasized over others.

Television journalists were equally clear in their explanations for player violence coverage. Commenting on live television broadcasts, a play-by-play man rationalized his channel's coverage, including replays of fist-fights, on the basis of possible audience desires, but additionally emphasized that his responsibility was to provide

> an entertaining package of something that is often tedious. We need to jazz things up a little. Also, the NHL is a private corporation and they are in the entertainment business, and they know what the guy sitting in the stands wants to see. I mean, if the guy didn't like the physical aspect of the NHL he wouldn't go to the games, and wouldn't buy his ticket. This is also true of the guy watching at home.

When asked to explain his programme's use of specially constructed packages of what can only be termed brutal body contact as, for instance, 'Fight of the week,' 'Plays (hits/fights) of the day,' 'Hits of the week/season,' a sports channel host again made reference to pressures to entertain and to audience expectations, this time quite adamantly:

Hey, it's there! If it's a good scrap or a fair one, it's entertaining. I'm not here to make moral judgements . . . The fans want it. The fans and the viewers are drawn to those 'cuts' [photographs] because somehow they make sense. These pictures may not be the game's best side. But if the fans want this stuff, what do you do?

Tellingly, when asked for evidence of audience expectations, journalists could provide very little of the kind of information one might expect to be available (such as demographic survey results, evidence of letters or phone calls of approval from consumers to TV channels and newspapers). Efforts had apparently been initiated to 'feel out' audience reactions by considering, for instance, viewers' calls or readers' letters and emails, but none of these efforts had been brought together in any systematic way. Many were still experimental and most seemed cursory at best. Rather than providing hard evidence to justify their coverage techniques, journalists tended to rely on information gathered anecdotally and observationally as demonstrated by the following explanation of a well-known Toronto talk-show host:

> Well, I would simply explain it this way. In all the years I've been around hockey, I've never seen a guy get up and leave the arena when a fight starts. I mean, I've seen all kinds leave when the hockey game is on. They don't [care] about what's going on, but in the situation of a fight, from the press box, I've never seen anyone leave.

In sum, journalists are often unable to compellingly justify claims of the so-called *rules of relevance* or audience expectations. This is not to say that the media's often brash and pro-aggression style of coverage is not received favourably by audiences, or that all journalists and sports news outlets see sports violence homogeneously. A steady sports media market suggests that many viewers probably *do* enjoy them, even though they may not always be accurate reflections of what actually took place. But, in general, if the question is 'for whom do the rules of relevance operate?,' the evidence points as much to journalists themselves as to audiences. As Desbarats (1990) has shown in his work on the self-reproducing institutional norms of Canadian newsrooms, newspaper coverage tends to show a level of 'concordance' with reporters' views of the world. The data reviewed here indicate that much the same is true of sports covered on television and in the popular press.

Economic and time constraints

Journalists also rationalize sports violence coverage in terms of budget and time constraints. With newspapers, for example, reference was often made to the varying demands and capabilities of 'high brow' versus lower quality papers. Where television coverage of hockey and football was concerned, journalists explained that both budget and time influenced broadcasting style and content. But precisely what kinds of constraints impact television and press coverage of sport and, more specifically, how are such constraints related to a disproportionate emphasis placed on sports aggression and violence?

While newspaper journalists also operate according to fairly strict deadlines, in a number of more obvious ways, the content of television broadcasts is linked directly to time constraints. As one well-known Canadian play-by-play commentator remarked in his account of televised coverage of hockey fighting:

> What are you going to . . . in the case of a fight or, more-so in the past, a bench-clearing brawl? I mean, it's fine to say that we'll go to a commercial that consumes 2 minutes, or if you have an entire block of commercials you might get 3 minutes. You've got to show the interruption in the game. So, more than a choice, it's an issue of what to do with the time we've been given. Yeah, we can cut away, but not for so long or so often in the case of a really nasty game. Gaps have to be filled. Simple as that.

Revealingly, the same respondent went on to explain that emotion also plays an important role in producing live sports events: 'Under pressure like that, there's not much time to think. You just react, and all of a sudden you get caught up in the action.'

Many of the differences in newspaper style and form are explained by journalists in terms of the financial capabilities of tabloids, dailies and 'broadsheets.' Workers at tabloids stated this condition in a number of different ways:

> We're a small outfit. We try to kick the other guy's butt whenever we can . . . To compensate for our lack of diverse coverage, we try to focus in on the local team more and gloss it up a bit. From time to time we run two page colour sections, pictures on the front page, you know. And we find that people respond positively to that. But we certainly can't compete with the column space written by double the staff down the road.

> We're quite proud of our staff but, well, it's small. We simply don't have the people or the agenda of the broader sheets. I don't like your term 'editing for impact,' but I think writing for impact is a way of compensating for scarce resources. I mean, on a tabloid paper you can't begin to start writing the length of copy that they do in the broadsheet newspapers, so we will take a long story and break it up into three stories or two and make them as bright and breezy as possible.

Several journalists hinted at the culture of tabloids or dailies, which has always involved, as one tabloid editor put it, 'jazzing it up.' While other respondents disagreed, this trend suggests that the traditional style of the tabloids would still exist if budget and time constraints were removed. For example, an assistant editor of a tabloid decried his paper's modest budget and resources, and implied that greater resources would inevitably lead to 'higher quality' reporting:

Sometimes we have an appalling scenario here . . . because, budget-wise, we simply can't go out and hire a [well known writer] simply because he costs too much. So we hire young people who we hope will learn and come along and grow into better journalists.

Ironically, some tabloids and dailies spend much more of their budgets than other 'high quality' papers on local sport coverage (this is particularly true of football and hockey in Canada) and, with greater resources available, *still* tend to treat their subject matter in graphic and sensational ways.

Similar contradictions exist in how journalists explain photographic content. While several employees of tabloids and dailies accounted for their use of photographic materials privileging roughness on the basis of constraints such as time deadlines ('We're a morning paper and have to meet deadlines'), and budget limitations ('sometimes we just have to depend on a part-time photographer'), in fact, for many years newspapers have received most of their photographs from the 'wire services' such as the Associated Press. Despite the availability of the latter to all newspapers, irrespective of tradition or type, tabloids and dailies continue to privilege violent photographic materials far more than high brow papers, which rarely show such graphic content. In this respect, the genre of the newspaper in question appears to be at least as important in *making violence news* as issues connected to constraints of money or time.

Professional ethics and social responsibility

In conversations with journalists, I was consistently struck by the seemingly haphazard manner in which some aspects of sports news were selected and organized, especially in the case of tabloid and daily newspapers. When one editor was asked to explain his newspaper's use of the kinds of headlines and captions described earlier, he remarked that his source liked 'to get a little "punnie," you know, have some fun with that stuff.' Another newspaper's hockey writer similarly underscored the element of levity in writing 'tag lines' and 'heads': 'we call them "community heads" because we all chip in over coffee and try to build in a joke or two. It's really become a case where we try to lighten this serious stuff up.'

Most journalists rejected the notion that media treatment may have broader social implications. For example, when questioned about ethical concerns of practices such as showing instant replays or ECUs of injurious football hits or hockey fist-fights, or of graphic newspaper headings and photographs, the following kinds of remarks were typical:

Our view is that the game is built on hitting and fans know it. When you have a hit like that, yes, we have to show it more than once. [*KY: But are four or six instant replay angles necessary?*] Probably not, but it happened like that, you know. Here we have something for the viewer . . . And these days the technology is so slick you just have to show it.

A number of journalists working for both television and newspapers went further in interpreting the use of the hockey fist-fight as a key news strategy:

> The worst you get in a hockey fight is the guy skating off the ice with blood streaming down his face from cuts or whatever. [*KY: Which, in your words, would be a dramatic photo?*] Which in our words *would* be a dramatic photograph, yes, and would be used without a second thought. I really don't believe it's in bad taste. It's part of the game and I guess at the base of the thing it sells papers. And if people see a shot on the front [page] of their hero coming off the ice with blood streaming down they're more likely to plunk a dollar into the machine and pull out a paper.

> I will grant you that if there's a picture of a guy who has a bloodied face, or a picture of a guy who's cocking back as if he's about to throw a punch, it connotes more action. Something is happening here, as opposed to a guy who's taking a breath between a face-off and they take a picture of that. If I have those two pictures I'm going to take the one of the guy with the blood streaming down his face because there's more going on in the picture, but I do not, nor does anybody else in my opinion, sit here and say 'that's a more violent picture, let's run it.'

Despite clear evidence to the contrary (as witnessed starkly by the last sentence of the first paragraph of the previous quotation), all journalists rejected the view that their own accounts represented a 'cashing in' on sports violence.

Surprisingly few journalists expressed concerns with the level of professionalism, ethics or responsibility underpinning their news practices. Those that were voiced came in all cases from senior and more experienced staff:

> Some of the people in our department I find have a tendency to write an inflamed headline, an insulting headline, because they're not accountable for it. They will write it and it's almost like 'I'm going to dare to see if I can get this past you.' And, whether or not you've got the editor who's up to speed that day will allow him to catch it and say 'no, we can't say that' and reject it, or rewrite it, or say 'go do it again.'

Hinting once more at the extravagant culture of the tabloids, the same editor went on to remark that this process was 'more than anything else a product of us being a "Tab."' Following an acknowledgement that his newspaper did tend to sensationalize reports on 'certain aspects' of violence in sports, an assistant editor with a different newspaper also accounted for this tendency by pointing to the format of his paper:

> The tabloid format which we have worked on [recently] has allowed us to take that extra little half-step wherever people think they can take it. And, sometimes it's hot and sometimes it's not, and I've maintained the last three

or four years there seem to be no ethics, there seems to be everything other than the s-word and the f-word, everyone, everything seems to be getting in on it. And, I'm not the least bit pleased about the way the industry is headed but, again, we're contributing to it, and we say 'that's fine.' We allow this to happen . . . but it's a changing world, we're trying to respond to the way people think, act, talk.

Other journalists working for tabloid newspapers similarly explained the graphic nature of their coverage (splatterings of colour photographs, pun-like headlines, blunt and abrupt language styles, a focus on dramatic aspects of the event etc.) on the basis of the tabloid format. Interestingly, while the content analysis showed coverage by dailies to be basically similar to the tabloids in all of the aforementioned categories, journalists working for them often explicitly denied such a parallel, preferring instead to align themselves with, in the words of one columnist, 'the more intellectual and thoughtful coverage of the broadsheets.'

Sports journalism: a masculinist occupational culture

In his research on youth subcultures, Brake (1985: 178) has referred to *masculinism* as the celebration of a particular brand of maleness. This may imply a number of things, beginning with the exclusion and/or marginalization of women, of women's perspectives or of alternative male perspectives. Despite the availability of qualified women who could occupy prominent roles, the sports media continue to be structured unequally. Here, we find the operationalization of another insidious 'rule of relevance.' As Spence (1988: 175) writes: 'Let there be no question that the predominantly male audience has some resistance to hearing from a female. That's male chauvinist piggism at its worst, but it's a fact.' Masculinism also implies the championing of a particular kind of male performance. With media representations of professional football and hockey we find a double dose of this. First, and as numerous sociologists have acknowledged, the structural character of modern elite sport is highly masculinist as, second, apparently are its mediated signifiers. Literally dozens of examples of notions of manliness based on force and physical dominance emerged in interviews, but space allows us to discuss only a few. The case of the controversial hockey fist-fight is used first for illustration.

It is clear that many journalists have 'bought into' what Dryden (1983: 189) refers to as the 'NHL theory of violence.' Based on the widely discredited notion of 'catharsis' (see Chapter 1), this theory not only views violence, such as fist-fighting, as inevitable, but as a necessary 'safety valve' in an intrinsically rough game. The theory, pervasive at all levels of the sport, contains a series of rationalizations for violence. The views of three journalists are illustrative:

I mean, hockey fighting is a very insignificant part of the action that takes place in a regular hockey game but, because of what it is, people have a tendency to remember it. I mean, there isn't a doubt in my mind that people go to the stadium to see a good fight as much as they do to see a good hockey game. And when they go home, if there has been a fight, and it was a good one, they'll say 'Jeez, you should have seen so-and-so kick the piss out of X.' I'm sure the guy at coffee break the next day will talk about the fight. But I don't know that that's not human nature.

I don't remember one serious injury that ever occurred because of a punch-up in a hockey game. [However, see numerous examples of fight-related injuries in Chapter 2.]

I think the whole question of fighting in hockey is silly. Most regulations are ostrich-like in their assessment of fighting in hockey. The people that seem to argue most strongly against it are the people you never see there. All I say is, go to a hockey game and when a fight breaks out check the stands, there's the reaction there. Everybody is up yelling, hollering, screaming 'kill 'em, fight 'em, smoke 'em.' It's entertainment. People go to Wrestlemania and MMA . . . to watch violence. I don't see anything wrong with it. Fighting is legislated as part of the rules of hockey.

While the norm was for journalists generally to hold fighting in high regard, the reasons for its appreciation varied. For some, fighting represented a less risky form of violence than other potential dangers such as high stick work while, for others, fighting actually took on the trappings of an art form:

Oh, the fighting thing, what's wrong with it? It's something the fans obviously want. They applaud, right? I suppose it is a little barbaric, but it's a part of the game. I have no objection to seeing a good fight, as long as it's clean and no one gets hurt. I think the fans see a clean fight, you know, a fair one with two players of the same size, as a thing of beauty.

In the NHL, you see, I like the fighting, I must admit it. I don't go out of my way to make it special in reports or anything though. It's just a fascinating part of the game. It's something you don't see in other sports, and I don't see anything wrong with it. But because I like NHL fights doesn't mean I promote violence in the sport. I mean . . . I'm not even close to it. I just think it's a fascinating part of the game. Maybe fascinating is too strong a word, but it's an interesting aspect of the game.

Pro-violence values were also demonstrated in respondents' answers to questions about the responsibility of using levity in captions and headlines accompanying photographs containing graphic violence:

I think that you'll find that most of those tag lines will be something like 'Let's Dance' or 'Dukes Up,' or whatever. I mean, I don't know if they're anything other than boxing terms or hockey terms for the most part. They're acceptable. We try to stay with the acceptable language. I don't think it matters unless it's a horribly serious situation where somebody is hurt badly. A lot of times nobody gets hurt in a hockey fight. If anything, the only thing that gets hurt are guys' hands from hitting a guy's helmet or shoulder pads. Mostly, it's just a little waltz out there.

A routine contradiction exists in these vantage points. On the one hand, appeals of innocence and professional responsibility prevailed ('players don't get injured in fights, you know'; 'we simply have to show it'). On the other hand, journalists' explanations were loaded with pro-violence rhetoric. As the interviews progressed, it became obvious that many journalists were simply unable or unwilling to identify the contradictory nature of their position on this issue. This was best-illustrated by three editors who spoke simultaneously of upholding responsible ethical standards, and not sensationalizing for profit, while referring to a fight picture appearing in one of their papers the previous week as, in their words, 'the best picture':

> I can't remember anybody ever making a decision or running a fight picture because it was a fight picture. If it ended up, in the judgement of our graphics editor and our slot man, being the best picture, that would be the one that we would run. But it wouldn't be run simply because it was a fight picture. It wouldn't be run at all unless it was the best picture we had.

> It's all a matter of good taste. The bad fights, leave them alone. But the clean ones really should be shown. In a clean fight, we've really gotta go with it.

> Many times a fight shot is not very exciting because by the time the photographer's got it, you know, they're just hanging on to each other, they're tired or whatever, and it's not a particularly dramatic shot. If he does happen to catch that instant where they're almost like two gladiators or two boxers aimed and primed to hit each other that is a dramatic shot. Now that tells the story!

Such claims of photographic 'representativeness' are based on a good deal of deception. Several editors acknowledged that choices are regularly made regarding photographs with marginal knowledge of the whole game that is rarely attended in person by the persons making decisions about it. The photo selection process, which remains largely unaltered over the past three decades despite widespread criticism and attention, clearly becomes an extremely subjective one based much more on dramatic content than representativeness. Further, the criteria for judging a 'good picture' were entirely consistent with traditional notions of aggressive masculinity. In the case of ice hockey, the image of men dominating others through force – the bloody fist-fight is the most literal translation – becomes the quintessential hockey moment. And, far from occasional or accidental, its consistently graphic depiction in Canadian sports news is patterned, routine and predictable.

Other indications that this occupational culture reveres dominant masculinities were evident in attitudes to such things as what it means to be a man in sport ('I think, in their own way, "enforcers" are every bit as important as the [great players]'), to the possibility of females and males playing football or hockey side-by-side ('It's just too rough for girls – they'd get hammered') and to female journalists poaching traditionally male-dominated sports *beats* ('They just don't seem to see or understand the game the same way as men do').

In brief, in a number of obvious ways, journalistic 'rules of relevance' act to galvanize the gender order through the Canadian media. Regarding both the inherently risky character of CFL football and NHL hockey, and the violence-approving media reporting process described here, journalists went out of their way to offer rationalizations or out-and-out fabrications. 'Beaters' working for tabloids and dailies particularly seemed so immersed in this masculinist orientation that they were quite blind to the routine contradictions of their own accounts. In Kidd's caustic but perceptive indictment of the world of sport: "'Ideology is like B.O.,'" a wag once said. "You can never smell your own!" That's certainly true for men in sports' (1987: 250).

Media effects

The question of the *effects* of mass media portrayals of violence on 'spill-over' or 'copycat' violence in society has also produced a substantial body of research, much of it in the 1970s and 1980s (Comisky et al. 1977; Gordon and Ibson 1977; Moriarty and McCabe 1977; Singer and Gordon 1977; Smith 1978, 1983; Russell 1979; Whannel 1979; Dupperault 1981; Goranson 1982). While this outpouring of energy has not resulted in the conclusive establishment of a direct cause-and-effect relationship between media and real-life violence, the bulk of the evidence, especially that pertaining to television, points strongly in this direction. Assuming that media presentations of aggressive sports disproportionately privilege violent aspects of play, to what extent do viewers, including presumably impressionable young athletes, consume and become affected by such material?

Several early laboratory and field experiments (cf. Geen and Berkowitz 1969; Baron 1977) showed that subjects exposed to filmed or televised models displaying aggression tend to exhibit similar behaviour when subsequently given the opportunity. Most of this work, however, took place in the laboratory raising inevitable questions about generalizing from artificial environments to the real world. Also, most experimental work has been concerned with immediate effects, subjects usually being tested within minutes of viewing the aggressive model. In real life, of course, opportunities to aggress do not usually present themselves quite so readily. For example, the young hockey player who views a professional game on television does not have an opportunity to engage in imitative aggression immediately afterward. However, though not replicated, Smith's early (1979a, 1979b) work with young ice-hockey players (which asked them where they learned skills such as 'tripping properly') did suggest long-term impacts on amateur players.

Recently, the 'media effects' research had tailed off, and the work that does exist is clearly out of date. That said, conclusions may be reached, especially with respect to attempts to ascertain the effects of media portrayals of sports violence that fall into several different theoretical camps. In particular, from a 'learning' point of view, modelling studies suggest that young athletes learn how to perform assaultive acts by watching elite models on television and subsequently enact what they have learned, especially in sports leagues where such conduct is rewarded. This effect seems to be cumulative and long-term. Legitimation studies, focusing more on the messages that accompany violence than on violent acts themselves, suggest that the media approve of sports violence and violence-doers in multiple ways, including selling products on the basis of their violence appeal. One suspects that such messages add up to one more way in which people learn that violence is acceptable sports behaviour. But this has not been demonstrated unambiguously. More research on the effects of this kind of media content on violence in amateur sport is needed.

Studies by Coakley (1988/1989), Young and Smith (1988/1989) and others have cautioned that a direct cause-and-effect relationship between media coverage of sports violence and imitative violence has not been validated empirically. Moreover, because audience readings of images and discourses in the sports media are likely heterogeneously linked to factors such as social class, gender, culture, regionality and ethnicity (Fiske 1987: 17), caution should also be exercised in assuming that media coverage affects all sports audiences in the same way or, indeed, at all. Sociologists also caution against over-simplistic 'false consciousness' approaches where audiences are assumed to be blindly duped by power-hungry media whose main motive is to trick consumers into receiving news uncritically and spending money. Nevertheless, Taylor (1982), Keen (1986), Young (1988), Young and Smith (1988/1989) and others have all shown that certain styles of sports violence coverage are associated with discourse effects (by promoting similar hyperbolized news coverage) and perhaps some limited behavioural effects – both of which suggest that social perspectives and behavioural patterns are reproduced through media representations. At the very least, the weight of the evidence suggests that media presentations of sports violence, particularly at the professional level, contribute to a social climate in sport conducive to violent behaviour. Once again, it is a fact that most people are exposed to sports violence both on-and-off the field, not directly, but indirectly through the media. For this reason alone the mass media are of considerable importance in any comprehensive attempt to understand violence in sport.

Towards a more responsible media

Following a flurry of late 1970s research into the inflammatory treatment of ice-hockey violence in the Canadian media, seminal Canadian sport scholars Michael Smith, Bruce Kidd and Rob Beamish wrote to the Ontario Press Council complaining of 'irresponsible' journalism (Smith 1983: 120). In particular, their 'protest' was aimed at an article published in the *Toronto Star* on professional hock-ey's toughest pugilists (Parish 1983) entitled 'Rating of the NHL's best fighters.' The article's lead caption read: 'Our panel of experts has a look at the NHL's top fighters now and then and recalls the best fights.' The letter carefully laid out how Canada's largest-circulation daily contributed to a climate of violence and sought a number of remedial actions including the paper acknowledging its error in pub-lishing the article and making a clear statement that it did not condone poten-tial injury-producing behaviour occurring outside the rules of the game. No such remedial action was taken.

Twenty-one years later, and in the immediate 2004 aftermath of Todd Bertuzzi of the Vancouver Canucks ending the career of Colorado Avalanche player Steve Moore by chasing and punching him from behind and viciously crushing his head face-first into the ice (Atkinson and Young 2008: 169), like many other Canadian newspapers, the *Calgary Herald* published numerous articles strongly condemning Bertuzzi, while at the same time continuing to publish fist-fight photographs, even on the same news pages. When I wrote to a (widely recognized and respected) columnist asking him to address, and hopefully protest, the ethics of this obvi-ously contradictory approach, he replied using two lines of text distancing himself from the photos, denying any culpability for production decisions and refusing to even raise the issue at his newspaper. A similar letter I sent to his editor went unresponded to.

Not every media outlet is unprofessional, and the world of sport is replete with responsible, critical and extremely differentiated journalism, but it is not difficult to find examples of irresponsible, unethical, inflammatory or violence-condoning styles and conventions in the sports media. These styles and conventions are rarely acknowledged, and almost never acknowledged as *patterned*, *intended* or *strategic* con-ventions that contribute to a gratuitous media culture where rule-breaking action is shown in a positive light and where images of brutal violence are hawked for profit. On the contrary – they are often rationalized as 'accidents' and are rarely accom-panied by the sort of embarrassment critical consumers might appreciate. After decades of research, public commissions, investigations into and reports on the role of the media in many countries, the fact of the matter is that, in North America at least, the sport sections of many nightly TV newscasts continue to blithely show-case violence, including fighting, in clusters and packages usually labelled 'Hits of the night/week,' and images of dangerous and injury-producing action continue to uncritically colour the sports pages of many tabloid and daily newspapers.

In a climate of increasing broadcasting, telecommunications and press legislation and control in many countries, the question thus becomes one of what can be done to promote a more responsible sport media. Whether this involves developing more effective and accessible channels for complaint, applying pressure on indi-vidual news outlets, sports leagues or media councils to more consistently condemn sports violence and violence-doers, or punishing irresponsible journalism glorifying sports violence by sanctioning violators, it is clear that far more could be done to a create a sports-media climate of violence *dis*approval. In the meantime, and in the absence of a media willing to play by a different (i.e. more consistently responsible) set of rules, we should expect both the patterns of coverage and coverage rationalization described in this chapter to continue.

Interestingly, however, traditional media treatment is not uncontested (Mahan III and McDaniel 2006: 409–410; Hall et al. 2007; Wilson 2007). Perhaps the most significant single change in the media industry in the age of the Internet is the opportunity for the public to oppose media viewpoints and offer challenging, alternative ones. Of course, the resulting discursive 'negotiations' are not always successful, and this chapter has shown how conventional styles and values may 'win out.' But the days of a fully autonomous, top-down media reporting in an uncontested way are gone and, today, bloggers, tweeters and other engaged consumers are increasingly taking the opportunity to interact with sport journalists whose messages they oppose.

Conclusion

As Boyle and Haynes (2000) argue, the mass media have had a profound and lasting effect on how we understand the society around us, including sport. While there may be little validity to the often-heard claim that the media *cause* sports violence, they certainly co-exist with it. Two dimensions of the relationship between SRV and the media seem obvious: (1) as with sport more broadly, much of what we know about SRV is choreographed through 'mediatized rituals' (Cottle 2006); and (2) conceiving of SRV news as either innocent or passive is naive. Research on media coverage has consistently showcased styles and conventions that, at best, disproportionately emphasize aggressive, confrontational, injurious or provocative components of the phenomena and, at worst, deliberately exploit (i.e. amplify, 'excite' or celebrate) it. In turn, while not all audiences consume it uncritically, exposure to sports violence news helps shape what we know and how we think about SRV. There are other factors involved, but it certainly seems reasonable to argue that media images and messages represent a principal channel through which children learn how to do sport, including dishing out and rationalizing violence, pain and injury.

Today, multiple media forms and outlets exist (from radio to magazines to newspapers to Internet sites to social media sources) in a multi-billion dollar industry, each varying from within. In this respect, it makes sense to exercise caution in generalizing to all media from particular sections of it. But there are more parallels than differences in media coverage of SRV, and most of these tend to underscore the ubiquity and influence of the 'edit for impact/legitimation' approach.

Using data from diverse media sources, this chapter has demonstrated some of the many ways in which the media are implicated in SRV. As three final examples, this may be seen in the ways in which television sports personalities on both sides of the Atlantic continue the tradition of bluster and bravado to legitimize aggression, and even injury. Whether one looks at the ways in which British television commentators routinely poke sexist humour at brawling soccer or rugby players

('It's just handbags at ten paces'), the approaches of CFL and NFL 'colour' men in trivializing belligerent rivalries between known 'tough guys' ('I don't think they'll be exchanging Christmas cards') or the entire career controversial Canadian ice-hockey icon Don Cherry[2] has made out of selling NHL violence (not just in his coverage *schtick*, but quite literally in his massively popular *Rock 'em Sock 'em* video[3] series currently in its twenty-second edition) (Gillett et al. 1996), it is clear that the sports media contribute to a climate conducive to violent behaviour.

Finally, this might all be easier to swallow if there were significant signs of a shift towards a safer and more responsible sports media where violence is concerned. But, as the case study of NHL photographs in six Canadian newspapers showed, this is not the case. Unfortunately, the letter of 'protest' Canadian scholars Smith, Kidd and Beamish sent to the Ontario Press Council almost 30 years ago calling for remedial change to widespread pro-violence media strategies is no less poignant, or applicable, today.

8

STRATIFIED SRV

Stasis and change

Introduction

Writing on the sociology of war, Siniša Malešević has written: 'If there is one unique feature that sets war apart from all other sociological phenomena this must be its staggering gender asymmetry' (2010: 275). In fact, there are other social phenomena that display stark gender disparities and imbalances, and sport is unambiguously one. But Malešević is certainly correct to point to the deep connection between men, conflict and violence, which is also visible in sport. Until relatively recently, in all of its different guises, SRV has been almost exclusively the domain of males, and it is abundantly clear from earlier chapters that men continue to feature centrally in SRV. Indeed, the notion of *masculinity* itself exists in the very engine-room of SRV, and likely operates as a cause of many SRV behaviours. What makes things complicated is that no one monolithic version of masculinity is involved, and the fact that masculinity is not *always* a contributing factor. As with femininity and sexuality, masculinity comes in multiple, varied and overlapping forms, but one goal of this chapter is to highlight the most problematic versions of gender identity and the behaviours associated with them. A principal line of thinking offered here is that, especially as they manifest themselves in SRV as high-risk, victimizing and other excessive ways, dominant masculinities are ultimately counter-productive, victimizing not only women, but men themselves, both individually and as an entire gender class. However, the chapter also sets out to offer a balanced perspective on the relationship between SRV and forms of social ordering. As such, it considers the changing roles of women, and of femininity, in SRV, as well as discussing other ways that SRV is stratified, such as religion, age and social class.

What is social stratification?

As with 'social control,' *social stratification* is one of the cornerstone concepts of sociology. The founding figures of sociological theory (including Marx (1867), Durkheim (1893) and Weber (1921)) wrote extensively on it, and it remains a core area of the discipline today. Social stratification refers to relatively permanent ranking systems where small groups, or entire societies, are ordered in terms of categories of difference, status or power. In most societies, social institutions, social structures and social processes are ordered hierarchically, although to different degrees (Ritzer 1992: 127). Some of the typical forms of such 'ordering' include gender, race, social class, religion and age. Since forms of social stratification intersect with power relations, social stratification often involves structures of inequality – or ways in which certain groups wield authority over others. Certain social groups are systematically exploited and marginalized, and the roles and functions performed by groups symbolize their respective superior or inferior status, identity or reputation in the overall social system. Such systematic inequalities may be intentional or unintentional, although the degree to which inequality is viewed as 'unintentional' typically depends on the theoretical perspective one adopts. The more critical approaches – such as Marxism, feminism, forms of critical theory and others – tend not to view structured inequality as 'accidental' but, rather, a deliberate and choreographed way that empowered groups can extend their influence over others (Ritzer 1992). Importantly, the various ways in which communities or societies are hierarchized are not mutually exclusive, and social categories such as gender, race and social class overlap. Thus, it becomes possible to understand sport participation, or involvement in certain types of sports, as an outcome of the interacting effects of, for example, social class and gender (Donnelly and Harvey 2007), or gender and race (e.g. Wilson 1997; Berry and Smith 2000; Newhall and Buzuvis 2008; Anderson and McCormack 2010), or religion and social class (e.g. Dunn and Stevenson 1998; Bairner and Shirlow 1998; Bairner 2001). As this chapter shows, these sorts of intersections are also visible in the respective cells of SRV.

SRV and gender rites: the counter-productive menace of masculinity

As noted previously, feminist work on sport and gender (e.g. Bryson 1987; Messner 1992; Theberge 1997) urges us to understand male tolerance of aggression and violence in sport, and elements of risk/pain/injury linked to it, not only as a *passive* social process that athletes and others are exposed to in the various settings of sport, but also as an *active* and *constituting* process enhancing masculine (individual or subcultural) identity. In this respect, playing or administering sport in a hyper-aggressive way, and causing or incurring injury, are means of establishing positive status in the form of reputational or material benefits. How strongly dominant codes of masculinity insert themselves into different sports and sports cultures varies, but it is clear that numerous sports contain what Connell (1995) calls 'patriarchal dividends' for males who are willing to dominate others through force, and 'sacrifice their body' in order to win and be considered a part of the group (Messner 1990, 1992, 2002; Messner and Sabo 1994; Young et al. 1994).

But the implications of behaving in ways that privilege physical force for men go beyond sport performance to wider forms of gender ordering. The cultural meaning of pro-violence attitudes and taking risks are linked with larger ideological issues of gender legitimacy and power. Theberge (1999, 2000) and Lenskyj (1990) argue that aggressive expressions of male power serve to consolidate the apparently compulsory heterosexualism of sport as well as to reproduce the subjugation of 'less forceful' femininity and less valued masculinities. For gender scholars, and feminists in particular, the risks of male sports aggression, including the hubris (Coakley and Donnelly 2009: 160) and rationalizing attitudes that are so often associated with male high-risk sport, carry enormous symbolic weight and, rather than being mere rituals associated with sport, now reflect centrally important forms of social stratification.

The diverse forms of *gendering* that males undergo in competitive sport settings have been widely researched (cf. Messner and Sabo 1994; McKay et al. 2000), as have the rather compliant reactions of the authorities when athletes break the rules, or hurt one another (see Chapters 2 and 6). As we saw in Chapter 4, away from the stadium, questions have been raised regarding the apparently disproportionate involvement of professional male athletes in common street crimes (Berry and Smith 2000; Coakley and Donnelly 2009), particularly in the US, where 'male athletes in conflict with the law' is a news theme of almost daily frequency. Research on this sub-strand of violence includes examinations of the intersections between sex, violence and sport (Lenskyj 1990; Messner and Sabo 1994), studies of male athletes and sexual assault (Melnick 1992; Crosset et al. 1995; Benedict and Klein 1997; Robinson 1998; Crosset 1999) and accounts of fraternal bonding and locker room 'rape cultures' (Curry 1991). One of the common threads in this body of research concerns the cultivation in many sport settings of what feminist scholar Raewyn Connell (1995) calls 'hegemonic masculinity,' where values such as prizing the ability to dominate others physically and resolving problems through force intersects with patriarchal, misogynist and homophobic values also present in those same settings leading, at times, to forms of violence against women, and to forms of intolerance towards homosexuality. Further, while this is complicated by matters such as disproportionate, or distorted, media coverage and racist policing, North American sociologists have underlined the link between race, poverty, gender, sport and violence, which also offers a partial explanation for why African-American (and African-Canadian) athletes find themselves in conflict with the law (Berry and Smith 2000; Coakley and Donnelly 2004). But the research is blurry on this matter, and the extent to which hegemonic masculinity interacts with race and violence, at or away from the stadium, remains unclear.

Men victimizing women

Urged by a huge literature on gender, rape and other forms of violence against women (e.g. Brownmiller 1975; Gartner 1993), it is both important, and justifiable, that the literature examining aspects of SRV has considered ways in which men victimize women, directly or indirectly through the sports process. As Reasons has argued, the effect of the cultural lionization of 'tough' men seems to spread well beyond the playing field: '[W]omen suffer . . . because the physically aggressive male is admired. Women are victimized, in part, because the culture emphasizes machismo though violence' (1992: 34). However, as Forbes et al. (2006: 441) have noted, there is reason for caution: 'Aggressive male sports have been criticized as bastions of sexism and training grounds for aggression against women, but there have been few empirical demonstrations of these alleged relationships.' But the research, and especially the feminist research, on the broader implications of male violence in sport is not *without* 'evidence.' For instance, examining dating attitudes among US college men, Forbes et al. (2006: 441) themselves found that, compared to other males, men who had played aggressive sport

> engaged in more psychological aggression, physical aggression, and sexual coercion toward their dating partners, caused their partners more physical injury, were more accepting of violence, had more sexist attitudes and hostility toward women, were more accepting of rape myths, and were less tolerant of homosexuality.

Few familiar with the sociology of sport literature would be surprised by these findings, which corroborate a still-modest, and understandably circumspect, body of work on the wider social implications of men learning about aggression, dominance and privilege in sport (e.g. Curry 1991; Lenskyj 1992; Melnick 1992; Messner and Sabo 1994; Crosset et al. 1995; Robinson 1998; Brackenridge 2001). Among other manifestations of men victimizing women, this body of research has examined the involvement of male athletes in forms of verbal and psychological violence, physical assault, sexual assault, rape, group or gang rape and sexual harassment. Buttressing so many of these behaviours is the existence, in many male sports cultures, of peer support networks that provide the ideological framework for misogynist or homophobic attitudes to develop and remain protected when challenged 'from the outside' (e.g. Curry 1991; Kane and Disch 1993; Welch 1997; Crosset 1999; Pappas et al. 2004).

Men victimizing men

If, as Jean Marie Brohm wrote in 1978, sport is a 'prison of measured time,' it is surely also a 'prison' of 'measured masculinities' – 'measured,' in this case, referring to 'excessive,' 'stereotypical' and judged against some cartoon-like version of maleness where every participant expects to have to be 'tough,' to act 'tough' and to get hit, hurt or injured. A classic example of the hegemony process (Whitson 1991; Young 1993) is how men hurt one another so frequently in sport that it is simply taken for granted. Men getting hit, hurt or injured represents what sport *is*. With few exceptions, the matrix of SRV cells describes a landscape of men victimizing other men.

Pro-violence, and injury-condoning, values pervade many sports, and at every level of play. As Chapters 2 and 7 illustrated, the authorities and the media have played contributing roles, too; sometimes shockingly exploitatively. For instance, following Eric Cantona's conviction for assault after jumping into a soccer crowd and kicking a fan in 1995, Nike ran an advertising campaign featuring an intimidating photograph of the Manchester United player about to enter the field, but hindered by what was meant to look like a jail door, with the caption: 'He's been punished for his mistakes. Now it's someone else's turn.' As we saw in Chapter 7, one of the common ways in which the media contribute to an ultra-macho climate of sports violence is by using humour and levity to trivialize serious, injurious and even (as in this case) criminal behaviours.

The outcomes of sport machismo: a graveyard of broken men

As Chapter 5 suggests, any scan, however brief, of the routine outcomes of the various levels of male sport, and certainly competitive elite amateur and professional sport, reveals that sport leaves behind a graveyard of battered and broken male bodies. But the institution of sport itself is only partly to blame. Just as culpable is *masculinity* itself.

In her candid and disturbing study, *The Hearts of Men*, Barbara Ehrenreich (1983: 140) warns about the dangers of the prefabricated male sex role. On men's health in general, she writes:

> The initial and irrefutable reason for men to transform themselves [is] not to improve their social status or expand their souls – but to save their lives. No treatise or document of men's liberation, no matter how brief, failed to mention the bodily injuries sustained by role abiding men, from ulcers to accidents to the most 'masculine' of illnesses, coronary heart disease.

In these ways, men pay a price for the privileged positions they occupy and enjoy, as Kimmel (1995: vii) also acknowledges:

> Most of the leading causes of death among men are the results of men's behaviors – gendered behaviors that leave men more vulnerable to certain illnesses and not others. Masculinity is one of the more significant risk factors associated with men's illness.

The evidence for the claims made by Ehrenreich, Kimmel and many other gender researchers is abundant. To be socialized into dominant forms of masculinity involves learning emotional denial and affective neutrality, and also the cultural importance of actions and attitudes that place the body at risk (Jackson 1990). Male prowess is often based on types of physicality that are destructive and that involve conspicuous silences around health (Hearn 1992; Rutherford 1992). As a result, sensitization to bodily wellbeing and matters of preventive health become viewed as the jurisdiction of women and 'ambiguous' men.

Oddly, deeply-rooted, and connected, destructive sport behaviours remain under-studied by sociologists. For instance, the place of anabolic steroids, other performance-enhancing drugs and recreational drugs as constituting features of 'masculinist' sports cultures has been glossed over by sport and gender research-ers. This is unfortunate because much can be learned from drug use of the ways in which the male athletic body is assumed to be masculinized even while it is injured, addicted, out of control and most at risk.

Sociological research on the topic may not be extensive, but North American sport has a long history linking the use of steroids with exaggerated versions of masculinity (Tricker and Cook 1990; Courson 1991; Monaghan 2001; Canseco 2005). Despite horrendous medical and psycho-emotional side effects including colitis, rectal bleeding, testicular shrinkage and becoming extremely violent and considering suicide, former varsity football player Tommy Chaikin spoke of how being relatively small challenged his sense of manhood and how team-mates 'in awe of [his] strength' (Chaikin and Telander 1988: 97) motivated him. Repeated and prolonged steroid cycles, which Chaikin described as 'rampant' at the US college level, became Chaikin's 'fix.' More recently, former professional baseball player Jose Canseco (2005) similarly reports how high-risk behaviours, and steroid use, not only enhanced his athletic identity, but also became the core of his sense of self, despite the personal turbulence that accompanied such behaviours.

Troublingly, elite level and professional sport leaves behind a very long trail of battered, broken and disabled former athletes. In addition to numerous other names mentioned and described in this book, consider the following list of athletes: Brian 'Spinner' Spencer (NHL, died 1988), Lyle Alzado (NFL, died 1992), John Kordic (NHL, died 1992), Fred Lane (NFL, 2000), Chris Antley (professional horse-racing, died 2000), Marco Pantani (professional road cycling, died 2004), Steve Courson (NFL, died 2005), Ryan Gracie (MMA, died 2007), Don Sanderson (Canadian amateur ice hockey, 2009) and Derek Boogaard (NHL, died 2011). This apparently random list of names represents cases of male athletes whose violence, drug problems, troubled personal lives or eventual death, may be been linked with conforming to ultra-macho principles. Sadly, the list represents only the proverbial tip of the iceberg – professional leagues such as the NFL, CFL and NHL *could* (but clearly never *would*) report lists of their own. No-one has bothered to collate or systematically study the similarly depressing sequences of serious illnesses, family tragedies or deaths of 'men out of control' in so many other sports. As suggested by the list above, conforming to excessive versions of mascu-linity in sport seems to come with risks related to drug and alcohol abuse, domestic conflict, street crime or interpersonal problems of one form or another. From a literal point of view, all the men on the list died because their hearts stopped. From another, more sociological, point of view, gender learning and gender identity killed them all.

Competitive sport in many countries is replete with male players who have carved out gladiatorial and exaggerated images for themselves in accordance with the expectations of their peer groups and hegemonic masculinity more broadly.

Messner's study of 20 years ago in which he describes the male athletic body as a 'weapon' is no less relevant today. For ice-hockey 'enforcers' and 'goons,' football 'warriors,' rugby 'hardmen' and the 'hunters,' 'snipers' and 'brawlers' of Aussie Rules etc., the costs of injury and disablement become mediated by the contributions they are assumed to make to masculine identity, male peer group solidarity and sport status and reputation more broadly.

In the sense that its product is simultaneously a culturally revered and extremely hazardous version of masculinity, the culture of modern male sport is fraught with paradox (Pringle 2001; Pringle and Markula 2005). Violent sports behaviour, and what Messner and Sabo (1990) have called the 'pain principle' of sport, appear to be defined by athletes as rich in rewards and masculinizing potential. Players allow their sport lives to be manipulated because salaries, public adoration and athletic identity make it seem worthwhile. But any *masculinization* emerging from pro-violence attitudes, including being willing to subject the body to high risk and play through injury, is ephemeral and comes with problems, either in the short- or long-term. As we have witnessed elsewhere in this book, this may be seen in the disproportionately high morbidity and even mortality rates of certain athletes (especially boxers and football players – Messner 1992: 101).

Much like the stereotypical but seductive images of feminine beauty and sexuality in Western cultures (Coward 1985), images of hyper-masculinity are ultimately impractical and literally incapacitating. The respective health risks associated with these images all too often include eating disorders for women and illnesses linked to violence, steroids and other drugs for men. The world of sport is filled with such cases, but the recent downward spiral and suicide of Canadian wrestler Chris Benoit, a fan favourite and known steroid user, is topical. Arguably more relevant is the utter chaos Benoit's drug habits caused to the people around him – before he took his own life, Benoit killed his wife and his son. Unfortunately, this is just one particularly disturbing example of the abuse that family members and loved ones become victims of when hyper-masculinity, violence and drugs overlap.

Tough girls and female warriors: how do women fit into SRV?

I swear to God I'll f****** take the ball and shove it down your f******
throat.[1]

Serena Williams' profane rant aimed at a line-judge at the 2009 US Open is not statistically significant, but it is emblematic of the fact that, in a number of both positive and negative ways, female athletes are 'catching up with men' (Pirinen 1997). While there is no evidence that females (as athletes, coaches, administrators or fans) have participated in aggressive and violent sports-related behaviours, or cultures, in anything like the numbers, the degree, or with the excessive hubris of their male counterparts, there is a growing body of literature, mostly written by women, representing many countries, which unambiguously demonstrates that behaving aggressively, violently or deviantly in sport settings *does* resonate with females (e.g. Rail 1992; Young and White 1995; Etue and Williams 1996; Nixon 1997; Avery and Stevens 1997; Denfeld 1997; Halbert 1997; Theberge 1997; Young 1997; Lowe 1998; Mennesson 2000; Merz 2000; Sekules 2000; Lawler 2002; Heywood and Dworkin 2003; Olsen 2003; Cohen 2005; Cove 2006; Keeler 2007; Fields 2008; Sisjord and Kristiansen 2009; Carlson 2010). The question is: 'why?'[2]

As opportunities for female athletes have increased in traditional 'male pre-serves' such as rugby, ice hockey, bodybuilding, boxing and martial arts, actions such as playing ultra-aggressively, hitting, being hit, becoming injured and injur-ing others are assuming an increasingly central place in female sport and female sport cultures (Denfeld 1997; Cove 2006). Earlier interview-based research with colleague Philip White (Young and White 1995; Young 1997) on the meanings elicited from involvement in aggressive and high-risk sport led us to reflect on the sport 'spaces' that were increasingly being occupied by female athletes in the fol-lowing way: '[M]any such spaces are being occupied by women who . . . appear to be contributing to a male-defined sports process replete with its violent, macho and health-compromising aspects' (Young and White 1995: 45). While, as with men's sport, this is not an exhaustive or exclusive process and, while the possibility that female athletes may be freshly defining the meanings of aggressive sport for themselves (Young and White 1995; Sekules 2000),[3] the trend towards women's involvement in aggressive, and sometimes violent, sport behaviours, on-and-off the pitch, cannot be denied. Nor can their debilitating outcomes. Predictably, as opportunities for women to 'play rough' have increased, so have women's experi-ences with injury. As Chapter 5 shows, a new research literature on this topic has expanded rapidly (e.g. Theberge 1997; King 2000; Charlesworth and Young 2004, 2006; Pike 2004; Safai 2004).

There are obvious problems in generalizing to all of female sport from isolated incidents such as the 2009 Serena Williams outburst cited above, the widespread critical attention that the 'laddish' Canadian female ice-hockey team received when they smoked celebratory cigars and drank beer at mid-ice after they won the Olym-pic gold medal in Vancouver 2010,[4] or episodes such as the 2009 hair-yanking/back-punching incident by a US college soccer player,[5] but to argue that females are not involved in SRV is inaccurate and misleading. For instance, let us briefly re-visit some of the SRV cells with respect to female involvement:

Cell 1 – player violence: As the literature cited above demonstrates, women are choosing to play combat, contact and other high-risk sports in growing numbers and, in turn, providing role models for younger girls. As with men, one inevitable outcome is injury, and sometimes serious injury (e.g. Young 1997; Mennesson 2000; Cove 2006). Female player violence is also increasingly being reported in the media (e.g. 'Punches, pushes and tackles in WNBA Brawl,' *Globe and Mail*, 23 July 2008: R7). And, as female sport becomes more competitive, in many respects, it is assuming the violent trappings and 'foul play' of men's sport (Comstock and Fields 2005; Patrick 2006: A3).

Cell 2 – crowd violence: In almost all settings, and with minor exceptions only (e.g. Cere 2002), crowd violence endures as a male domain, but one wonders why the question of females either directly involved in, or behind the scenes of, crowd disorder have so rarely been taken seriously from a research point of view. For instance, the extensive literature on British soccer hooliganism has rarely addressed the ways in which girlfriends, wives, mothers and sisters of participants might approve of, or be willing to live with, their male significant others validating their masculinity in violent and criminal ways; no sociologist has explored why so many NHL fans standing up and yelling during fist-fights are female; and, to date, no sociologist has examined why MMA or UFC events bear cultural meaning for women who attend in large numbers. In 2009, a *Toronto Star–Angus Reid* online poll asked 1,004 randomly selected Canadian adults (who are regular Angus Reid forum participants) how they felt about fist-fighting in the game. Overall, more men (52 per cent) than women supported fighting and keeping it as part of the game, but almost one-third (30 per cent) of female respondents voted to keep fighting 'in.'[6]

Cell 4 – player violence away from the game: As Wheatley's 1984 study of the female rugby subculture, and an entire strand of popular literature on female boxing (e.g. Denfeld 1997; Halbert 1997; Mennesson 2000; Merz 2000; Sekules 2000; Cohen 2005; Cove 2006) has shown, that female athletes form, and enjoy, subcultures whose behaviours can be lewd, disruptive and unlawful is not, in any way, new.

Cell 5 – street crimes: During an era of popular movies such as *Million Dollar Baby* and *Fight Club*, and of 'she-roes' from any number of other popular films and sources, female fight clubs have begun to emerge. These include 'Extreme Chickfights' – an underground, unsanctioned and unregulated organization for female street fighting in Los Angeles. Although such groups are cloaked in secrecy and next to no research exists, underground female fighting is suspected to be on the rise (*Sports Illustrated*, 2 May 2005: 102–118; Reilly 2005: 72).

Cell 6 – violence against the self: An extensive literature in the sociology of sport demonstrates how sport interfaces not only with injury (see Chapter 5), but also with dangerous body perceptions and habits. Most athletic anorexics and bulimics are female (Kirkland and Lawrence 1986; Ryan 1995; Davis 1999; McEwen and Young 2011). Such 'violence against the self' is a problem throughout sport, especially in the so-called 'appearance' sports, such as gymnastics and figure skating. Further, only the most naive observer could possibly think that the use of performance-enhancing drugs in numerous sports is restricted to men and to problems created by 'masculinity.'

Cell 7 – athlete initiation/hazing: From the available empirical research on hazing in Canada, the US and England, the evidence is clear – female athlete cultures are involved in hazing, they condone hazing and participate in hazing in ways similar to men, including highly dangerous and illegal forms of the practice (Bryshun and Young 1999, 2007; King 2000; Johnson and Holman 2004).

Cell 8 and 9 – harassment, stalking and threat/sexual assault: As the highly publicized 2003 and 2010 cases involving a well-known professional basketball player (Kobe Bryant), golfer (Tiger Woods) and football player (Brett Favre) suggest, the mediated world of professional sport is awash in examples of sexually promiscuous male athletes who cheat on their partners and, usually through being 'caught' and the often sordid news accounts that follow, embarrass themselves and their families. As McKay (1993) has cautioned, it is unfair to consider this behaviour in sport solely as a matter of 'wanton women' pursuing 'marked men.' However, while the research is lacking, it seems reasonable to acknowledge that females in sport, including female fans, can also be involved in predatory and sexually aggressive behaviours (e.g. Olson 2003; Mewett and Toffoletti 2008) and what Ariel Levy (2005) would call 'raunch culture.' Of course, this does not address the questions either of why male athlete infidelity occurs in such a seemingly patterned and opportunistic way, or how 'obsessive sports groupie' (Olson 2003) cultures are part of the larger web of male sports. Of equal interest is why sociologists have ignored questions of female 'stalking' when it is such a recognized aspect of many male sports, and at many levels.

Cell 12 – parental abuse: As noted in Chapter 4, there is a conspicuous absence of empirical work on the negative influence of overbearing and abusive parents in the lives of child athletes, as well as of referees and other game officials. Although both fathers *and* mothers are involved in this practice (e.g. Engh 1999; Baron 2007; Hennessy and Schwartz 2007; Hyman 2009; Thompson 2010), we know almost nothing from a research point of view about how mothers are involved in such behaviour, or the 'mother wounds' they leave behind.

Cell 15 – animal abuse: In our research on greyhound racing (Atkinson and Young 2005a), Michael Atkinson and I found that abusive and inhumane practices in the industry were enacted, condoned and disguised by *both* male and female insiders. A scattered 'blood sport' literature also highlights the complicity of females in 'sport' activities that involve extreme violence and death, such as forms of hunting. For instance, Smalley (2005) shows how the relationship between women and hunting is historically grounded in the US, although she describes it as a 'softening influence.'

Cell 18 – crimes against the environment: The history of sport is a history of male privilege and male power. However, as females have moved into powerful sport positions, such as those making decisions on how to use stadia or venues, public funding and community involvement, it is clear that harmful corporate and exploitative values and practices are not restricted to men. Women support bids to replace pristine wilderness with golf courses, to persuade reluctant home owners to sell their homes to build new stadia, and ride mountain bikes off-trail and 'out of bounds.' If these things are problems when men are involved, surely they are problems when they are initiated, funded, administered and enjoyed by women?

As suggested in all of these ways, and by rapidly expanding popular and academic literatures, aggression of one kind or another, and risk, are becoming increasingly meaningful to, and possible for, women. Women appear to have an expanding presence in SRV. But, again, caution and *scale* are critical here, even if we speak (as we must) in 'approximates.' There are no adequate 'counting methods' – or studies – that enable us to claim with certainty that, where any of the SRV cells are concerned, as many women are involved as men. It may be that women are not *increasingly* involved in SRV at all, but are increasingly *reported* to be involved in SRV, though this seems unlikely given the expanding range and diversity of 'evidence' gradually emerging. Where female involvement in SRV is concerned, most questions simply remain unanswered.

The SRV literature strongly points in the direction of one conclusion – women's participation is increasing on a number of fronts, but the vast majority of SRV offenders are men. And, because learning about hegemonic masculinity in sport starts early for boys (Dunning et al. 1988; West 1996; Armstrong 1998; Atkinson 2011a), the more accurate way of stating this is, 'the vast majority of SRV offenders are *male*.' Malešević's (2010) argument about 'staggering gender asymmetry' is all too pertinent here. With only minor exceptions and evidence to the contrary, there are no sweeping cultures of homophobia in women's sport as there are, for example, in so many men's sports, there is no widespread or patterned problem among female athletes with 'street' drugs, weapons and violent behaviours, and no-one has been given cause to consider whether female athletes are more involved in domestic violence than non-sporting women. In other words, at the core of SRV is *maleness* and *masculinity*. Shifting opportunity and power structures where gender relations are concerned may be prompting changes in certain expressions of SRV (as we saw in Chapter 5 with the willingness of female athletes to subject themselves to risk), but SRV remains squarely, and disproportionately, associated with men.

Other ways in which SRV is stratified

Gender represents a principal way that SRV is 'striated,' but it is not the only way. SRV appears to be stratified by age, but unevenly. For example, while police reports in North America, and a combination of official reports and academic research in the UK, indicate that the majority of crowd violence offenders (cell 2) are young men, there are complications in trusting available figures, and difficulties making general statements. The British work shows that, along with young men in their teens, twenties and thirties, older men have been involved, and that age factors are likely linked with specific roles, locales and age-segregation cultures associated with particular teams (e.g. Dunning et al. 1988; Young 1988; Armstrong 1998).

Meanwhile, in North America, the age of spectators ejected from, or arrested at, professional football and baseball games seems higher than those ejected from, or arrested at, college sports (e.g. Young 1988). But this is all vague and, again, more work needs to be done on the specific question of age of offenders in crowd violence. Where the remainder of the SRV cells are concerned, scant research is available on the relevance of age but, as the illustrations in Chapter 4 suggest, it seems apparent that SRV offenders span age categories. As inexact as it sounds, the most certain conclusion in an under-researched area is that offender age varies by SRV context, as one might expect, for example, when one considers the typical ages of coaches in various areas, animal trainers in various settings, and parents of young child athletes, etc.

The research on the relationship between some aspects of SRV and race and ethnicity is clearer and, on certain axes, there are well-researched processes and patterns. Where North America sports crowd disorder is concerned, Young (1988) found that most fans ejected at college and university games were white, but that non-white participants were involved in conflicts with police during post-event disturbances. There is little evidence to suggest that violent North American sports crowds are racially organized, although there have been some exceptions to the rule where crowd riots have been prompted by ethnic tensions. The aforementioned 1955 riots in Montreal grew out of hostilities between francophone and anglophone Canadians (Duperrault 1981), but they occurred half a century ago and are hardly relevant today. The European work has been far clearer on the impact of race as a factor in crowd violence. For example, hooliganism is *racialized* in that it so often pits stereotypical, jingoistic and xenophobic notions of national identity against 'others,' including racist attacks against players (e.g. House 1992; Endean 1993; van der Kraan 1993; Müller et al. 2006). Where ethnicity is concerned, there is a modest literature not only on hooliganism as an outgrowth of sectarian and territorial tensions (e.g. Bairner and Shirlow 1998), but also on the interface between hooliganism, sectarianism and masculinity (e.g. Giulianotti 1993; Bairner 1999, 2001).

Where player violence on and off the field is concerned, research has investigated how SRV may be 'racialized' in a number of ways. For instance, Collings and Condon (1996) discuss how ice-hockey violence carries special meaning in aboriginal Canadian communities (cell 1 – player violence); Blackshaw and Crabbe (2005) and Wilson (1997) explore racist media depictions of athletes involved in crimes (cell 5 – street crimes); Berry and Smith (2000) examine the difference between perception and incidence in public mis-understandings of African Americans involved in street crimes (cell 5 – street crimes); Anderson and McCormack (2010) discuss the link between homophobia and racism for gay black atheletes (cell 14 – other identity violence); and, in a case that best fits into cell 17 (offences against workers and the public), Dufur and Feinberg (2009) examine the 'symbolic discrimination' done to minority sport merchandise workers. And where race and racism itself becomes a centrally stratifying element of sport more broadly (cell 14 – other identity violence), there is a deep, compelling and expanding literature (Goram 2007; Bradbury 2010; Burdsey 2010; Hylton 2010; Massao and Fasting 2010).

Strangely, outside of crowd violence, and soccer hooliganism in particular (where it is not only a research element, but also a central point of contention among researchers – see Chapter 3), the relationship between SRV and social class has not been explored extensively. Using police and sports team records, Young (2000) showed how fans ejected or arrested for crowd violence in North America come from a combination of working-class and middle-class backgrounds. This is complicated by the fact that US college crowds, which represent relatively high levels of education, also pose a routine problem for the authorities, often due to alcohol-related disorders (Young 1988; Wann et al. 2001; Russell 2008). Almost all of the British and European work on hooliganism has pointed to the relationship between hooliganism and working-class participants, with two caveats: first, many fans with 'respectable' middle-class jobs have been involved, and many offenders are not unemployed; second, researchers have disagreed as to which particular socio-economic strands of the 'working-class' offenders come from, as was discussed in Chapter 3.

Finally, although 'type of sport' is not normally seen as a determining social institutional factor such as gender or race, where player violence on and off the field of play is concerned, the research suggests a relationship between the levels of aggression learned and expected in certain sports and pro-aggression attitudes 'off the pitch.' Among others, Nixon (1997), Tucker and Parks (2001), Brown et al. (2002) and Pappas et al. (2004) all identified differences in attitudes towards social aggressivity on the basis of type of sport played – specifically, athletes in the more aggressive sports displayed more aggressive social values. But, in their Canadian study of varsity initiation practices, Bryshun and Young (1999) did not find type of sport to be a reliable predictor of hazing severity. Indeed, in a cluster of varied sports, for both women and men, including ice hockey, gridiron football, wrestling, volleyball, soccer, swimming and synchronized swimming, they discovered only small variations in willingness to haze, and type of hazing, finding some of the more dangerous and coercive practices among swimmers and synchronized swimmers.

Conclusion

The purpose of this chapter has been to show that SRV does not happen randomly, or in some scattered way, unaffected by the sorts of organizing influences that affect the rest of society. Although the research is not definitive and our understanding of it is not exhaustive, SRV is often socially stratified according to factors such as gender, religion, age, social class and even type of sport. None of these factors has so galvanized the subject matter that it is completely fixed or static. SRV does indeed display patterns, and *predictable* patterns, of social stratification, but these patterns change. Thus, elements of both *social reproduction* and *social transformation*, or what I have called 'stasis and change,' are at work in SRV.

Where specific dimensions of this social stratification process are concerned, that SRV is affected by, for instance, race and ethnicity, age and social class is important but not, at this point, crystal clear. By contrast, that SRV is heavily *gendered* is difficult to miss. SRV has operated over time as a 'male preserve.' Much of sport and SRV is explainable by looking at traditional notions of masculinity, aggressive male roles and identities in sport, and the principle of dominating others through force. Further, many sports are enmeshed in widespread and impacting climates of male 'groupthink' – 'a mind-set that makes men incapable of believing that there is anything wrong with their misogynist and violent behaviour towards women' (McKay and Middlemiss 1995: 42). Even violence against animals seems to be entangled in masculinity-validating processes (Evans et al. 1998; Cashmore 2000: 39–43).

Men no longer have a monopoly on the use, benefits and sense-making of aggression and violence related to sport. What Malešević argues about the gender asymmetry of war remains applicable to sport today, but less so than ever before. Thinking back to the definition of SRV in Chapter 1, today, women are involved in every cell of SRV, although not to the extent of men. Moreover, to take Malešević's (2010) argument in another militaryesque direction, as with female soldiers at war, just because females in sport are pushing back frontiers where various forms of 'aggro' are concerned does not mean that they do not continue to face marginalization, harassment, sexual violence and rage at the hands of men (Benedict 2009), or that forms of men's aggression change.

Widely researched processes of *masculinization* occurring through player violence are complicated by the fact that studies demonstrate that many female athletes also revere risk and the use of aggression (Rail 1992; Young and White 1995; Theberge 1997; Cove 2006). As noted previously, female involvement in high-risk, aggressive and violent sport values thus suggests that sport socialization per se may be at least as important as gender socialization but, on this important question, more research is needed.

On the basis of what we do know so far, several conclusions may be arrived at regarding the gender stratification of SRV. First, in many societies, the recorded history of aggression and violence is a history of men. However, in addition to overlooking the existing 'violences' of women, as opportunities have opened up for women to aggress in institutions such as sport, women are taking them. Simply put, female SRV exists and requires further study. Second, mainstream disciplinary and sub-disciplinary literatures have paid insufficient attention to the roles of women in many forms of social violence. In sport, this attention is astonishingly thin. Third, as is evident from the matrix of SRV forms, there are ways in which females are involved in violence directly and indirectly, as victims and also as offenders, and there are likely ways in which they are both at the same time. But again, very little sociological research is available on female involvement, especially as it pertains to women as violence-*doers*. Finally, sociologically, it is unclear whether female violence in sport is contributing to an ongoing subjugation of women in sport and in society, to forms of self-victimization or to a re-definition of what *gender* is, what it means and how it may be lived out. Time, as they say, will tell.

CONCLUSION

Violence in sport is a complex and multi-dimensional topic that has generated a huge volume of research and writing. The principal goal of this book is to offer a fresh perspective on how we think about the social structures, processes and behaviours involved. So far, almost all of the research in this area has zoned in on a particular dimension of the subject matter, such as, for example, soccer hooliganism, player violence or sexual harassment. This approach is both understandable and necessary, and the field remains in desperate need of concrete in-depth investigations into the varied manifestations of SRV, especially those captured by cells 3–18.

However, a single-subject approach to SRV is problematic in at least two different ways. First, it tends to disassociate, or de-contextualize, the topic under scrutiny from what I have called the broader landscape of SRV and, in so doing, creates the impression that the various elements of SRV are 'stand-alone' entities, unconnected to other elements and other parts of the violence process. This is not true, and any sociological study of even the most narrowly-defined aspect of SRV must explain how, in cause, expression or outcome, the subject matter does not operate in isolation from other aspects of the SRV process. Second, even if the research offers a thorough in-depth empirical examination of a given topic (luckily, such work *is* available), it is not always easy to teach from. Very few colleges and universities offer entire courses on the individual dimensions of SRV (courses on soccer hooliganism in the UK represent one exception to the rule), and a consideration of how any one aspect of SRV fits into a broader picture seems both more sociological and more pedagogically useful.

As noted in Chapter 1, the concept of 'sports violence' is elusive and difficult to 'pin down.' Everyone has an opinion on it, everyone considers some elements more important and pressing than others, and everyone has ideas about how they would 'fix' it. This is true not only for ordinary members of the public, but also for sports organizations themselves, and those responsible for policing sport, including the courts.

When I ask my students what they think constitutes 'violence in sport' and how to define the subject matter, almost invariably they define, describe and label it in ways that very closely resemble the matrix of cells. Indeed, this is where the matrix of cells, and the 'SRV wheel,' come from. Even before they start reading what scholars have to say on the matter, the list of topics and issues that emerges from these debates is long and varied. Together with my own sociological inclination towards thinking more broadly about SRV, it is this fact that has encouraged me to write this book. For good or ill, the scope of this book is far broader than most treatments of the subject matter currently available in the literature. As noted at the outset, this necessarily means the literature available in the subdiscipline of the Sociology of Sport. Mainstream sociology and criminology apparently have little interest in matters of aggression, violence, victimization, health, safety or justice *related to sport*. The absence of 'sports violence' from the colossal mainstream literatures on studies of aggression and violence is conspicuous, frustrating and, ultimately, *asociological*. Despite the very obvious sociological fact that sport remains one of the most culturally important social institutions in all developed countries that touches almost everyone's lives, and (rightly or wrongly) is being used by governments and interventionists as a panacea and instrument of progress and peace in developing societies all over the world, the disinclination of sociologists to take sport seriously clearly endures.

Part of the complexity of explaining SRV is that it is not easy to study. Since so much of the subject matter is deviant, criminal, harmful or punishable, or could lead to embarrassment, loss of reputation or discipline, SRV is a world cloaked in secrecy and disguise. In my own work on the various dimensions of the phenomenon, I have found that while, for example, getting athletes and others to speak about risk, pain and injury in sport is relatively uncomplicated, all the fieldwork experience and savvy in the world still leaves so many other parts of the SRV puzzle tough to access and penetrate. Using my own forays into the SRV field as illustrations:

- Where North American crowd violence is concerned, I have found that professional teams often minimize violence or security problems that their own security personnel acknowledge. In fact, the only way I came to be aware of fan disorder at certain clubs was through security personnel violating club policy and risking their jobs by making their records available to me, verbally or in hard copy, and often only after strict assurances of confidentiality had been elicited (Young 1988, 2002a).
- In both the UK and Canada, I have discovered a clear shift in athlete willingness to talk openly about hazing over time. In the 1980s in Canada (Young 1983), it was relatively easy to encourage athletes to open up about how they 'initiated.' However, by the time of the much more tightly policed 1990s and current period (Bryshun and Young 1999, 2007), college athletes concerned not only about the possible implications of being caught for themselves but also for their coaches had become far more wary, and many had even 'closed

shop.' In many settings, hazing is now fully subterranean and athletes refuse to engage outsiders or betray insider trust.

- If getting male or female athletes to speak openly about risk, pain and injury in sport is relatively uncomplicated, getting them to speak about such matters as coaching style, intimidation, coercion, bullying and pressure is not, and I have found that many male and female athletes become noticeably, and understandably, guarded around these issues (e.g. Young et al. 1994; Young and White 1995; Young 1997).

- In my work on animal abuse with Michael Atkinson, we have jointly (and perhaps predictably) found that researching the world of training, kennelling and racing dogs comes with access, deception and trust difficulties (Atkinson and Young 2005a).

- Despite the apparent candour and transparency of views offered by journalists on player violence coverage discussed in Chapter 7, even the most staunch supporter of 'old fashioned' 'rock 'em, sock 'em' ice hockey tempers his views in the presence of a prying social scientist (Young 1990, 1991b).

Of course, the sociology of sport literature is replete with admirable examples of potentially 'tricky' and even iconoclastic SRV research on important, but delicate, disguised or potentially explosive SRV topics which would never be possible without the fieldwork acumen of the researchers themselves. In this connection, the respective ventures of colleagues Michael Atkinson (in Canada) and John Sugden (in the UK) stand out as exemplars of savvy fieldwork producing knowledge on difficult-to-research SRV issues. Examples include Atkinson's studies of abuse in animal sports (Atkinson and Young 2005a), oppositional uses of the environment (2009), violence against the self (2007, 2008b, 2011b), the link between dangerous masculinities and high-risk practices (2009) and criminal activity in the ticket scalping subculture (2000), and Sugden's exposés of corruption in the world's most powerful soccer body (Sugden and Tomlinson 2003), innovative underground economies that build on soccer hooligan culture (2002), as well as his exploration of how sport can be used to mediate ethnic conflict and nationalistic hostility (Sugden and Wallis 2007; Sugden 2010). Without these sorts of research ventures, which come with risks for the researchers themselves (ranging from status and identity risks to personal safety risks) we would understand SRV communities less, and be far less well-prepared to deal with them from a practical point of view.

Most of the examples of SRV in this book derive from North America and the UK. But the fact of the matter is that, at the present time, SRV remains a thorn in the side of sports organizations, activist communities and governments all over the world. Representing a critical barometer of this are the multiple and varied empirical inquiries into respective 'cells' of the phenomenon across the globe. In addition to the many other international examples provided throughout the book, these include studies of racism and aboriginal identity in Australia (Hallinan and Judd 2007), masculinity and violence against the self in New Zealand (Pringle 2004), soccer hooliganism in Italy (Scalia 2009), offences against workers in the sports garment industry in Bangladesh

(Rock 2003), offences against the environment in the build-up to the next Winter Olympic Games in Russia (Gajewski 2010), the link between street crime and corruption in Sumo wrestling in Japan (Duggan and Steven 2002; McCurry 2011), sexual abuse and harassment in Greece and other European countries (Chroni et al. 2010) and stadium disasters and crowd violence in South Africa (Alegi 2004). While it may not be true that work is being conducted on *all* of the SRV cells in *all* countries of the world, *many* cells are being studied in *many* countries, and there seems little doubt that SRV research is as vibrant and expansive as it has ever been.

But, despite the volume and variance of research underway, I would caution against complacency and suggest that, overall, we still know relatively little about SRV. As noted several times throughout the book, the bulk of the research on SRV can easily be slotted into cells 1 (player violence) and 2 (crowd violence). On the remaining 16 cells, our knowledge and understanding remain limited.

Where the future of SRV is concerned, there are reasons to feel both optimistic *and* pessimistic. On the pessimistic side, there is, by now, abundant evidence to make us question the integrity of sport, the power structures of sport and the leaders of sport, at all levels. When one considers the matrix of cells and ponders, for instance, how steroids and other more sophisticated drugs are hidden, how player violence and injury are easily rationalized, a persistently exploitative media, the 'soft' treatment of athletes who violate rules and laws, the low priority of the environment relative to building glitzy new stadiums and expensive golf courses, it is hard to conceive of a better, safer, more responsible sports world.

Even when challenged, embarrassed and disciplined, we know from the past that sport changes slowly and that its hegemonic structures, processes and value systems show astonishing 'elasticity' that allows them to 'bounce back' and enable the practices embodied in the respective cells to persist, and even flourish. If this were not true, how else could we explain, for example, what appears to be (and is argued by insiders to be) a transformed and more responsible world of ice hockey whose violence, and media coverage of violence, has not changed much at all over the past 30 years? At the end of the day, the NHL remains a dangerous place to 'work,' concussions and other serious injuries are common, it sends out less-than-responsible messages to youngsters about how to hit and how to establish revered male identity, even respectable news outlets continue to use photographs of fist-fights, many TV stations continue to exploit violence, pain and injury in the form of 'hits of the night' content, and a shocking number of fans continue to support practices that would be illegal in any other walk of life. As Coakley and Donnelly (2009: 160) suggest, the hubris of sport is palpable at every level, and it is sometimes difficult to see that sport has any integrity in dealing with SRV at all. Once again, if this were not true, how else might we explain, for example, the audacity of professional football teams hiring convicted sex offenders under the guise of 'second-chance' philanthropy, the denial of corruption by so many sports bodies, even at the highest level of organization, influence and power, or the supreme arrogance that might lead a privileged elite high school athlete to attempt to set fire to a police cruiser in broad daylight in full view of the world during a post-event sports riot?[1]

But this darker downside is countered by reasons to think positively about the future of SRV. On all of the aforementioned issues and examples there is dialogue, and more transparent and wide-ranging dialogue than ever before. That dialogue might come in the form of angry 'whistle-blowing,' or casual interactive blogging, or it might come in the form of rational organized opposition from within sport, or outside. As Chapters 2, 3 and 6 showed, social control operates informally as well as at the formal level of policy and law. All of the SRV cells are experiencing some version of formal intervention – some successfully. For example, even the most jaded critic of heavy-handed forms of social control has to admit that, coupled, as it has been, with a prudent use of what the academic research has found and recommended, the soccer hooliganism scenario in the UK has, at least, been contained. There is no doubt that, while our knowledge and understanding of many elements of SRV remain uncertain, there is work being done to understand, and intervene on, behaviours encompassed in every one of the SRV cells.

This book has been written mostly for my students, with whom I share a passionate and sociological fascination for SRV. To me and to them, this is not a field of research that is isolated to any one subdiscipline, or exclusive to the narrow and confining borders of a traditionally defined sociology of sport. In principle at least, there is no reason why SRV, or any one sub-element of it, could not be explored in a class on the sociology of race, the sociology of gender, in women's or men's studies or, of course, in any number of criminology and sociology of deviance classes. Admittedly, notions such as 'SRV,' a 'matrix of cells' or an 'SRV wheel' do not really mean very much in and of themselves. They are conceptual and meant, in the first instance, as tools for accessing a world filled with intrigue and social relevance, and not always welcoming to outsiders. Hopefully readers will find some sense and some practical, explanatory use in these conceptual 'tools.'

Whatever approach is used and whichever concepts seem appropriate, if you are reading this book, it is likely because you share this fascination with SRV. In that case, and notwithstanding the underpinning overall purpose – which is to demonstrate that apparently disparate and unconnected SRV behaviours share sociological things in common – the important 'beginning-point' question becomes: 'What kind of changes to SRV might *you* envision?' After teaching and researching in this field for some time, I imagine someone out there might suggest that your version of sport unwittingly reveals your own complicity in SRV. It might be accepting an elite model of sport; it might be some gendered version or sport where certain behaviours are viewed as appropriate or inappropriate, or enjoyable or reprehensible; it might be that you are willing to accept the risky and dangerous character of sport as a player, a coach or a fan; it might be the video game you play whose graphic violence seems, to you, removed from everyday reality; or, it might be that you like to wear certain sports brands, or ski certain hills. It is highly unlikely that you are *none* of these things. *All* of them have implications for what this book calls 'SRV.' The point here is that understanding SRV is not a matter of thinking in stereotypes that caricature and pathologize the everyday practices of particular people in sport. SRV is not solely the jurisdiction of uber-violent soccer hooligans, flagrantly abusive and shrewdly 'grooming' coaches, or highly paid bratty athletes running dog-fighting operations. At all levels, including those we do not read about in the daily newspaper, SRV is about gender, race, culture, social class, religion, ethnicity and so many other fundamentally *social* factors that render SRV meaningful, poignant and *ordinary*. For these reasons, it is equally likely that, in our own social allegiances, indulgences with, and preferences for, modern sport, we may be complicit in keeping SRV safe and hidden, too.

NOTES

1 A history of violence: definitions, theories and perspectives

1   http://www.who.int/violenceprevention/approach/definition/en/index.html.

2 Player violence: the drift to criminalization

1   In countries such as Canada, the US and the UK, for example, there has been a swing
    to the political 'right' since the 1970s with respect to punitive responses to street crime
    such as common assault and sexual assault (Bell 2007).

2   *Sports Illustrated*, 1 October 2004: 18.

3   Most sports violence/sports injury cases that become litigated occur in the 'predictable'
    sports – that is, contact, collision and otherwise physically high-risk sports such as grid-
    iron football, ice hockey, rugby, boxing etc. However, some perhaps more surprising
    sports, such as horse-racing, have also been litigated (e.g. 'Jockeys cleared of ending
    rival's career in fall,' *The Independent*, 2 February 2001: 13). Similarly, following a series
    of high-profile accidents in auto-racing, such as the death of Canadian driver Greg
    Moore at the 1998 Molson Toronto Indy (*Calgary Herald*, 1 November 1999: C6) and
    the horrifying crash of Italian Formula One driver Alex Zanardi who lost both legs in a
    200 mph smash at an event in Germany in the same year (*News of the World*, 10 February
    2002: 64), drivers and racing aficionados are asking increasingly critical questions regard-
    ing whether sponsor and fan requirements for speed meet reasonable risk expectations.
    Perhaps the best-known litigated case from the world of Formula One auto racing relates
    to the 1994 death of Brazilian driver Ayrton Senna. As one newspaper wrote of litiga-
    tion connected to the case: 'Senna, a three-time world champion, died when his Wil-
    liams-Renault car slammed into a concrete wall during the San Marino Grand Prix. The
    prosecution contended [that] a poorly modified steering column broke as the Brazilian
    driver entered a curve, causing him to lose control. Newey, now with the McLaren team
    Head, team owner Frank Williams and three race officials were accused of manslaughter
    but were cleared in December 1997' (*Calgary Herald*, 29 January 2003: F4).

4   http://www.canada.com/Courts+wrong+place+deal+with+hits+lawyers/4424603/
    story.html.

5   In response to injuries in ice hockey, including numerous paralyses, the government of
    Canada released an advertisement in the late 1980s that contained a photograph of an

empty hockey arena and the caption: 'The scene of the crime.' The Ministry of Fitness and Amateur Sport has since allowed this particular advertising campaign to lapse, but it remains a fascinating attempt by the state to re-label and transform public thinking on the Canadian national game in light of its less-than-impressive record where player health and safety is concerned.

3 Crowd violence: from hooliganism to post-event riots

1   Arguing that '[a] surprisingly large proportion of fans feel frightened when visiting certain football stadiums,' John Bale (1993: 95) used this phrase to refer to the state of 'hooligan' affairs in Britain before the turn of the millennium.
2   Putting a different (i.e. less anxious) 'spin' on football hooligan statistics, which they call 'troublesome' (2006: 403), Frosdick and Newton indicate that such figures translate in England and Wales into approximately one hooligan incident in every 20 matches, and that only 0.011 per cent of spectators are arrested for football-related offences.
3   In March 1955, francophone sports icon, Maurice Richard of the Montreal Canadiens, was suspended by anglophone NHL President, Clarence Campbell, for a stick-swinging incident, and was thus prevented from reaching what looked like a certain single-season goal-scoring record. When Campbell attended the Canadiens' next home game, he was subjected to verbal and physical abuse, and a smoke bomb was deployed in the stadium (Mark et al. 1983: 84). A two-day riot ensued on the streets of Montreal.
4   Of course, caution should be exercised on this matter since not everyone who attends college football games is a college student or a college graduate. Many locals also attend these events, with varying levels of education.
5   Caused by dissonant sets of crowd dynamics and cultural circumstances, and despite the fact that property destruction was not a central feature in either the Heysel or the Hillsborough cases, these incidents nevertheless resulted in unacceptable human losses. As with the two British tragedies, most of the persons victimized by the Wisconsin incident had no unlawful intentions but were simply caught up in the crowd surge and eventual crush.
6   For example, 'penning' in English soccer was initially part of an anti-pitch invasion policy and was introduced after invasions forced a number of games to be abandoned. Especially in light of the Bradford and Hillsborough disasters, where thousands of fans were trapped against wire fences and lives were lost in the ensuing crushes and panic, many would argue that enclosing sport 'terraces' has a deleterious effect on crowd safety.

4 Formations of sports-related violence: widening the focus

1   I am indebted to the students of Sociology 425 ('Sociology of Violence') at the University of Calgary, and Dan Christie in particular, for their help in thinking through the sociological purpose and merits of the 'SRV wheel.'

5 Risk, pain and injury in sport: a cause or effect of violence?

1   http://www.nytimes.com/2008/12/17/sports/football/17vecsey.html.
2   According to *Newsweek* magazine (13 August 2001: 53), Stringer's death followed 19 other deaths of high school and college football players in the US between 1995 and 2001.
3   http://news.bbc.co.uk/sport2/hi/funny_old_game/7067348.stm.
4   http://today.msnbc.msn.com/id/35327155/ns/today-today_in_vancouver/t/lindsey-vonn-reveal-serious-injury-shin/.
5   On this matter, while it may be unfair to directly blame flamboyant media personalities for sports-related injury such as concussions (e.g. 'MD blames Don Cherry for hockey

violence' – http://www.cbc.ca/news/canada/saskatchewan/story/2009/12/12/sk-head-injuries-don-cherry-charles-tator-91212.html), as both this chapter and Chapter 7 demonstrate, the media's role in bringing the phenomenon to the public is, once again, unambiguously 'active.'

6   In this respect, sociologists could benefit from a more thoughtful use of media or bio-graphical accounts of the long-term injury problems encountered by former athletes. Three cases from English soccer stand out. First, former Charlton Athletic player, Garry Nelson, has noted that '[i]njuries are a player's way of life' (1996: 246); second, former 'hardman' and captain of Liverpool FC, Tommy Smith, now in his 60s, is 40 per cent disabled by osteoarthritis and lives with constant pain (*The Independent*, 3 October 2000: 11); and third, a 2002 inquest into the death of former West Bromwich Albion striker, Jeff Astle, disclosed that Astle, known in his playing years as one of the hardest headers of the ball in the game, died from illnesses brought on by his repeated heading of heavy leather-encased soccer balls. Interestingly, the coroner in the case recorded a verdict of 'death by industrial disease' (*The Guardian*, 12 November 2002: 5).

7   The concept of 'edgework' is used by Lyng (1990) to refer to the experience of partici-pants in dangerous and high-risk activities, as well as to 'social places' where norms and boundaries are contested and negotiated.

6 Sport in the panopticon: the social control of SRV

1   While not strictly the way it was originally used by Foucault (1977), the notion of the panopticon has come to be understood in a similar way to the axioms 'all-seeing' or 'the whole world is watching.'

2   'Bengals CB Jones' plea deal includes anger management,' NFL.com, 24 February 2011. http://www.nfl.com/news/story/09000d5d81e74e3f/article/bengals-cb-jones-plea-deal-includes-anger-management.

3   http://www.hockeycalgary.ca/ris.php.

4   http://saskatoonyouthsoccer.ca/uploads/files/Rules%20Field%20Marshal%20Program.pdf.

5   *Intercollegiate Sport Student-Athlete Administrative Information (2010–2011)*. Department of Athletics, McGill University, Montreal, Quebec. http://www.mcgill.ca/files/athlet-ics/Administrative_Meeting_PowerPoint_2010-11.pdf.

6   http://www.eteamz.com/calgaryblizzard/files/CSMA-Letter.pdf.

7   http://www.halifaxswimmingclub.co.uk/index.php/images/modules/mod_jw_ucd/mod_jw_ucd/images/phocagallery/biathlonpics/thumbs/index.php?option=com_content&view=article&id=9&Itemid=6www.webmai.

8   Australian Sport Commission. 2004. *Code of Conduct*. http://www.ausport.gov.au/__data/assets/pdf_file/0011/151004/codeofconduct2.pdf.

9   http://www.thestar.com/sports/wrestling/mixedmartialarts/article/847995.

7 An eye on SRV: the role of the media

1   Specifically, the data derive from in-depth interviews with crews of television and news-paper journalists across Canada, and from content analyses of television coverage of CFL and NHL games.

2   For at least two decades, his outspoken, pro-violence and often xenophobic views on such issues as fist-fighting, masculinity and the role played by 'foreign' players has made Don Cherry a household name in Canada. Despite constant public complaints and apparent disagreements within his network, CBC has obviously 'cashed in' on the pop-ular appeal of this presiding iconoclast of [*Hockey Night in Canada's*] 'Coach's corner.' This raises serious questions regarding the integrity of Canada's publicly-funded net-work vis-à-vis promoting a cleaner, less violent and less racist version of ice hockey in Canada.

3 In a clear instance of what Blackshaw and Crabbe (2004) would call the 'consumptive aspects of sports deviance,' one of the most telling ways in which mediated pro-violence values interact and overlap with real life behaviours may be seen in the massively popular video games industry, where caricatured forms of sports brutality and violence are routinely championed in video games such as 'Madden Football 12' and 'NHL 11' (both by EA Sports).

8 Stratified SRV: stasis and change

1 http://www.guardian.co.uk/sport/2009/sep/13/serena-williams-tirade-us-open.
2 The changing meanings of aggression and violence for women in society in general have garnered some mainstream attention in criminology (e.g. see Anne Campbell's *Men, Women, and Aggression*, 1993) and psychology (e.g. see James Garbarino's *See Jane Hit: Why Girls Are Growing More Violent and What We Can Do about It*, 2006), and certainly some popular attention in the form of autobiographies of female boxers and other athletes, as noted in this chapter. But sociologists of sport have been relatively slow in turning to this issue so far. The research suggests that some female athletes do find aggression, and even violence, 'empowering' and 'emancipatory' as so much of the research with men has shown. However, at this stage, the only safe conclusion in this still-developing research area is that 'sports experiences can be ambiguous and contradictory regardless of gender' (Young and White 1995: 55).
3 Boxer Kate Sekules (2000) even goes so far as to argue that aggressive sport for women has 'a purity and a purpose' ('I like hitting women,' *The Times*, 21 October 2007: 19).
4 http://www.telegraph.co.uk/sport/othersports/winter-olympics/7326057/Canadian-womens-ice-hockey-team-apologise-for-beer-and-cigars-on-ice.html.
5 http://sports.espn.go.com/ncaa/news/story?id=4629837.
6 'Hockey fans love fighting, survey says,' *The Star*, 17 March 2009. http://www.thestar.com/Sports/article/603432.

Conclusion

1 Recently, the Edmonton Eskimos of the CFL have hired a general manager who admitted to sexually assaulting his 16-year-old babysitter (http://www.cbc.ca/news/story/2010/09/14/edm-tillman-hired-eskimos.html); the Calgary Stampeders of the CFL have hired a player who is a known sex offender (*Calgary Herald*, 19 June 2011: E5); amid the usual denials from senior officials, FIFA has again been widely accused of corruption (http://www.telegraph.co.uk/sport/football/international/8535640/Fifa-corruption-and-bribery-allegations-a-timeline.html); and a 17-year-old national-level Canadian athlete has been suspended by his federal sport association for participating in the 2011 Vancouver NHL riots (*Calgary Herald*, 19 June 2011: A4).

BIBLIOGRAPHY

Aalten, A. (2007). Listening to the dancer's body. *Sociological Review Monograph*, 55, 1: 109–125.

Adams, S. (1987). Liability and negligence. In S. Adams, M. Adrian and M. Bayless (eds), *Catastrophic Injuries in Sport: Avoidance Strategies*. Indianapolis: Benchmark: 3–7.

Adams, S., Adrian, M. and Bayless, M. (Eds) (1987). *Catastrophic Injuries in Sport: Avoidance Strategies*. Indianapolis: Benchmark.

Albert, E. (1999). Dealing with danger: The normalization of risk in cycling. *International Review for the Sociology of Sport*, 34, 2: 157–171.

Alegi, P. (2004). 'Like cows driven to a dip': The 2001 Ellis Park Stadium disaster in South Africa. *Soccer and Society*, 5, 2: 233–247.

Anderson, E. (2000). *Trailblazing: America's First Openly Gay Track Coach*. Hollywood, CA: Alyson.

Anderson, E. (2005). *In the Game: Gay Athletes and the Cult of Masculinity*. New York: SUNY.

Anderson, E. and McCormack, M. (2010). Intersectionality, critical race theory, the American sporting oppression: Examining black and gay male athletes. *Journal of Homosexuality*, 57, 8: 949–967.

Apter, M.J. (1989). *Reversal Theory: Motivation, Emotion and Personality*. London: Routledge.

Archetti, E.P. and Romero, A.C. (1994). Death and violence in Argentinian football. In R. Giulianotti, N. Bonney and M. Hepworth (eds), *Football Violence and Social Identity*. London: Routledge: 37–72.

Arms, R.L., Russell, G.W. and Sandilands, M.L. (1979a). Effects on the hostility of spectators of viewing aggressive sports. *Review of Sport and Leisure*, 4: 115–127.

Arms, R.L., Russell, G.W. and Sandilands, M.L. (1979b). Effects of viewing aggressive sports on the hostility of spectators. *Social Psychology Quarterly*, 42, 3, 275–279.

Armstrong, G. (1998). *Football Hooligans: Knowing the Score*. New York: Berg.

Atkinson, M. (2000). Brother, can you spare a seat: Developing recipes of knowledge in the ticket scalping subculture. *Sociology of Sport Journal*, 17, 2: 151–170.

Atkinson, M. (2001). 'It's just part of the game': Toward a typology of sports crime. Paper presented at North American Society for the Sociology of Sport, San Antonio, TX, 31 October–4 November.

Atkinson, M. (2002). Fifty million viewers can't be wrong: Professional wrestling, sports-entertainment and mimesis. *Sociology of Sport Journal*, 19: 47–66.

Atkinson, M. (2005). You are what you eat: Sports supplementation in endurance athlete figurations. Paper presented at North American Society for the Sociology of Sport, Winston-Salem, NC, 27 October.

Atkinson, M. (2007). Playing with fire: Masculinity and exercise supplements. *Sociology of Sport Journal*, 24, 2: 165–186.

Atkinson, M. (2008a). *Battleground: Sports*. Westport, CT: Greenwood Publishing.

Atkinson, M. (2008b). Triathlon, suffering and exciting significance. *Leisure Studies*, 27, 2: 165–180.

Atkinson, M. (2009). Parkour, anarcho-environmentalism and poiesis. *Journal of Sport and Social Issues*, 33, 2: 169–194.

Atkinson, M. (2011a). *Deconstructing Men and Masculinities*. Toronto: Oxford University Press.

Atkinson, M. (2011b). Male athletes and the culture of thinness in sport. *Deviant Behavior*, 32, 3: 224–256.

Atkinson, M. and Young, K. (2003). Terror games: Media treatment of security issues at the 2002 winter Olympic games. *OLYMPIKA: The International Journal of Olympic Studies*, XI: 53–78.

Atkinson, M. and Young, K. (2005a). Reservoir dogs: Greyhound racing, mimesis and sports-related violence. *International Review for the Sociology of Sport*, 40, 3: 335–356.

Atkinson, M. and Young, K. (2005b). Political violence, terrorism and security at the Olympic games. In K. Young and K. Wamsley (eds), *Global Olympics: Historical and Sociological Studies of the Modern Games*. Oxford: Elsevier Press: 269–294.

Atkinson, M. and Young, K. (2008). *Deviance and Social Control in Sport*. Champaign, IL: Human Kinetics.

Atkinson, M. and Young, K. (2011). Cracking 'the (male) code' of player violence. In P. Donnelly (ed.), *Taking Sport Seriously: Social Issues in Canadian Sport* (3rd edition). Toronto: Thompson Educational Publishing: 145–148.

Atkinson, M. and Young, K. (2012). Shadowed by the corpse of war: Sport spectacles and the spirit of terrorism. *International Review for the Sociology of Sport* (forthcoming).

Atyeo, D. (1979). *Violence in Sports*. Toronto: Van Nostrand Reinhold.

Avery, J. and Stevens, J. (1997). *Too Many Men on the Ice: Women's Hockey in North America*. Victoria: Polestar Publishers.

Bairner, A. (1995). Soccer, masculinity and violence in Northern Ireland. Paper presented at the North American Society for the Sociology of Sport, Sacramento, CA, 1–4 November.

Bairner, A. (1999). Soccer, masculinity, and violence in Northern Ireland: Between hooliganism and terrorism. *Men and Masculinities*, 1, 3: 284–301.

Bairner, A. (2001). *Sport, Nationalism, and Globalization: European and North American Perspectives*. Albany, NY: SUNY Press.

Bairner, A. and Shirlow, P. (1998). Loyalism, Linfield and territorial politics of soccer fandom in Northern Ireland. *Space and Polity*, 2, 3: 163–177.

Baker, N. (1996). Going to the dogs – Hostility to greyhound racing in Britain: Puritanism, socialism and pragmatism. *Journal of Sport History*, 23: 97–119.

Bale, J. (1993). *Sport, Space and the City*. London: Routledge.

Bale, J. (1994). *Landscapes of Modern Sport*. London: Leicester University Press.

Ball-Rokeach, S. (1971). The legitimation of violence. In J.F. Short and M.E. Wolfgang (eds), *Collective Violence*. Chicago: Aldine: 100–111.

Ball-Rokeach, S. (1980). Normative and deviant violence from a conflict perspective. *Social Problems*, 28: 45–62.

Ballard, C., O'Brien, R. and Bechtel, M. (2003). Female Kobe? *Sports Illustrated*, 25 August: 20.

Bandura, A. (1973). *Aggression: A Social Learning Analysis*. Englewood Cliffs, NJ: Prentice-Hall.

Bandura, A. (1977). *Social Learning Theory*. Englewood Cliffs, NJ: Prentice-Hall.

Barker-Ruchti, N. and Tinning, R. (2010). Foucault in leotards: Corporeal discipline in women's artistic gymnastics. *Sociology of Sport Journal*, 27, 3: 229–249.

Barnes, J. (1988). *Sports and the Law in Canada*. Toronto: Butterworths.

Barnes, J. (1991). Recent developments in Canadian sports law. *Ottawa Law Review*, 23: 623–706.

Baron, L. (2007). *Contemporary Issues in Youth Sports*. New York: Nova Sciences Publishers.

Baron, R.A. (1977). *Human Aggression*. New York: Plenum.

Barthes, R. (1972). *Mythologies*. London: Jonathan Cape.

Bechtel, M. and Cannella, S. (2006). T-Ball coach trial. *Sports Illustrated*, 25 September: 26.

Becker, H. (1963). *Outsiders: Studies in the Sociology of Deviance*. Chicago: The Free Press.

Beecher, C. (1994). Crowd control: When sports fanatics turn violent. *Illinois Quarterly* (University of Illinois Alumni Association Magazine), May/June: 22–25.

Beisser, A.R. (1967). *The Madness in Sports*. New York: Appleton Century Crofts.

Bélanger, A. (1999). The last game? Hockey and the experience of masculinity in Quebec. In P. White and K. Young (eds), *Sport and Gender in Canada*. Toronto: Oxford University Press: 293–309.

Bell, S.J. (2007). *Young Offenders and Youth Justice: A Century after the Fact* (3rd edition). Toronto: Thomson Nelson.

Benedict, H. (2009). *The Lonely Soldier: The Private War of Women Serving in Iraq*. Boston: Beacon Press.

Benedict, J. and Keteyian, A. (2011). College football and crime. *Sports Illustrated* online. Internet source: (http://sportsillustrated.cnn.com/2011/writers/the_bonus/02/27/cfb.crime/index.html).

Benedict, J. and Klein, A. (1997). Arrest and conviction rates for athletes accused of sexual assault. *Sociology of Sport Journal*, 14, 1: 86–95.

Benedict, J. and Yaeger, D. (1998). *Pros and Cons: The Criminals Who Play in the NFL*. New York: Warner Books.

Benidickson, J. (1997). *Environmental Law*. Concord, ON: Irwin Law.

Berczeller, E. (1967). The aesthetic feelings and Aristotle's catharsis theory. *Journal of Psychology*, 65: 261–267.

Berkowitz, L. (1978). Whatever happened to the Frustration–Aggression Hypothesis? *The American Behavioural Scientist*, 21, 5: 691–709.

Berkowitz, L. (1993). The problem of aggression. In L. Berkowitz (ed.), *Aggression: Its Causes, Consequences and Control*. New York: McGraw Hill: 1–24.

Berry, B. and Smith, E. (2000). Race, sport and crime: The misrepresentation of African Americans in team sports and crime. *Sociology of Sport Journal*, 17, 2: 171–197.

Bianchi, M. (2005). For celebrities justice is blind. *Calgary Herald*, 27 September: F2.

Birrell, S. (2000). Feminist theories for sport. In J. Coakley and E. Dunning (eds), *Handbook of Sports Studies*. London: Sage: 61–76.

Blackshaw, T. and Crabbe, T. (2004). *New Perspectives on Sport and Deviance*. London: Routledge.

Blackshaw, T. and Crabbe, T. (2005). Leeds on trial: Soap opera, performativity and the racialization of sports-related violence. *Patterns of Prejudice*, 39, 3: 327–342.

Blair, T. (2009). Glubiak shocked, 22 August. Internet source: (http://blogs.news.com.au/dailytelegraph/timblair/index.php/dailytelegraph/comments/glubiak_shocked/asc/).

Bonk, T. (1999). A new hazard: Fans. *Calgary Herald*, 2 February: C1.

Bonnell, K. (2007). Benoit's doctor dispensed drugs 'like candy.' *Calgary Herald*, 3 July: A8.

Booth, D. (1996). Athletes with disabilities. In M. Harries, C. Williams, W. Stanish and L. Micheli (eds), *Oxford Textbook of Sports Medicine*. New York: Oxford University Press: 634–645.

Bourdieu, P. (1978). Sport and social class. *Social Science Information*, 17, 6: 819–840.

Bouton, J. (1970). *Ball Four: My Life and Hard Times Throwing Knuckleball in the Big Leagues*. New York: Dell.

Bowker, L.H. (1998). The coaching abuse of teenage girls: A betrayal of innocence and trust. In *Masculinities and Violence* (Chapter 6). London: Sage.

Boyle, R. and Haynes, R. (2000). *Power Play: Sport, the Media and Popular Culture*. Harlow: Pearson Education.

Brackenridge, C. (1996). *Child Protection in Sport: Politics, Procedures and Systems. Report on a Sport Council Seminar for National Governing Bodies*. Cheltenham: CandGCHE.

Brackenridge, C. (2001). *Spoilsports: Understanding and Preventing Sexual Exploitation in Sport*. London: Routledge.

Bradbury, S. (2010). From racial exclusions to new inclusions: Black and minority ethnic participation in football clubs in the East Midlands of England. *International Review for the Sociology of Sport*, 46, 1: 23–44.

Brake, M. (1985). *Comparative Youth Culture*. Boston: Routledge and Kegan Paul.

Branscombe, N.R. and Wann, D.L. (1992). Role of identification with a group, arousal categorization processes, and self-esteem in sports spectator aggression. *Human Relations*, 45, 10: 1013–1033.

Brill, A.A. (1929). The way of the fan. *North American Review*, 226: 400–434.

Brimson, D. and Brimson, E. (1996). *Everywhere We Go: Behind the Matchday Madness*. London: Headline.

Brimson, E. (1999). *Tear Gas and Ticket Touts: With the England Fans at the World Cup*. London: Headline.

British Columbia Police Commission (1994). *Report on the Riot that Occurred in Vancouver on June 14–15, 1994*. Vancouver.

Brittain, I. (2009). *The Paralympic Games Explained*. London: Routledge.

Brock, S.C. and Kleiber, D.A. (1994). Narrative in medicine: The stories of elite college athletes' career-ending injuries. *Qualitative Health Research*, 4, 4: 411–430.

Bronfenbrenner, U. (1979). *The Ecology of Human Development: Experiments by Nature and Design*. Cambridge, MA: Harvard University Press.

Brown, T.J., Summer, K.E and Nocera, R. (2002). Understanding sexual aggression against women: An examination of the role of men's athletic participation and related variables. *Journal of Interpersonal Violence*, 17: 937–952.

Brownmiller, S. (1975). *Against Our Will: Men, Women and Rape*. New York: Simon and Schuster.

Bryant, J. and McElroy, M. (1997). *Sociological Dynamics of Sport and Exercise*. Englewood Cliffs, NJ: Morton.

Bryant, J. and Zillmann, D. (1983). Sports violence and the media. In J.H. Goldstein (ed.), *Sports Violence*. New York: Springer-Verlag: 195–208.

Bryshun, J. (1997). Hazing in sport: An exploratory study of veteran/rookie relations. Unpublished MA thesis, Department of Sociology, University of Calgary, Canada.

Bryshun, J. and Young, K. (1999). Sport-related hazing: An inquiry into male and female involvement. In P. White and K. Young (eds), *Sport and Gender in Canada*. Toronto: Oxford University Press: 269–292.

Bryshun, J. and Young, K. (2007). Hazing as a form of sport and gender socialization. In K. Young and P. White (eds), *Sport and Gender in Canada* (2nd edition). Don Mills: Oxford University Press: 302–327.

Bryson, L. (1987). Sport and the maintenance of masculine hegemony. *Women's Studies International Forum*, 10, 4: 349–360.

Buckley, W. (2002). Here comes the judge. *The Observer*, 20 January: 13.

Buford, B. (1991). *Among the Thugs*. London: Mandarin.

Burdsey, D. (2010). British Muslim experiences in English first-class cricket. *International Review for the Sociology of Sport*, 45, 3: 315–334.

Burstyn, V. (1999). *The Rites of Men: Manhood, Politics, and the Culture of Sport*. Toronto: University of Toronto Press.

Bushman, B.J. and Anderson, C.A. (2001). Is it time to pull the plug on hostile versus instrumental aggression dichotomy? *Psychological Review*, 108: 273–279.

Caine, D.J., Caine, C.G. and Lindner, K.J. (Eds) (1996). *Epidemiology of Sports Injuries*. Champaign, IL: Human Kinetics.

Caluya, G. (2010). The post panoptic society? Reassessing Foucault in surveillance studies. *Social Identities*, 16, 5: 621–633.

Campbell, A. (1993). *Men, Women, and Aggression: From Rage to Marriage to Violence in the Streets – How Gender Affects the Way We Act*. New York: Basic Books.

Canetti, E. (1981). *Crowds and Power*. New York: Penguin.

Canseco, J. (2005). *Juiced: Wild Times, Rampant 'Roids, Smash Hits, and How Baseball Got Big*. New York: ReganBooks.

Card, D. and Dahl, G. (2009). Family violence and football: The effect of unexpected emotional cues on violent behavior. National Bureau of Economic Research Working Paper no. 15497, November (http://www.nber.org/papers/w15497).

Carlson, J. (2010). The female significant in all-women's amateur roller derby. *Sociology of Sport Journal*, 27, 4: 428–440.

Case, R.W. and Boucher, R.L. (1981). Spectator violence in sport: A selected review. *Journal of Sport and Social Issues*, 5, 2: 1–15.

Cashmore, E. (1998). *Making Sense of Sports*. London: Routledge.

Cashmore, E. (2000). *Sports Culture: An A–Z Guide*. New York: Routledge.

Cashmore, E. (2005). *Tyson – Nurture of the Beast*. Malden: Polity Press.

Cauldwell, J. (2007). *Sport, Sexualities and Queer Theory*. London: Routledge.

Center for Problem-Oriented Policing (2010). Responses to the problem of spectator violence in stadiums. Internet source: (http://www.popcenter.org/problems/spectator_violence/3).

Centre for Health Promotion and Research (1990). Sports injuries in Australia: Causes, costs, and prevention. A report to the National Better Health Program. Sydney: National Better Health Program.

Cere, R. (2002). 'Witches of our age': Women Ultras, Italian football and the media. *Culture, Sport, Society*, 5, 3: 166–188.

Chaikin, T. and Telander, R. (1988). The nightmare of steroids. *Sports Illustrated*, 24 October: 83–102.

Charlesworth, H. (2004). Sports-related injury, risk and pain: The experiences of English female university athletes. Unpublished doctoral dissertation, Loughborough University, UK.

Charlesworth, H. and Young, K. (2004). Why English female university athletes play with pain: Motivations and rationalisations. In K. Young (ed.), *Sporting Bodies, Damaged Selves: Sociological Studies of Sports-related Injury.* Oxford: Elsevier Press: 163–180.

Charlesworth, H. and Young, K. (2006). Injured female athletes: Experiential accounts from England and Canada. In S. Loland, B. Skirstad and I. Waddington (eds), *Pain and Injury in Sport: Social and Ethical Analysis.* London: Routledge: 89–106.

Chase, L.F. (2008). Running big: Clydesdale runners and technologies of the body. *Sociology of Sport Journal*, 25, 1: 130–147.

Chibnall, S. (1981). The production of knowledge by crime reporters. In S. Cohen and J. Young (eds), *The Manufacture of News.* London: Constable: 75–98.

Chroni, S., Fasting, K., Hervik, S.E. and Knorre, N. (2010). Sexual harassment in sport toward females in three European countries. *International Review for the Sociology of Sport*, 48, 1: 76–89.

City of Vancouver (1994). *Review of Major Events – Riots: A Background Paper.* Vancouver.

Clarke, J. (1978). Football and working class fans: Tradition and change. In R. Ingham (ed.), *Football Hooliganism: The Wider Context.* London: Inter-Action Inprint: 37–61.

Coakley, J. (1988/1989). Media coverage of sports and violent behavior: An elusive connection. *Current Psychology: Research and Reviews* 7, 4: 322–330.

Coakley, J. (1998). *Sports in Society: Issues and Controversies* (6th edition). New York: McGraw Hill.

Coakley, J. and Donnelly, P. (2004). *Sports in Society: Issues and Controversies* (1st Canadian edition). Toronto: McGraw-Hill Ryerson.

Coakley, J. and Donnelly, P. (2009). *Sports in Society: Issues and Controversies* (2nd Canadian edition). Toronto: McGraw-Hill Ryerson.

Cohen, L. (2005). *Without Apology: Girls, Women, and the Desire to Fight.* New York: Random House.

Cohen, S. (1973). *Folk Devils and Moral Panics: The Creation of the Mods and Rockers.* St Albans: Paladin.

Collings, P. and Condon, R. (1996). Blood on ice: Status, self-esteem and ritual injury among Innuit hockey players. *Human Organizations*, 55, 3: 253–262.

Collins, A., Flynn, A., Munday, M. and Roberts, A. (2007). Assessing the environmental consequences of major sporting events: The 2003/04 FA Cup Final. *Urban Studies*, 44, 3: 457–476.

Collinson, J. (2003). Running into injury: Distance running and temporality. *Sociology of Sport Journal*, 20, 4: 331–351.

Collinson, J. (2005). Emotions, interaction and the injured sporting body. *International Review for the Sociology of Sport*, 40, 2: 221–240.

Comisky, P., Bryant, J. and Zillman, D. (1977). Commentary as a substitute for action. *Journal of Communication*, 27, 3: 150–153.

Comstock, R.D. and Fields, S.K. (2005). The fair sex? Foul play among female rugby players. *Journal of Science and Medicine in Sport*, 8, 1: 101–110.

Connell, R.W. (1992). A very straight gay: Masculinity, homosexuality and the dynamics of gender. *American Sociological Review*, 57, 6: 735–751.

Connell, R.W. (1995). *Masculinities.* Berkeley, CA: University of California Press.

Connors, E.T. (1981). *Educational Tort Liability and Malpractice.* Bloomington, IN: Phi Delta Kappa.

Cook, K. and Mravic, M. (1999). The catcher's father hit him. *Sports Illustrated*, 24 May: 36.

Cooper, M., Brockman J. and Hoffar, I. (2004). Final report on equity and diversity in Alberta's legal profession. Report completed for the joint Committee on Equality, Equity and Diversity. Calgary: Alberta Law Foundation.

Coram, S. (2007). Race formations (evolutionary hegemony) and the 'aping' of the Australian indigenous athlete. *International Review for the Sociology of Sport*, 42, 4: 392–409.

Cottle, S. (2006). Mediatized rituals: Beyond manufacturing consent. *Media, Culture and Society*, 28, 2: 411–432.

Courson, S. (1991). *False Glory*. Stamford, CT: Longmeadow.

Cove, L. (2006). Negotiating the ring: Reconciling gender in women's boxing. Unpublished MA thesis, Department of Sociology, University of Calgary, Canada.

Coward, R. (1985). *Female Desires: How They Are Sought, Bought, and Packaged*. New York: Grove Press.

Crisfield, P. (1996). *Protecting Children: A Guide for Sportspeople*. Leeds: The National Coaching Foundation.

Crosset, T. (1999). Male athletes' violence against women: A critical assessment of the athletic affiliation violence against women debate. *Quest*, 52, 3: 244–257.

Crosset, T., Benedict, J. and MacDonald, M. (1995). Male student-athletes reported for sexual assault: Survey of campus police departments and judicial affairs. *Journal of Sport and Social Issues*, 19, 2: 126–140.

Cruise, D. and Griffiths, A. (1991). *Net Worth: Exploding the Myths of Pro Hockey*. Toronto: Viking.

Curry, T. (1991). Fraternal bonding in the locker room: A feminist analysis of talk about competition and women. *Sociology of Sport Journal*, 8: 119–135.

Curry, T. (1993). A little pain never hurt anyone: Athletic career socialization and the normalization of sports injury. *Symbolic Interaction*, 16, 3: 273–290.

Curry, T. and Strauss, R.H. (1994). A little pain never hurt anyone: A photo-essay on the normalization of sports injuries. *Sociology of Sport Journal*, 11, 2: 195–208.

David, P. (2005). *Human Rights in Youth Sport*. London: Routledge.

Davies, S. (2011). Aintree day of horror as TV audience of millions see two horses die at the National. *Daily Mail* online. 10 April. Internet source: (http://www.dailymail.co.uk).

Davis, C. (1999). Eating disorders, physical activity, and sport: Biological, psychological, and sociological factors. In P. White and K. Young (eds), *Sport and Gender in Canada*. Toronto: Oxford University Press: 85–106.

Davis-Delano, L.R. (2007). Eliminating Native American mascots: Ingredients for success. *Journal of Sport and Social Issues*, 31: 340–373.

de Garis, L. (1997). 'Be a buddy to your buddy': Violence, aggression and masculinity in boxing. Paper presented at the North American Society for the Sociology of Sport, Toronto, 5–8 November.

Denfeld, R. (1997). *Kill the Body and the Head Will Fall: A Closer Look at Women, Violence and Aggression*. New York: Warner.

Desbarats, P. (1990). *Guide to the Canadian Mass Media*. Toronto: Harcourt, Brace, Jovanovich.

Deutschmann, L. (1998). *Deviance and Social Control* (2nd edition). Toronto: Nelson.

Deutschmann, L. (2007). *Deviance and Social Control* (4th edition). Toronto: Nelson.

Dewar, C.K. (1979). Spectator fights at professional baseball games. *Review of Sport and Leisure*, 4, 12: 12–26.

Dollard, J., Doob, L., Miller, N., Mower, O. and Sears, R. (1939). *Frustration and Aggression*. New Haven: Yale University Press.

Donaldson, M. (1993). What is hegemonic masculinity? *Theory and Society*, 22: 643–657.

Donnelly, P. (1999). Who's fair game? Sport, sexual harassment and abuse. In P. White and K. Young (eds), *Sport and Gender in Canada*. Toronto: Oxford University Press.

Donnelly, P. (2003). Marching out of step: Sport, social order, and the case of child labour.

Keynote address, Second World Congress of the Sociology of Sport, Cologne, Germany, 18–21 June.

Donnelly, P. (2007). Who's fair game? Sport, sexual harassment and abuse. In K. Young and P. White (eds), *Sport and Gender in Canada* (2nd edition). Don Mills, ON: Oxford University Press: 279–301.

Donnelly, P. and Harvey, J. (2007). Social class and gender: Intersections in sport and physical activity. In K. Young and P. White (eds), *Sport and Gender in Canada* (2nd edition). Don Mills, ON: Oxford University Press: 95–119.

Donnelly, P. and Young, K. (1985). Reproduction and transformation of cultural forms in sport: A contextual analysis of rugby. *International Review for the Sociology of Sport*, 20 (1/2): 19–39.

Donnelly, P. and Young, K. (1988). The construction and confirmation of identity in sport subcultures. *Sociology of Sport Journal*, 5, 3: 223–240.

Donnelly, P. and Young, K. (2004). 'Sports-related violence' as an outcome of cultures of control in sport. Paper presented at the Pre-Olympic Scientific Congress, Thessaloniki, Greece, 6–10 August.

Downey, G. (2007). Producing pain: Techniques and technologies in no-holds-barred fighting. *Social Studies of Science*, 37, 2: 201–226.

Dryden, K. (1983). *The Game*. Toronto: Macmillan.

Dubbert, J.L. (1979). *A Man's Place: Masculinity in Transition*. Englewood Cliffs, NJ: Prentice Hall.

Dubin, C. (1990). *Commission of Inquiry into the Use of Drugs and Banned Practices Intended to Increase Athletic Performance*. Ottawa: Canadian Government Publishing Centre.

Dufur, M. and Feinberg, S. (2009). Race and the NFL draft: View from the Auction Block, *Qualitative Sociology*, 32, 1: 53–73.

Duggan, M. and Steven, D.L. (2002). Winning isn't everything: Corruption in sumo wrestling. *American Economic Review*, 92, 5: 1594–1605.

Dunn, R. and Stevenson, C. (1998). The paradox of the church hockey league. *International Review for the Sociology of Sport*, 33, 2: 131–144.

Dunning, E. (1986). Sport as a male preserve: Notes on the social sources of masculine identity and its transformations. In N. Elias and E. Dunning (eds), *Quest for Excitement: Sport and Leisure in the Civilizing Process*. Oxford: Basil Blackwell: 267–283.

Dunning, E. (1994). Sport in space and time: Civilizing processes, trajectories of state-formation and the development of modern sport. *International Review for the Sociology of Sport*, 29: 331–345.

Dunning, E. (1997). Sport in the quest of excitement: Norbert Elias's contribution to the sociology of sport. *Group Analysis*, 30: 477–487.

Dunning, E. (1999). *Sport Matters: Sociological Studies of Sport, Violence and Civilization*. London: Routledge.

Dunning, E., Murphy, P. and Waddington, I. (2002a). Towards a sociological understanding of football hooliganism as a world phenomenon. In E. Dunning, P. Murphy, I. Waddington and A. Astrinakis (eds), *Football's Fighting Fans: Soccer Hooliganism as a World Social Problem*. Dublin: University College Dublin Press: 1–22.

Dunning, E., Murphy, P., Waddington, I. and Astrinakis, A. (Eds) (2002b). *Fighting Fans: Football Hooliganism as a World Phenomenon*. Dublin: University College Dublin Press.

Dunning, E., Murphy, P. and Williams, J. (1988). *The Roots of Football Hooliganism: An Historical and Sociological Study*. London: Routledge and Kegan Paul.

Duperrault, J.R. (1981). l'affaire Richard: A situational analysis of the Montreal hockey riot. *Canadian Journal of History of Sport*, XII: 66–83.

Duprez, C. (2006). Regulations changing in Patagonia, *Climbing Magazine Online*, 19 December. Internet source: (http://www.climbing.com/news/hotflashes/patagonia06/).

Durkheim, E. (1893). *The Division of Labour in Society*. New York: Free Press.

Eaves, N. and Phillips, A. (2000). Last orders. *Stadia*, 5: 84–87.

Edwards, H. (1973). *The Sociology of Sport*. Homewood, IL: Dorsey Press.

Edwards, H. and Rackages, V. (1977). The dynamics of violence in sport. *Journal of Sport and Social Issues*, 1: 3–31.

Ehrenreich, B. (1983). *The Hearts of Men: American Dreams and the Flight from Commitment*. New York: Doubleday.

Eitzen, S. and Sage, G. (2003). *Sociology of North American Sport*. London: McGraw Hill.

Elias, N. (1994). *The Civilizing Process*. Oxford: Basil Blackwell.

Elias, N. (1996). *The Germans: Studies of Power Struggles and the Development of Habitus in the Nineteenth and Twentieth Centuries*. Oxford: Polity Press.

Elias, N. and Dunning, E. (1971). Folk football in medieval and early modern Britain. In E. Dunning (ed.), *The Sociology of Sport: A Selection of Readings*. London: Frank Cass: 116–132.

Elias, N. and Dunning, E. (Eds) (1986). *Quest for Excitement: Sport and Leisure in the Civilizing Process*. Oxford: Basil Blackwell.

Elias, R. (1986). The hidden dimensions of victimization: Victims, victimology, and human rights. In *The Politics of Victimization: Victims, Victimology and Human Rights*. New York: Oxford University Press: 3–8.

Eller, J.D. (2006). *Violence and Culture: A Cross Cultural and Interdisciplinary Perspective*. Toronto: Thomson Wadsworth.

Elliot, P., Murdock, G. and Schlesinger, P. (1983). Terrorism and the state: A case study of the discourses of television. *Media, Culture and Society*, 5, 2: 155–177.

Endean, C. (1993). Racism takes a turn for the worse. *The European*, 23–26 September: 4.

Engh, F. (1999). *Why Johnny Hates Sports*. New York: Avery.

Etue, E. and Williams, M.K. (1996). *On the Edge: Women Making Hockey History*. Toronto: Second Story Press.

Evans, R. A. (1974). A conversation with Konrad Lorenz about aggression, homosexuality, pornography and the need for a new ethic. *Psychology Today*, 8: 82–93.

Evans, R., Gauthier, D.K. and Forsyth, C.J. (1998). Dogfighting: Symbolic expression and validation of masculinity. *Sex Roles*, 39, 11/12: 825–838.

Ewald, K. and Jiobu, R.M. (1985). Explaining positive deviance: Becker's model and the case of runners and bodybuilders. *Sociology of Sport Journal*, 2, 2: 144–156.

Farber, M. (2004). Code red. *Sports Illustrated*, 22 March: 56–60.

Farber, M. (2005). Skating on. *Sports Illustrated*, 7 November: 20–23.

Fasting, K., Brackenridge, C. and Sundgot Borgen, J. (2000). *Sexual Harassment In and Outside Sport*. Oslo: Norwegian Olympic Committee.

Faulkner, R. (1973). On respect and retribution: Toward an ethnography of violence. *Sociological Symposium*, 9: 17–36.

Faulkner, R. (1974). Making violence by doing work: Selves, situations, and the world of professional hockey. *Sociology of Work and Occupations*, 1: 288–312.

Featherstone, M., Hepworth, M. and Turner, B.S. (Eds) (1991). *The Body: Social Processes and Cultural Theory*. London: Sage.

Feldman, A. (1991). *Formations of Violence: The Narrative of the Body and Political Terror in Northern Ireland*. London: University of Chicago Press.

Ferguson, E. (2009). Minor hockey fights ref abuse. *Calgary Herald*, 6 March: B1–B2.

Fields, S. (2008). *Female Gladiators: Gender, Law, and Contact Sport in America*. Champaign, IL: University of Illinois Press.

Fimrite, R. (1976). Take me out to the brawl game. In A. Yiannakis (ed.), *Sport Sociology: Contemporary Themes*. Dubuque, IA: Kendall/Hunt: 200–203.

Fiske, J. (1987). *Television Culture*. London: Methuen.

Fleming, T. (1983). Mad dogs, beasts and raving nutters: The presentation of the mentally disordered in the British press. In T. Fleming and L. Visano (eds), *Deviant Designations: Crime, Law and Deviance in Canada*. Toronto: Butterworths: 153–184.

Fletcher, J. (1997). *Violence and Civilization: An Introduction to the Work of Norbert Elias*. Oxford: Polity Press.

Fleury, T. (2009). *Playing with Fire: The Highest Highs and Lowest Lows of Theo Fleury*. Toronto: Harper Collins.

Fogel, C. (2009). Discerning consent on the gridiron: Violence, hazing, and performance-enhancing drug use in Canadian football. Unpublished PhD dissertation, University of Calgary, Canada.

Fontana, A. (1978). Over the edge: A return to primitive sensation in play and games. *Urban Life*, 7: 213–229.

Forbes, G.B, Adams-Curtis, L.E, Pakalka, A.H. and White, K. (2006). Dating aggression, sexual coercion, and aggression: Supporting attitudes among college man as a function of participation in aggressive high school sports. *Violence Against Women*, 12, 5: 441–455.

Foucault, M. (1977). *Discipline and Punish: The Birth of the Prison*. New York: Pantheon.

Francis, C. (1991). *Speed Trap*. New York: St Martin's Press.

Francis, M. and Walsh, P. (1997). *Govnors: The Shocking True Story of a Soccer Hooligan Gang Leader*. Preston: Milo.

Frank, A.W. (1991). For a sociology of the body: An analytic review. In M. Featherstone, M. Hepworth and B.S. Turner (eds), *The Body: Social Processes and Cultural Theory*. London: Sage: 36–110.

Frank, A.W. (1995). *The Wounded Storyteller: Body, Illness, and Ethics*. Chicago: University of Chicago Press.

Frank, A.W. (1996). Reconciliatory alchemy: Bodies, narratives and power. *Body and Society*, 2, 3: 53–71.

Freund, P.E.S. (1991). *Health, Illness and the Social Body: A Critical Sociology*. London: Prentice Hall.

Frey, J. (1991). Social risk and the meaning of sport. *Sociology of Sport Journal*, 8, 2: 136–145.

Frey, J., Preston, F.W. and Bernhard, B. (1997). Risk and injury: A comparison of football and rodeo subcultures. Paper presented at the North American Society for the Sociology of Sport, Toronto, 5–8 November.

Frosdick, S. and Newton, R. (2006). The nature and extent of football hooliganism in England and Wales. *Soccer and Society*, 7, 4: 403–422.

Fuller, C. (1995). Implications of health and safety legislation for the professional sportsperson. *British Journal of Sports Medicine*, 29, 1: 5–9.

Gajewski, K.A. (2010). Worth noting. *Humanist*, 70, 3: 48.

Garbarino, J. (2006). *See Jane Hit: Why Girls Are Growing More Violent and What We Can Do about It*. New York: Penguin Press.

Garcia, R.S. and Malcolm, D. (2010). Decivilizing, civilizing or informalizing: The international development of mixed martial arts. *International Review of the Sociology of Sport*, 45, 1: 39–58.

Gardiner, S., Felix, A., James, M., Welch, R. and O'Leary, J. (1998). *Sports Law*. London: Cavendish.

Garfinkel, H. (1967). Conditions of successful degradation ceremonies. In J. Manis and B.

Meltzer (eds), *Symbolic Interaction: A Reader in Social Psychology*. Boston: Allyn & Bacon: 205–213.

Garland, D. (2001). *The Culture of Control: Crime and Social Order in Contemporary Society*. New York: Oxford University Press.

Garland, J. and Rowe, M. (2000). The hooligan's fear of the penalty. *Soccer and Society*, 1, 1: 144–156.

Gartner, R. (1993). Studying woman abuse: A comment on Dekeseredy and Kelly. *Canadian Journal of Sociology*, 18, 3: 312–320.

Geen, R.G. and Berkowitz, L. (1969). Some conditions facilitating the occurrence of aggression after observation of violence. In L. Berkowitz (ed.), *Roots of Aggression: A Re-examination of the Frustration–Aggression Hypothesis*. New York: Atherton.

Geen, R.G. and O'Neal, E.C. (1976). *Perspectives on Aggression*. New York: Academic Press.

Geertz, C. (1972). Deep play: Notes on Balinese cockfight. In C. Geertz (ed.), *Interpretation of Cultures*. New York: Basic Books: 1–37.

Gerber, B. and Young, K. (2011). Of horses and humans: Public discourses on animal rights and social justice in Canada. Paper presented at the Pacific Sociological Association, Seattle, 10–13 March.

Gibson, O. (2011). Andy Gray sacked by Sky for 'unacceptable and offensive behaviour.' *The Guardian* online, 25 January. Internet source: (http://www.guardian.co.uk/football/2011/jan/25/andy-gray-sacked-sky).

Gilbert, B. and Twyman, L. (1983). Violence: Out of hand in the stands. *Sports Illustrated*, 31 January: 62–74.

Gillett, J., White, P. and Young, K. (1996). The Prime Minister of Saturday night: Don Cherry, the CBC, and the cultural production of intolerance. In H. Holmes and D. Taras (eds), *Seeing Ourselves in Canada: Media Power and Policy* (2nd edition). Toronto: Harcourt Brace & Company Canada: 59–72.

Giulianotti, R. (1993). Soccer casuals as cultural intermediaries. In S. Redhead (ed.), *The Passion and the Fashion: Football Fandom in the New Europe*. Aldershot: Avebury: 153–205.

Giulianotti, R. (1994). Taking liberties: Hibs casuals and Scottish law. In R. Giulianotti, N. Bonney and M. Hepworth (eds), *Football, Violence and Social Identity*. London: Routledge: 229–261.

Giulianotti, R. (1995). Football and the politics of carnival: An ethnographic study of Scottish fans in Sweden. *International Review for the Sociology of Sport*, 30, 2: 191–217.

Giulianotti, R. (1999). *Football: A Sociology of the Global Game*. Cambridge: Polity.

Giulianotti, R., Bonney, N. and Hepworth, M. (Eds) (1994). *Football, Violence and Social Identity*. London: Routledge.

Giulianotti, R. and Williams, J. (1994). *Games without Frontiers: Football, Identity and Modernity*. Aldershot: Arena.

Glendinning, M. (2001). Sport surveys security risk. *SportBusiness International*, December: 25.

Goffman, E. (1959). *The Presentation of Self in Everyday Life*. Garden City, NY: Doubleday–Anchor.

Goffman, E. (1963). *Stigma*. Englewood Cliffs, NJ: Prentice Hall.

Goffman, E. (1974). *Frame Analysis*. Cambridge, MA: Harvard University Press.

Goldman, B. and Klatz, R. (1992). *Death in the Locker Room II: Drugs and Sport*. Chicago: Elite Sports Medicine Inc.

Goldstein, J. (1986). The nature of human aggression. In J. Goldstein (ed.), *Aggression and Crimes of Violence*. New York: Oxford University Press: 3–29.

Goldstein, J.H. (1989). Sports violence. In D.S. Eitzen (ed.), *Sport in Contemporary Society: An Anthology*. New York: St. Martin's Press.

Goldstein, J.H. and Arms, R.L. (1971). Effects of observing athletic contests on hostility. *Sociometry*, 34, 1: 83–90.

Gonzales, L. (2003). *Deep Survival: Who Lives, Who Dies, and Why*. New York: W.W. Norton and Company.

Goodger, J. and Goodger, B. (1989). Excitement and representation: Toward a sociological explanation of the significance of sport in modern society. *Quest*, 41: 257–272.

Goranson, R. E. (1982). The impact of television hockey violence. *LaMarsh Research Program Reports on Violence and Conflict Resolution*. Toronto: York University Press.

Gordon, D.R. and Ibson, L. (1977). Content analysis of the news media, radio. *Report of the Royal Commission on Violence in the Communication Industry*. Toronto: Ontario Government Bookstore.

Gramling, S. (2001). The FHM definitive guide to football fanatics. *FHM Magazine*, September: 140–148.

Grayson, E. (1988). *Sport and the Law*. London: Butterworths.

Green, L. (1984). *Sportswit*. New York: Harper and Row.

Greenberg, P.S. (1977). Wild in the stands. *New Times*, 9, 11 November: 24–63.

Guschwan, M. (2006). Riot in the curve: Soccer fans in twenty-first century Italy. *Soccer and Society*, 7, 2: 250–266.

Guttmann, A. (1986). *Sports Spectators*. New York: Columbia University Press.

Habib, D.G., Kim, A. and Mravic, M. (2001). Cruel and unusual. *Sports Illustrated*, 12 February: 23.

Hack, D. (2007). Tragedies that speak to a larger issue. *Sports Illustrated*, 31 December: 47.

Hagan, J. (1991). *The Disreputable Pleasures: Crime and Deviance in Canada*. Toronto: McGraw-Hill Ryerson.

Halbert, C. (1997). Tough enough and woman enough: Stereotypes, discrimination and impression management among women professional boxers. *Journal of Sport and Social Issues*, 21, 1: 7–37.

Hall, A., Nichols, W., Moynahan, P. and Taylor, J. (2007). *Media Relations in Sport* (2nd edition). Morgantown, WV: Fitness Information Technology.

Hall, S. (1978). The treatment of football hooliganism in the press. In R. Ingham (Ed.), *Football Hooliganism: The Wider Context*. London: Inter-Action Inprint: 15-37

Hall, S., Critcher, C., Jefferson, T., Clarke, J. and Roberts, B. (1978). *Policing the Crisis: Mugging, the State, and Law and Order*. London: Macmillan.

Hall, V. (2009). Football's forgotten warrior. *Calgary Herald*, 26 November: B1.

Hall, V. (2011). Day of vindication finally arrives for female ski jumpers. *Calgary Herald*, 7 April: F2.

Hallinan, C.J., Bruce, T. and Coram S. (1999). Up front and beyond the centre line: Australian Aborigines in elite Australian Rules football. *International Review for the Sociology of Sport*, 34, 4: 369–383.

Hallinan, C. and Judd B. (2007). 'Blackfellas' basketball: Aboriginal identity and Anglo-Australian race relations in regional basketball. *Sociology of Sport Journal*, 24: 421–436.

Hans, V.P. and Lofquist, W.S. (1992). Jurors' judgments of business liability in tort cases: Implications for the litigation explosion debate. *Law & Society Review*, 26, 1: 85–112.

Hanstad, D.V., Smith A. and Waddington, I. (2008). The establishment of World Anti-Doping Agency: A study of the management of organizational culture an unplanned outcomes. *International Review for the Sociology of Sport*, 43: 228–249.

Hardman, A.E. and Stensel, D.J. (2003). *Physical Activity and Health*. London: Routledge.

Hargrove, T. (2006). Supersized in the NFL: Many ex-players dying young. Scripps Howard News Service, 31 January. Internet source: ⟨http://nflretirees.blogspot.com/2006/02/supersized-in-nfl-many-ex-players.html⟩.

Harries, M., Williams, C., Stanish, W. and Micheli, L. (Eds) (1996). *Oxford Textbook of Sports Medicine*. New York: Oxford University Press.

Harrington, J.A. (1968). *Soccer Hooliganism*. Bristol: John Wright.

Harris, M. (2009). Mixed martial arts' popularity inspires fight club boom. *Calgary Herald*, 26 September: A3.

Harris, N. (2002). The first rugby hooligans? *The Observer*, 20 January: 10.

Hartill, M. (2010). The sexual subjection of boys in sport: Toward a theoretical account. In C. Brackenridge and D. Rhind (eds), *Elite Child Athlete Welfare: International Perspectives*. London: Brunel University Press: 85–92.

Hartley, J. (1982). *Understanding News*. London: Methuen.

Hawkins, R.D. and Fuller, C.W. (1998). A preliminary assessment of professional footballers' awareness of injury prevention strategies. *British Journal of Sports Medicine*, 32, 2: 140–143.

Hawkins, R.D. and Fuller, C.W. (1999). A prospective epidemiological study of injuries in four English professional clubs. *British Journal of Sports Medicine*, 33: 196–203.

Hearn, J. (1992). *Men in the Public Eye: The Construction and Deconstruction of Public Men and Public Patriarchies*. New York: Routledge.

Hechter, W. (1976/1977). Criminal law and violence in sports. *Criminal Law Quarterly*, 19: 425–453.

Hennessy, D.A. and Schwartz, S. (2007). Personal predictors of spectator aggression at little league baseball games. *Violence and Victims*, 22, 2: 205–215.

Herbert, T. (1994). Setting the tone: Sportsmanship in intercollegiate athletics. Paper presented at conference on 'Sports Violence: Issues for Law Enforcement,' University of Illinois, Chicago, 28–30 March.

Herzog, H. and Golden, L. (2009). Moral emotions and social activism: The case of animal rights. *Journal of Social Issues*, 65, 3: 485–498.

Heywood, L. and Dworkin, S. (2003). *Built to Win: The Female Athlete as Cultural Icon*. Minneapolis: University of Minnesota Press.

Hobbes, T. (1957). *Leviathan*. New York: Oxford University Press.

Hoch, P. (1979). *White Hero, Black Beast: Racism, Sexism, and the Mask of Masculinity*. London: Pluto Press.

Holmes, D. and Frey, J. (1990). The kind of people who skydive. *Parachutist*, February: 28–32.

Home Office (2008). *Statistics on Football-related Arrests and Banning Orders, Season 2007–8*. London: HMSO.

Hornby, N. (1992). *Fever Pitch*. London: Victor Gollancz.

Horrow, R. (1980). *Sports Violence: The Interaction between Private Lawmaking and the Criminal Law*. Arlington, VA: Carrollton Press.

Horrow, R. (1982). Violence in professional sport: Is it part of the game? *Journal of Legislation*, 9, 1: 1–15.

Houlihan, B. (1991). The development of policy for football hooliganism. In B. Houlihan (ed.), *The Government and Politics of Sport*. London: Routledge: 174–200.

House, P. (1992). Fanning flames of hatred. *The European*, 10–13 December: 30.

Howe, P.D. (2001). An ethnography of pain and injury in professional rugby union: The case of Pontypridd RFC. *International Review for the Sociology of Sport*, 36, 3: 289–303.

Howe, P.D. (2004). *Sport, Professionalism and Pain: Ethnographies of Injury and Risk*. London: Routledge.

Howe, P.D. (2008). *The Cultural Politics of the Paralympic Movement: Through the Anthropological Lens*. London: Routledge.

Hoyle, J. and White, P. (1999). Sport, women and disability: Some exploratory notes. In P. White and K. Young, *Sport and Gender in Canada*. Toronto: Oxford University Press: 254–268.

Hrudey, K. (2005). Playing hurt – A fact of NHL life. *Calgary Herald*, 23 October: D2.

Hughes, R. and Coakley, J. (1991). Positive deviance among athletes: The implications of overconformity to the sport ethic. *Sociology of Sport Journal*, 8, 4: 307–325.

Huizenga, R. (1994). *You're Ok, It's Just a Bruise: A Doctor's Sideline Secrets about Pro Football's Most Outrageous Team*. New York: St Martin's Griffin.

Hume, P. and Marshall, S. (1994). Sports injuries in New Zealand: Exploratory analyses. *New Zealand Journal of Sports Medicine*, 22: 18–22.

Hunt, J. (1996). Diving the wreck: Risk and injury in the sport of scuba diving. *Psychoanalytic Quarterly*, 65, 3: 591–621.

Hylton, K. (2010). How a turn to critical race theory can contribute to our understanding of 'race,' racism and anti-racism in sport. *International Review for the Sociology of Sport*, 45, 3: 335–354.

Hyman, M. (2009). *Until it Hurts: America's Obsession with Youth Sports and How it Harms our Kids*. Boston: Beacon Press.

Hyndman, J. (1996). The growing athlete. In M. Harries, C. Williams, W. Stanish and L. Micheli (eds), *Oxford Textbook of Sports Medicine*. New York: Oxford University Press.

Jackson, D. (1990). *Unmasking Masculinity: A Critical Autobiography*. London: Unwin Hyman.

The Jockey Club (2010). *Equine Injury Database Statistic Released by the Jockey Club*, 6 February. Internet source: (http://www.thejockeyclub.com/).

Johns, D. (1998). Fasting and feasting: Paradoxes of the sport ethic. *Sociology of Sport Journal*, 15, 1: 41–63.

Johns, D. and Johns, J.S. (2000). An analysis for the discursive practice of high performance sport. *International Review for the Sociology of Sport*, 35, 2: 219–234.

Johnson, J. and Holman, M. (Eds) (2004). *Making the Team: Inside the World of Sport Initiations and Hazing*. Toronto: Canadian Scholars Press.

Johnson, W.O. (1993). The agony of victory. *Sports Illustrated*, 5 July: 30–37.

Joukowsky, A. and Rothstein, L. (2002). *Raising the Bar: New Horizons in Disability Sports*. New York: Umbrage.

Kahn, J. and Barboza, D. (2007). China passes a sweeping labor law. *New York Times*, 30 June. Internet source: (http://www.nytimes.com/2007/06/30/business/worldbusiness/30chlabor.html).

Kane, L. and Sinoski, K. (2011). Anarchists, criminals blamed for cup riot. *Calgary Herald*, 17 June: A1–A7.

Kane, M.J. and Disch, L.J. (1993). Sexual violence and the reproduction of male power in the locker room: 'The Lisa Olson incident.' *Sociology of Sport Journal*, 10, 4: 331–352.

Karmen, A. (2004). The rediscovery of crime victims and the rise of victimology. In A. Karmen (ed.), *Crime Victims: An Introduction to Victimology*. Toronto: Thomson/Wadsworth: 1–41.

Katz, S. (1955). Strange forces behind the Richard hockey riot. *Maclean's*, 17 September: 11–110.

Keeler, L.A. (2007). The difference in sport aggression, life aggression and life assertion among adult male and female collision, contact and non-contact sport athletes. *Journal of Sport Behavior*, 30, 1: 57–77.

Keen, D. (1986). Exterminate them. *New Statesman*, 31 January: 16.

Kelley, W.D. (1994). Developing security plans for the 1996 Olympics. Paper presented at conference on 'Sports Violence: Issues for Law Enforcement,' University of Illinois, Chicago, 28–30 March.

Kennedy, K. and Bechtel, M. (2003). Welcome to rush week. *Sports Illustrated*, 13 October, 99, 14: 22–23.

Kennedy, K. and McEntegart, P. (2003). For the record. *Sports Illustrated*, 17 February: 22.

Kennedy, K. and O'Brien, R. (1997). Court of public opinion. *Sports Illustrated*, 2 June: 20.

Kerr, J.H. (2004). *Rethinking Violence and Aggression in Sport*. London: Routledge.

Kerr, J.H. and de Kock, H. (2002). Aggression, violence and the death of a Dutch soccer hooligan: A reversal theory explanation. *Aggressive Behaviour*, 28: 1–10.

Kidd, B. (1987). Sports and masculinity. In M. Kaufman (ed.), *Beyond Patriarchy Essays by Men on Pleasure, Power and Change*. Toronto: Oxford University Press: 250–266.

Kidd, B. and Donnelly, P. (2000). Human rights in sports. *International Review for the Sociology of Sport*, 35, 2: 131–148.

Kim, A., Kennedy, K. and Habib, D.G. (2002). Blood sport. *Sports Illustrated*, 2 April, 1: 30.

King, A. (1997). The lads: Masculinity and the new consumption of football. *Sociology*, 31, 2: 329–346.

King, A. (1998). *The End of the Terraces: The Transformation of English Football in the 1990s*. London: Leicester University Press.

King, J. (1996). *The Football Factory*. London: Vintage.

King, C. (2000). Trial by fire: A study of initiation practices in English sport. Unpublished MSc thesis. School of Sport and Exercise Sciences, Loughborough University, UK.

Kirby, S. and Fusco, C. (1998). 'Are your kids safe?' Media representations of sexual abuse in sport. Paper presented at the International Conference of the Leisure Studies Association, Leeds, 16–20 July.

Kirby, S. and Greaves L. (1996). Athletes admit abuse. *Herizons*, 10, 4: 12–20.

Kirby, S., Greaves, L. and Hankivsky, O. (2000). *The Dome of Silence: Sexual Harassment and Abuse in Sport*. Halifax, NS: Fernwood Publishing.

Kirkby, R. (1995). Psychological factors in sport injuries. In T. Morris and J. Summers (eds), *Sport Psychology: Theory, Applications and Issues*. New York: John Wiley: 456–473.

Kirkland, G. and Lawrence, G. (1986). *Dancing on My Grave*. New York: Doubleday.

Kodas, M. (2008). *High Crimes: The Fate of Everest in an Age of Greed*. New York: Harper Collins.

Kotarba, J.A. (1983). *Chronic Pain: Its Social Dimensions*. Beverly Hills, CA: Sage.

Krakauer, J. (1997). *Into Thin Air: A Personal Account of the Mount Everest Disaster*. New York: Anchor Books.

Kreager, D.A. (2007). Unnecessary roughness? School sports, peer networks and male adolescence violence. *American Sociological Review*, 72, 5: 705–772.

Kuper, S. (1997). *Football against the Enemy*. London: Phoenix Books.

Kwak, S. (2006). Timeline of trouble. *Sports Illustrated*, 26 June: 78–79.

Lang, Sir J. (1969). *Report of the Working Party on Crowd Behaviour at Football Matches*. London: HMSO.

Larson, M., Pearl, A.J., Jaffet, R. and Rudowsky, A. (1996). Soccer. In D.J. Caine, C.G. Caine and K.J. Lindner (eds), *Epidemiology of Sports Injuries*. Champaign, IL: Human Kinetics: 387–398.

Lawler, J. (2002). *Punch! Why Women Participate in Violent Sports*. Terre Haute, IN: Wish Publishing.

Layder, D. (1986). Social reality as figuration: A critique of Elias's conception of sociological analysis. *Sociology*, 20: 367–386.

Lenskyj, H. (1990). Power and play: Gender and sexuality issues in sport and physical activity. *International Review for the Sociology of Sport*, 25, 3: 235–246.

Lenskyj, H. (1992). Unsafe at home base: Womens' experiences of sexual harassment in university sport and physical education. *Women's Sport and Physical Activity Journal*, 1, 1: 19–33.

Lenskyj, H. (2000). *Inside the Olympic Industry: Power, Politics and Activism*. New York: SUNY Press.

Leonard, W. (1993). *A Sociological Perspective of Sport*. New York: Macmillan.

Leonard, W. (1998). *A Sociological Perspective of Sport* (5th edition). Boston: Allyn and Bacon.

Lever, J. (1983). *Soccer Madness*. Chicago: University of Chicago Press.

Levitt, C. and Shaffir, W. (1987). *The Riot at Christie Pits*. Toronto: Lester and Orpen Dennys.

Levy, A. (2005). *Female Chauvinist Pigs: Women and the Rise of Raunch Culture*. New York: Free Press.

Lewis, J.M. (1982). Fan violence: An American social problem. *Research in Social Problems and Public Policy*, 12: 175–206.

Listiak, A. (1981). 'Legitimate deviance' and social class: Bar behavior during Grey Cup week. In M. Hart and S. Birrell (eds), *Sport in the Sociocultural Process*. Dubuque, IO: Wm. C. Brown: 532–563.

Llanos, M. (2006). Muted environmental concerns at Olympics. MSNBC online, 24 February. Internet source: ⟨http://www.msnbc.msn.com/id/9993547/⟩.

Llosa, L.F. and Wertheim, L.J. (2008). Sins of a father, *Sports Illustrated*, 21 January, 108: 30–34.

Lorenz, K. (1966). *On Aggression*. London: Routledge.

Lowe, M.R. (1998). *Women of Steel: Female Body Builders and the Struggle for Self-definition*. New York: New York University Press.

Lowrey, B. (2011). Alleged cockfighting ring busted. *North County Times*, 20 February. Internet source: ⟨http://www.nctimes.com/news/local/sdcounty/article_9dcf8f30-023f-5561-b22f-fb21364b1e57.html⟩.

Lubell, A. (1989). Questioning the athlete's right to sue. *The Physician and Sports Medicine*, 17, 3: 240–244.

Lupton, D. (1995). *The Imperative of Health: Public Health and the Regulated Body*. London: Sage.

Lyng, S. (1990). Edgework: A social psychological analysis of voluntary risk taking. *American Journal of Sociology*, 95, 4: 851–886.

McCallum, J. (2003). The dark side of a star. *Sports Illustrated*, 28 July: 42–45.

McCurry, J. (2011). Sumo wrestling hit by match-fixing scandal. *The Guardian*, 2 February.

McCutcheon, T., Curtis, J. and White, P. (1997). The socioeconomic distribution of sport injuries: Multivariate analyses using Canadian national data. *Sociology of Sport Journal*, 14, 1: 57–72.

MacDonald, G.J. (2004). After the big game why is there a riot going on? *USA Today*, 1 November. Internet source: ⟨http://www.usatoday.com/news/health/2004-11-01-riot_x.htm⟩.

McEwen, K. and Young, K (2011). Ballet and pain: Reflections on a risk-dance culture. *Qualitative Research in Sport, Exercise and Health* (forthcoming).

McKay, J. (1993). 'Marked men' and 'wanton women': The politics of naming sexual 'deviance' in sport. *The Journal of Men's Studies*, 2, 1: 69–87.

McKay, J., Messner, M. and Sabo, D. (Eds) (2000). *Masculinities, Gender Relations and Sport*. Thousand Oaks, CA: Sage.

McKay, J. and Middlemiss, I. (1995). 'Mate against mate, state against state': A case study of media constructions of hegemonic masculinity in Australian sport. *Masculinities*, 3, 3: 28–45.

McLaughlin, M. (1999). Salt Lake City bribery scandal: The buying of the Olympic games. *World Socialist* online. Internet source: (http://wsws.org/articles/1999/jan1999/olym-j13.shtml).

McNamee, M. (2004). Pain and trust in sport. Paper presented at workshop on 'Pain and Injury in Sport: Social and Ethical Perspectives.' Oslo, 12–13 February.

McPherson, B., Curtis, J. and Loy, J. (Eds) (1989). *The Social Significance of Sport: An Introduction to the Sociology of Sport*. Champaign, IL: Human Kinetics.

Maguire, J. (1999). *Global Sport: Identities, Societies, Civilizations*. Cambridge: Polity Press.

Maguire, J., Jarvie, G., Mansfield, L. and Bradley, J. (2002). *Sport Worlds: A Sociological Perspective*. Windsor, ON: Human Kinetics.

Mahan III, J.E. and McDaniel, S.R. (2006). The new online arena: Sport, marketing, and media converge in cyberspace. In A.A. Raney and J. Bryant (eds), *Handbook of Sports and Media*. Mahwah, NJ: Lawrence Erlbaum Associates, Publishers: 409–431.

Maisel, I., Dohrmann, G. and Yaeger, D. (2001). Open secret. *Sports Illustrated*, 11 June: 50–54.

Malcolm, D. (2009). Medical uncertainty and clinician–athlete relations: The management of concussion injuries in rugby union. *Sociology of Sport Journal*, 26: 191–210.

Malcolm, D. and Sheard, K. (2002). 'Pain in the assets': The effects of commercialization and professionalization on the management of injury in English rugby union. *Sociology of Sport Journal*, 19, 2: 149–169.

Malešević, S. (2010). *The Sociology of War and Violence*. New York: Cambridge University Press.

Manning, F. (1983). *The Celebration of Society*. Bowling Green, KY: Bowling Green State University Press.

Mansfield, L. (2009). Fitness cultures and environmental (in)justice. *International Review for the Sociology of Sport*, 44, 4: 345–362.

Mark, M., Bryant, F.B. and Lehman, D.R. (1983). Perceived injustice and sports violence. In J.H. Goldstein (ed.), *Sports Violence*. New York: Springer Verlag: 83–109.

Markula, P. and Pringle, R. (2006). *Foucault, Sport, and Exercise: Power, Knowledge and Transforming the Self*. New York: Routledge.

Marsh, P., Fox, K., Carnibella, G., McCann, J. and Marsh, J. (1996) *Football Violence in Europe*. London: The Amsterdam Group.

Marsh, P., Rosser, E. and Harré, R. (1978). *The Rules of Disorder*. London: Routledge and Kegan Paul.

Martin's Annual Criminal Code [of Canada] (2011). Aurora: Canada Law Book.

Massao, P.B. and Fasting K. (2010). Race and racism: Experiences of black Norwegian athletes. *International Review for the Sociology of Sport*, 45, 2: 147–162.

Marx, K. (1867/1967). *Capital: A Critique of Political Economy*. Vol. 1. New York: International Publishers.

May, R. (1972). *Power and Innocence: A Search for Causes of Violence*. New York: W.W. Norton.

Meggyesy, D. (1971). *Out of their League*. Berkeley, CA: Ramparts Press.

Melnick, M. (1989). The sports fan: A teaching guide and bibliography. *Sociology of Sport Journal*, 6, 2: 167–175.

Melnick, M. (1992). Male athletes and sexual assault. *Journal of Physical Education, Recreation and Dance*, May/June: 32–35.

Menard, D. (1996). The ageing athlete. In M. Harries, C. Williams., W. Stanish and L. Micheli (eds), *Oxford Textbook of Sports Medicine*. New York: Oxford University Press: 596–620.

Mennell, S. (2006). Civilizing process. *Theory Culture and Society*, 23: 429–431.

Mennesson, C. (2000). 'Hard' women and 'soft' women: The social construction of identities among female boxers. *International Review for the Sociology of Sport*, 35, 1: 21–35.

Merz, M. (2000). *Bruising: A Journey through Gender*. Sydney: Picador.

Messner, M. (1990). When bodies are weapons: Masculinity and violence in sport. *International Review for the Sociology of Sport*, 25, 3: 203–219.

Messner, M. (1992). *Power at Play: Sports and the Problem of Masculinity*. Boston: Beacon.

Messner, M. (2002). *Taking the Field: Women, Men, and Sports*. Minneapolis: University of Minneapolis Press.

Messner, M. and Sabo, D. (Eds) (1990). *Sport, Men, and the Gender Order: Critical Feminist Perspectives*. Champaign, IL: Human Kinetics.

Messner, M. and Sabo, D. (1994). *Sex, Violence, and Power in Sports: Rethinking Masculinity*. Freedom, CA: The Crossing Press.

Mewett, P. and Toffoletti, K. (2008). Rouge men and predatory women: Female fans' perceptions of Australian footballers' sexual conduct. *International Review of the Sociology of Sport*, 43: 165–180.

Mills, C. Wright. (1940). Situated actions and vocabularies of motive. *American Sociological Review*, 5: 904–913.

Mills, C. Wright (1959). *The Sociological Imagination*. New York: Oxford University Press.

Miller, M.A., Croft, L.B., Belanger, A.R., Romero-Corral, A., Somers, V.K., Roberts, A.J. and Goldman, M.E. (2008). Prevalence of metabolic syndrome in retired National Football League players. *The American Journal of Cardiology*, 1281–1284.

Miller, N.E. (1941). The Frustration Aggression Hypothesis. *Psychological Review*, 48, 4: 337–342.

Mintah, J., Huddleston, S. and Doody, S.G. (1999). Justification of aggressive behaviors in contact and semi-contact sports. *Journal of Applied Psychology*, 29: 597–605.

Moffat, K.H. (2002). Book review of David Garland: *The Culture of Control: Crime and Social Order in Contemporary Society*. *Contemporary Sociology*, 31, 5: 597–599.

Monaghan, L. (2001). *Bodybuilding, Drugs and Risk*. London: Routledge.

Moorhouse, H. (2000). Book review of G. Armstrong: *Football Hooligans: Knowing the Score* (1998). *Urban Studies*, 37, 8: 1463–1464.

Moran, R. (2000). Racism in football: A victim's perspective. *Soccer and Society*, 1, 1: 190–200.

Moriarty, D., Holman, M., Brown, R. and Moriarty, M. (1994). *Canadian/American Sport, Fitness and the Law*. Toronto: Canadian Scholars' Press Inc.

Moriarty, R. and McCabe A. (1977). Studies of television and youth sports. *Report of the Royal Commission on Violence in the Communication Industry*. Toronto: Ontario Government Bookstore.

Morris, D. (1967). *The Naked Ape*. New York: McGraw Hill.

Morris, D.B. (1991). *The Culture of Pain*. Los Angeles: University of California Press.

Morse, M. (1983). Sport on television: Replay and display. In E.A. Kaplan (ed.), *Regarding Television: Critical Approaches*. Los Angeles: American Film Institute: 44–66.

Mottl, R. (1980). Paper presented before the US Congressional Subcommittee on Crime, 30 September.

Mouzelis, N. (1993). On figurational sociology. *Theory and Culture Society*, 10: 239–253.

Mueller, F., Cantu, R. and Van Camp, S. (1996). *Catastrophic Injuries in High School and College Sports*. Champaign, IL: Human Kinetics.

Muir, K.B. and Seitz, T. (2004). Machismo, misogyny, and homophobia in a male athletic subculture: A participant-observation study of deviant rituals in collegiate rugby. *Deviant Behaviour*, 25: 303–327.

Müller, F., de Roode, L. and van Zoonen, L. (2007). Accidental racists: Experiences and contradictions of racism in local Amsterdam soccer fan culture. *Soccer and Society*, 8, 2/3, 336–351.

Müller, F., van Zoonen, L. and de Roode, L. (2008). We can't 'Just do it' alone! An analysis of Nike's (potential) contributions to anti-racism in soccer. *Media Culture Society*, 30, 1: 23–39.

Mullins, A. (2010). North America: Home to the world's deadliest racetracks. *PETA – The PETA Files*, 10 February. Internet source: ⟨http://www.peta.org⟩.

Munson, L., Chadiha, J., Kennedy, K. and Bechtel, M. (2003). End of the line? *Sports Illustrated*, 7 July: 22.

Muraskin, R. and Domash, S.F. (2007). *Crime and the Media – Headlines vs. Reality*. Upper Saddle River, NJ: Pearson Education.

Murphy, P., Dunning, E. and Williams, J. (1988). Soccer crowd disorder and the press: Processes of amplification and de-amplification in historical perspective. *Theory, Culture and Society*, 5, 3: 645–693.

Murphy, P. and Williams, J. (1979). *Football Hooliganism: An Illusion of Violence*. Leicester: University of Leicester Press.

Murphy, P., Williams, J. and Dunning, E. (1990). *Football on Trial: Spectator Violence and Development in the Football World*. London: Routledge.

Murray, B. (1984). *The Old Firm: Sectarianism, Sport and Society in Scotland*. Edinburgh: John Donald.

Murray, B. (1988). *Glasgow Giants: A Hundred Years of the Old Firm*. London: Mainstream.

Nack, W. (2000). Hell on wheels. *Sports Illustrated*, 10 January: 72–82.

Nack, W. and Munson, L. (1995a). Out of control. *Sports Illustrated*, 24 July: 86–93.

Nack, W. and Munson, L. (1995b). Sports' dirty secret. *Sports Illustrated*, 31 July: 62–72.

Nack, W. and Yaeger, D. (1999). Every parent's nightmare. *Sports Illustrated*, 13 September: 40–51.

Nash, R.P. and Auerhahn, K. (1998). Alcohol, drugs, and violence. *Annual Review of Sociology*, 24: 291–311.

Nelson, G. (1996). *Left Foot Forward: A Year in the Life of a Journeyman Footballer*. London: Headline.

Nelson, S. (1994). Celebration riots: A retrospective. Paper presented at conference on 'Sports Violence: Issues for Law Enforcement,' University of Illinois, Chicago, 28–30 March.

Newhall, K.E. and Buzuvis, E.E. (2008). (e)Racing Jennifer Harris: Sexuality and race, law and discourse in Harris v. Portland. *Journal of Sport and Social Issues*, 32, 4: 345–368.

Nixon, H.L. II (1992). A social network analysis of influences on athletes to play with pain and injury. *Journal of Sport and Social Issues*, 16, 2: 127–135.

Nixon, H.L. II (1993). Accepting the risks of pain and injury in sport: Mediated cultural influences on playing hurt. *Sociology of Sport Journal*, 10, 2: 183–196.

Nixon, H.L. II (1994a). Coaches' views of risk, pain, and injury in sport with special reference to gender differences. *Sociology of Sport Journal*, 11, 1: 79–87.

Nixon, H.L. II (1994b). Social pressure, social support, and help seeking for pain and injuries in college sports networks. *Journal of Sport and Social Issues*, 18, 4: 340–355.

Nixon, H.L. II (1996). The relationship of friendship networks, sports experiences, and gender to expressed pain thresholds. *Sociology of Sport Journal*, 13, 1: 78–87.

Nixon, H.L. II (1997). Gender, sport, and aggressive behaviour outside sport. *Journal of Sport and Social Issues*, 21, 4: 379–391.

Nixon H.L. II (2000). Sport and disability. In J. Coakley and E. Dunning (eds) *Handbook of Sports Studies*. London: Sage: 422–438.

Noden, M. (1994). Dying to win. *Sports Illustrated*, 8 August: 52–60.

Norris, C. (2007). The intensification and bifurcation of surveillance in British criminal justice policy. *European Journal on Criminal Policy and Research*, 13, 1/2: 130–158.

O'Brien, R. and McCallum, J. (1993). Himalayan trash heap. *Sports Illustrated*, 29 November: 12.

Okada, C. and Young, K. (2011). Sport and social development: Promise and caution from an incipient Cambodian football league. *International Review for the Sociology of Sport* (forthcoming).

Olsen, M. (2003). *Women Who Risk: Profiles of Women in Extreme Sports*. New York: Hatherleigh Press.

Olson, L. (2003). For the love of the game: Obsessive sports groupies are predators with a dream. *Calgary Herald*, 13 September.

O'Malley, J. (1994). Preparations for the 1994 World Cup games. Paper presented at conference on 'Sports Violence: Issues for Law Enforcement,' University of Illinois, Chicago, 28–30 March.

Oppliger, R.A., Utter, A.C., Scott, J.R., Dick, R.W. and Klossner, D. (2006). NCAA rule change improves weight loss among national championship wrestlers. *Medicine and Science in Sport and Exercise*, 38: 963–970.

Owen, O. (2001). Ravens face a walk on the wild side. *The Observer*, 14 January: 16.

Owens, A.M. (2004). Triumph and tragedy. *Calgary Herald*, 30 August: A1, A5.

Oxley, B. and Kramer, L. (1986). Chuck-wagon controversy. CBC Digital Archives, 10 July. Internet source: 〈http://archives.cbc.ca/version_print.asp?page=1&IDLan=1&IDClip=4573&IDDossier=0&IDCatPa=263〉.

Pappas, N., McKenry, P.C. and Catlett, B.S. (2004). Athlete aggression on the rink and off the ice. *Men and Masculinities*, 6, 3: 291–312.

Parrish, W. (1983). Rating of the NHL's best fighters. *Toronto Star*, 25 February: B1–3.

Parry, J. (2004). Infliction of pain in sport – Ethical perspectives. Paper presented at workshop on 'Pain and Injury in Sport: Social and Ethical Perspectives.' Oslo, 12–13 February.

Patrick, K. (2006). Blood on the ice in women's hockey. *National Post*, 1 December: A3.

Pike, E. (1997). Self, stigma, and significant others: Some preliminary thoughts on the social construction of sport-related injury. In P. de Nardis, A. Mussino and N. Porro (eds), *Sport: Social Problems and Social Movements*. Rome: Edizioni Seam: 249–259.

Pike, E. (2000). Illness, injury and sporting identity: A case study of women's rowing. Unpublished doctoral dissertation, Loughborough University, UK.

Pike, E. (2004). Risk, pain and injury: 'A natural thing in rowing'? In K. Young (ed.), *Sporting Bodies, Damaged Selves: Sociological Studies of Sports-related Injury*. Oxford: Elsevier Press: 151–162

Pirinen, R. (1997). Catching up with men? Finnish newspaper coverage of women's entry into traditionally male sports. *International Review for the Sociology of Sport*, 32, 3: 239–249.

Pemberton, K. (2011). BC dog slaughter prompts stiffer law. *Calgary Herald*, 6 April: A3.

Petryszak, N. (1977). The bio-sociology of joy in violence. *Review of Sport and Leisure*, 2: 1–16.

Pietersen, B. and Kristensen, B.H. (1988). *An Empirical Survey of Danish Hooligans during the European Championships '88*. Copenhagen: The Danish State Institute of Physical Education. CHEK.

Popplewell, O. Lord Justice (Chairman) (1985). *Committee of Inquiry into Crowd Safety and Control at Sports Grounds*. London: HMSO.

Pirks, M. (2010). Does frustration lead to violence? Evidence from the Swedish hooligan scene. *Kyklos*, 63, 4: 450–460.

Price, S.L., Kennedy, K., Bechtel, M. and Cannella, S. (2008). The big red machine. *Sports Illustrated*, 3 March: 14–15.

Pringle, R. (2001). Competing discourses: Narratives of a fragmented self, manliness and rugby union. *International Review for the Sociology of Sport*, 36, 4: 426–439.

Pringle, R. (2004). A social-history of the articulations between rugby union and masculinities within Aotearoa/New Zealand. *New Zealand Sociology*, 19, 1: 102–128.

Pringle, R. and Markula P. (2005). No pain is sane after all: A Foucauldian analysis of masculinities and men's experiences in rugby. *Sociology of Sport Journal*, 22: 472–497.

Pronger, B. (1990). *The Arena of Masculinity: Sports, Homosexuality, and the Meaning of Sex*. London: GMP Publishers Ltd.

R. v. Bertuzzi [2004] BCPC 472, B.C.J. No. 2692 (B.C. Prov. Ct.).

R. v. Ciccarelli [1989] O.J. No. 2388, 54 C.C.C. (3d) 121 (Ont. Dist. Ct.).

R. v. Green [1970] O.J. No. 1699, [1971] 1 O.R. 591 (Ont. Prov. Ct.).

R. v. McSorley [2000] BCPC 117, B.C.J. No. 1994 (B.C. Prov. Ct.).

R. v. Maki [1970] O.J. No. 1607, 3 O.R. 780 (Ont. Prov. Ct.).

R. v. Starratt [1971] O.J. No. 1762, [1972] 1 O.R. 227 (Ont. C.A.).

R. v. Watson [1975] O.J. No. 2681, 26 C.C.C. (2d) 150 (Ont. Prov. Ct.).

R. v. Wildfong and Lang [1911] 17 C.C.C. 256, (Ont. County Ct.).

Rail, G. (1990). Physical contact in women's basketball: A first interpretation. *International Review for the Sociology of Sport*, 25, 4: 269–285.

Rail, G. (1992). Physical contact in women's basketball: A phenomenological construction and contextualization. *International Review for the Sociology of Sport*, 27, 1: 1–27.

Rail, G. and Bridel, W. (2007). Sport, sexuality, and the production of (resistant) bodies: De-/re-constructing the meanings of gay male marathon corporeality. *Sociology of Sport Journal*, 24, 2: 127–144.

Reasons, C. (1992). The criminal law and sports violence: Hockey crimes. Unpublished manuscript, University of British Columbia, Vancouver.

Redhead, S. (1996). *Post-fandom and the Millennial Blues: The Transformation of Soccer Culture*. London: Routledge.

Redhead, S. (2008). Firms, crews and soccer thugs: The slight return of the football hooligan. In M. Atkinson and K. Young (eds), *Tribal Play: Subcultural Journeys through Sport*. Bingley: Emerald: 67–82.

Rees, D. and Schnepel, K.T. (2009). College football games and crime. *Journal of Sports Economics*, 10: 68–86.

Reilly, R. (1994). Dealt a bad hand. *Sports Illustrated*, 30 May: 82–92.

Reilly, R. (2005). 200-dollar babies. *Sports Illustrated*, 2 May: 72.

Remnick, D. (1987). Still on the outside. *Sports Illustrated*, 5 October: 42–54.

Report of a Joint Sports Council/Social Science Research Council Panel (1978). *Public Disorder and Sporting Events*. London: Social Sciences Research Council.

Riseling, S. (1994). Law enforcement responds to sports violence. Paper presented at conference on 'Sports Violence: Issues for Law Enforcement,' University of Illinois, Chicago, 28–30 March.

Ritzer, G. (1992). *Sociological Theory* (3rd edition). New York: McGraw Hill.

Robidoux, M. (2001). *Men at Play: A Working Understanding of Professional Hockey*. Montreal: McGill-Queen's University Press.

Robins, D. (1984). *We Hate Humans*. Markham: Penguin.

Robinson, L. (1998). *Crossing the Line: Violence and Sexual Assault in Canada's National Sport.* Toronto: McClelland and Stewart.

Rock, M. (2003). Labour conditions in the export-oriented garment industry in Bangladesh. *Journal of South Asian Studies*, 26, 3: 391–407.

Roderick, M. (1998). The sociology of risk, pain and injury: A comment on the work of Howard Nixon II. *Sociology of Sport Journal*, 15: 64–79.

Roderick, M. (2006a). *The Work of Professional Football: A Labour of Love?* London: Routledge.

Roderick, M. (2006b). Adding insult to injury: Workplace injury in English professional football. *Sociology of Health and Illness*, 28, 1: 76–97.

Roderick, M., Waddington, I. and Parker, G. (2000). Playing hurt: Managing injuries in English professional football. *International Review for the Sociology of Sport*, 35, 2: 165–180.

Rojek, C. (1985). *Capitalism and Leisure Theory.* London: Tavistock.

Rose, N. and O'Malley, P. (2006). Governmentality. *Annual Review for Law and Social Sciences*, 2: 83–104.

Runfola, R. (1976). Violence in sports: Reflections of the violence in American society. *New York Times*, 11 January: 304–305.

Russell, G. (1979). Hero selection by Canadian ice hockey players: Skill or aggression? *Canadian Journal of Applied Sports Sciences*, 4: 309–313.

Russell, G. (2008). *Aggression in the Sports World: A Social Psychological Perspective.* Toronto: Oxford University Press.

Russell, G.W. and Drewry, B.R. (1976). Crowd size and competitive aspects of aggression in ice hockey: An archival study. *Human Relations*, 29, 8: 723–735.

Rutherford, J. (1992). *Men's Silences: Predicaments in Masculinity.* New York: Routledge.

Ryan, J. (1995). *Little Girls in Pretty Boxes: The Making and Breaking of Elite Gymnasts and Figure Skaters.* New York: Doubleday.

Sabo, D. (1986). Pigskin, patriarchy and pain. *Changing Men: Issues in Gender, Sex, and Politics*, 16 (Summer): 24–25.

Sabo, D. (1994). The body politics of sports injury: Culture, power and the pain principle. Paper presented at the National Athletic Trainers Association, Dallas, TX, 6 November.

Safai, P. (2001). Healing the body in the 'culture of risk,' pain and injury: Negotiations between clinicians and injured athletes in Canada's competitive intercollegiate sport. Unpublished MA thesis, University of Toronto, Canada.

Safai, P. (2004). Negotiating with risk: Exploring the role of the sports medicine clinician. In K. Young (ed.), *Sporting Bodies, Damaged Selves: Sociological Studies of Sports-related Injury.* Oxford: Elsevier Press: 269–286.

Sage, G. (1999). Justice do it! The Nike transnational advocacy network: Organization, collective actions, and outcomes. *Sociology of Sport Journal*, 16, 3: 206–233.

Salamone, J.J. (2001). Social control. In C.D. Bryant (ed.), *Encyclopedia of Criminology and Deviant Behavior.* Philadelphia: Brunner-Routledge: 360–363.

Savelsberg, J. (2002). Book review: *The Culture of Control: Crime and Social Order in Contemporary Society. Law and Social Inquiry*, 27, 3: 685–710.

Scalia, V. (2009). Just a few rouges? Football Ultras, clubs and politics in contemporary Italy. *International Review for the Sociology of Sport*, 22: 41–53.

Schwarz, A. (2001). *Stadia*, 9: 47–48.

Scraton, P., Jemphrey, I. and Coleman, I. (1995). *No Last Rights: The Denial of Justice and the Promotion of Myth in the Aftermath of the Hillsborough Disaster.* Liverpool: Alden Press.

Sekules, K. (2000). *The Boxer's Heart: Lessons from the Ring.* New York: Random House.

Selden, M.A., Helzberg, J.H., Waeckerle, J.F., Browne, J.E., Brewer, J.H., Monaco, M.E.,

Tang F. and O'Keefe, J.H. (2009). Cardiometabolic abnormalities in current National Football League players. *The American Journal of Cardiology*, 969–971.

Sellers, C.S., Cochcan, J.K. and Branch, K.A. (2005). Social learning theory and partner violence: A research note. *Deviant Behaviour*, 26: 379–395.

Shaw, G. (1972). *Meat on the Hoof*. New York: St Martin's.

Sheard, K. (1999). A stitch in time saves nine: Birdwatching, sport, and civilizing processes. *Sociology of Sport Journal*, 16: 181–205.

Shepherd, D.J., Lee, B. and Kerr, J.H. (2006). Reversal theory: A suggested way forward for an improved understanding of interpersonal relationship in sport. *Psychology of Sport and Exercise*, 7: 143–157.

Sheridan, A. (Trans). (1995). *Discipline and Punish: The Birth of the Prison*. New York: Vintage Books.

Shilling, C. (1993). *The Body and Social Theory*. London: Sage.

Simpson, J.C., Chalmers, D.J., Williams, T.M. and Williams, S.M. (1999). Evaluating tackling rugby injury: The pilot phase for monitoring injury. *Australian and New Zealand Journal of Public Health*, 23, 1: 86–89.

Singer, B. and Gordon, D.R. (1977). Content analysis of the news media: Newspapers and television. In J. LaMarsh, L.A. Beaulieu and S.A. Young (commissioners), *Report of the Royal Commission on Violence in the Communications Industry*. Vol. 5. Toronto, ON: Ontario Government Bookstore.

Sipes, R.G. (1973). War, sports and aggression: An empirical test of the two rival theories. *American Anthropologist*, 75: 64–86.

Sir Norman Chester Centre for Football Research (1984). *All Sit Down: A Report on the Coventry City All-seated Stadium 1982/3*. Leicester: Sir Norman Chester Centre for Football Research.

Sir Norman Chester Centre for Football Research (1995). *Fact Sheet 4: Black Footballers in Britain*. Leicester: Sir Norman Chester Centre for Football Research.

Sisjord, M.K. and Kristiansen, E. (2009). Elite women wrestler's muscles: Physical strength and social burden. *International Review for the Sociology of Sport*, 44: 231–246.

Sluiter, L. (2009). *Clean Clothes: A Global Movement to End Sweatshops*. London: Pluto Press.

Smalley, A. (2005). 'I just like to kill things': Women, men and the gender of sport hunting in the United States, 1940–1973. *Gender and History*, 17, 1: 183–209.

Smelser, N.J. (1962). *The Theory of Collective Behavior*. New York: Free Press.

Smith, B. (2008a). Spinal cord injury, the body, and narratives of recovery in mental distress. *SCI PsychoSocial Process*, 20, 2: 18–30.

Smith, B. (2008b). Imagine being disabled through playing sport: The body and alterity as limits to imagining others' lives. *Sport, Ethics and Philosophy*, 2, 2: 142–157.

Smith, E. (1989). *Not Just Pumping Iron: On the Psychology of Lifting Weights*. Springfield, IL: Charles C. Thomas.

Smith, M.D. (1975). Sport and collective violence. In D.W. Ball and J.W. Loy (eds), *Sport and Social Order: Contributions to the Sociology of Sport*. Reading, MA: Addison-Wesley: 277–333.

Smith, M.D. (1976). Hostile outbursts in sport. In A. Yiannakis (ed.), *Sport Sociology: Contemporary Themes*. Dubuque, IO: Kendal/Hunt: 203–205.

Smith, M.D. (1978). Precipitants of crowd violence. *Sociological Inquiry*, 48, 2: 121–131.

Smith, M.D. (1979a). Hockey violence: A test of the violent subculture thesis. *Social Problems*, 27, 235–247.

Smith, M.D. (1979b). Towards an explanation of hockey violence. *Canadian Journal of Sociology*, 4, 105–124.

Smith, M.D. (1983). *Violence and Sport*. Toronto: Butterworths.

Smith, M.D. (1987). Violence in Canadian amateur sport: A review of literature. *Report for the Commission for Fair Play*. Ottawa: Government of Canada.

Smith, M.D. (1991). Violence and injuries in ice hockey. *Clinical Journal of Sports Medicine*, 1: 104–109.

Snyder, E. (1990). Emotion and sport: A case study of collegiate women gymnasts. *Sociology of Sport Journal*, 7, 3: 254–270.

Snyder, E. and Spreitzer, E. (1983). *Social Aspects of Sport*. Englewood Cliffs, NJ: Prentice Hall.

Snyder, E. and Spreitzer, E. (1989). *Social Aspects of Sport* (3rd edition). Englewood Cliffs, NJ: Prentice Hall.

Sorensen, C. and Sonne-Holm, S. (1980). Social costs of sport injuries. *British Journal of Sports Medicine*, 14, 1: 24–25.

Spaaij, R. (2006). Football hooliganism in the Netherlands: Patterns of continuity and change. *Soccer and Society*, 7, 2: 316–334.

Sparkes, A.C. (1996). The fatal flaw: A narrative of the fragile body-self. *Qualitative Inquiry*, 2, 4: 463–494.

Sparkes, A.C. (1999). Exploring body narratives. *Sport, Education and Society*, 4, 1: 17–30.

Sparkes, A.C. and Smith, B. (2008). Men, spinal cord injury, memories and the narrative performance of pain. *Disability and Society*, 23, 7: 679–690.

Spence, J. (1988). *Up Close and Personal: The Inside Story of Network Television Sports*. New York: Atheneum.

Sports Council (1991). *Injuries in Sport and Exercise*. London: The Sports Council.

Stead, D. (2003). Sport and the media. In B. Houlihan (ed.), *Sport and Society: A Student Introduction*. London: Sage: 184–200.

Stebbins, R.A. (1987). *Canadian Football: The View from the Helmet*. London: Centre for Social and Humanistic Studies of the University of Western Ontario.

Stollenwerk, H. and Sagurski, R. (1989). *Spectator Conduct during the 1988 European Football Championships with Special Consideration of Pertinent News Coverage in the Printed Media*. Paper for the Council of Europe.

Sugden, J. (2002). *Scum Airways: Inside Football's Underground Economy*. London: Mainstream Press.

Sugden, J. (2006). Teaching and playing sport for conflict resolution and co-existence in Israel. *International Review for the Sociology of Sport*, 41: 221–240.

Sugden, J. (2010). Critical left realism and sport interventions in divided societies. *International Review for the Sociology of Sport*, 45, 3: 258–272.

Sugden, J. and Tomlinson, A. (2003). *Badfellas: FIFA Family at War*. London: Mainstream Press.

Sugden, J. and Wallis, J. (Eds) (2007). *Football for Peace? The Challenges of Using Sport for Co-existence in Israel*. Aachen: Meyer.

Sutherland, E. (1947). *The Professional Thief*. Chicago: University of Chicago Press.

Sutherland, E. (1973). *Principles of Criminology*. Chicago: University of Chicago Press.

Syal, R. (2004). Bodyguards for Magnier family as Manchester United fans are blamed for threats. *Sunday Telegraph*, 1 February: 5.

Sykes, G. and Matza, D. (1957). Techniques of neutralization: A theory of delinquency. *American Sociological Review*, 22: 664–670.

Sykes, G. and Matza, D. (1989). Techniques of neutralization: A theory of delinquency. In D. Kelly (ed.), *Deviant Behaviour: A Text-reader in the Sociology of Deviance*. New York: St Martin's Press.

Tanner, J. (2010). Ski jumper sentenced to 16 months. *Calgary Herald*, 25 August: C1.

Tator, C.H. (Ed.) (2008). *Catastrophic Injuries in Sports and Recreation: Causes and Prevention*. Toronto: University of Toronto Press.

Taylor, I. (1971). Soccer consciousness and soccer subculture. In S. Cohen (ed.), *Images of Deviance*. New York: Penguin: 134–165.

Taylor, I. (1982). On the sports violence question: Soccer hooliganism revisited. In J. Hargreaves (ed.), *Sport, Culture and Ideology*. Boston: Routledge and Kegan Paul: 152–197.

Taylor, I. (1987). Putting the boot into a working-class sport: British soccer after Bradford and Brussels. *Sociology of Sport Journal*, 4, 2: 171–191.

Taylor, I. (1989). Hillsborough: 15 April 1989. Some personal contemplations. *New Left Review*, 177.

Taylor, P. Lord Justice (Chairman) (1990). *Inquiry into the Hillsborough Stadium Disaster: Final Report*. London: HMSO.

Terkel, S. (1974). *Working*. New York: Avon.

Theberge, N. (1989). A feminist analysis of responses to sports violence: Media coverage of the 1987 World Junior Hockey Championship. *Sociology of Sport Journal*, 6, 3: 247–256.

Theberge, N. (1997). 'It's part of the game': Physicality and the production of gender in women's hockey. *Gender and Society*, 11, 1: 69–87.

Theberge, N. (1999). Being physical: Sources of pleasure and satisfaction in women's ice hockey. In J. Coakley and P. Donnelly (eds), *Inside Sports*. London: Routledge: 146–155.

Theberge, N. (2000). *Higher Goals: Women's Ice Hockey and the Politics of Gender*. Albany, NY: State University of New York Press.

Thomas, C.E. and Rintala, J. (1989). Injury as alienation in sport. *Journal of the Philosophy of Sport*, 16, 1: 44–58.

Thompson, K. (2010). On and off the ice: The involvement of parents in competitive youth hockey from a symbolic interactionist perspective. Unpublished PhD dissertation, University of Ottawa, Canada.

Tiger, L. (1969). *Men in Groups*. London: Thomas Nelson and Son.

Tolliver, G. (1994). Celebration riots: A retrospective. Paper presented at conference on 'Sports Violence: Issues for Law Enforcement,' University of Illinois, Chicago, 28–30 March.

Tricker, R. and Cook, D.L. (1990). *Athletes at Risk: Drugs and Sport*. Dubuque, IO: Wm. C. Brown.

Tucker Center for Research on Girls and Women in Sport (2011). Female athletes and concussions: The untold and unexamined story. Spring newsletter. Tucker Center, University of Minnesota.

Tucker, L.W. and Parks, J.B. (2001). Effect of gender and sport type on intercollegiate athletes' perceptions of the legitimacy of aggressive behaviours in sport. *Sociology of Sport Journal*, 18: 403–413.

Van Bottenburg, M. and Heilbron, J. (2006). De-sportization of fighting contests: The origins and dynamics of no-holds-barred events and the theory of sportization. *International Review for the Sociology of Sport*, 41 (3/4): 259–281.

Vancouver Police Department (1995). *Review of the Stanley Cup Riot, June 14, 1994*. Vancouver.

Van der Kraan, M. (1993). Ajax lead the fight against racial thugs. *The European*: 30.

Van Limbergen, K. and Walgrave, L. (1988). Euro '88: Fans and hooligans. *Youth Criminology Research Group Commissioned by the Belgian Minister of the Interior*. Brussels: Belgium.

Van Zunderd, P. (1994). Law enforcement responds to sports violence. Paper presented at conference on 'Sports Violence: Issues for Law Enforcement,' University of Illinois, Chicago, 28–30 March.

Vaz, E. (1982). *The Professionalization of Young Hockey Players*. Lincoln, NE: University of Nebraska Press.

Vine, C. and Challen, P. (2002). *Gardens of Shame: The Tragedy of Martin Kruze and the Sexual Abuse at Maple Leaf Gardens*. Vancouver: Douglas and Mcintyre.

Vinger, P.F. and Hoerner, E.F. (1981). *Sports Injuries: The Unthwarted Epidemic*. Littleton, MA: PSG Publishing Company.

Voumvakis, S. and Ericson, R. (1984). News accounts of attacks on women: A comparison of three Toronto newspapers. Research report of the Centre of Criminology, University of Toronto.

Vulliamy, E. (1985). Live by agro, die by agro. *New Statesman*, 7 June: 8–10.

Waddington, I. (2000). *Sport, Health and Drugs: A Critical Sociological Perspective*. London: Routledge.

Wade, M. (1990). Animal liberationism, ecocentrism, and the morality of sport hunting. *Journal of the Philosophy of Sport*, 17, 1: 15–27.

Wade, M. (1996). Sports and speciesism. *Journal of the Philosophy of Sport*, 23: 10–29.

Wahl, G. and Wertheim, L.J. (2003). A rite gone terribly wrong. *Sports Illustrated*, 22 December: 68–77.

Wainwright, S. and Turner, B. (2006). 'Just crumbling to bits'? An exploration of the body, ageing, injury and career in classical ballet dancers. *Sociology*, 40, 2: 237–255.

Walk, S. (1997). Peers in pain: The experiences of student athlete trainers. *Sociology of Sport Journal*, 14, 1: 22–56.

Walvin, J. (1986). *Football and the Decline of Britain*. Basingstoke: Macmillan.

Wann, D.L. (1993). Aggression among highly identified spectators as a function of their need to maintain positive social identity. *Journal of Sport and Social Issues*, 17, 2: 134–143.

Wann, D.L., Melnick, M., Russell, G. and Pease, D. (2001). *Sport Fans: The Psychology and Social Impact of Spectators*. London: Routledge.

Wann, D.L., Peterson, R.R., Cothran, C. and Dykes, M. (1999). Sport fan aggression and anonymity: The importance of team identification. *Social Behavior and Personality*, 27, 6: 596–602.

Ward, C. (1996). *All Quiet on the Hooligan Front: 8 Years that Shook Football*. London: Headline.

Watson, R.C. and MacLellan, J.C. (1986). Smitting to spitting: 80 years of ice hockey in the Canadian courts. *Canadian Journal of History of Sport*, 17, 2: 10–27.

Wazir, B. (2001). Nike accused of tolerating sweatshops. *The Observer*, 20 May: 12.

Weber, M. (1921/1968). *Economy and Society* (3 vols). Totowa, NJ: Bedminster Press.

Weber, M. (1947). *The Theory of Social and Economic Organization*. A. M. Henderson and T. Parsons (trans.). T. Parsons (ed.). Glencoe, IL: Free Press.

Weber, R. (2009). Protection of children in competitive sport: Some critical questions for London 2012. *International Review for the Sociology of Sport*, 44: 55–69.

Weinstein, M., Smith, M. and Wiesenthal, D. (1995). Masculinity and hockey violence. *Sex Roles*, 33, 11/12: 831–847.

Weiss, O., Norden, G. and Hilscher, P. (1998). Ski tourism and environmental problems: Ecological awareness among different groups. *International Review for the Sociology of Sport*, 33, 4: 367–379.

Welch, M. (1997). Violence against women by professional football players: A gender analysis of hyper-masculinity, positional status, narcissism, and entitlement. *Journal of Sport and Social Issues*, 21: 392–411.

Wenner, L. (1997). Blowing whistles: Mediated sports violence and gender relations. Paper presented at conference on 'Sport, Youth, Violence and the Media.' University of Southern California, 3–4 April.

Wertheim, L.J. (2001). King of fools. *Sports Illustrated*, 30 April: 26.

West, G. (1996). Youth sports and violence: A masculine subculture? In G. O'Bireck (ed.), *Not a Kid any More: Canadian Youth, Crime and Subcultures*. Toronto: Nelson: 309–348

Whannel, G. (1979). Football crowd behavior and the press. *Media, Culture and Society*, 1, 327–342.

Wheatley, E.E. (1984). A woman's rugby subculture: Contesting on the 'wild' side of the pitch. Unpublished MA thesis, University of Illinois, Urbana-Champaign.

Wheatley, J., Right Honorable Lord (1972). *Report of the Inquiry into Crowd Safety at Sports Grounds*. London: HMSO.

Wheaton, B. (2008). From the pavement to the beach: Politics and identity in 'Surfers Against Sewage.' In M. Atkinson and K. Young (eds), *Tribal Play: Subcultural Journeys through Sport*. Bingley: Emerald: 113–134.

White, C. (1970). Analysis of hostile outbursts in spectator sports. *Dissertation Abstracts International*, 31: 6390A.

White, D. (1986). Sports violence as criminal assault: Development of the doctrine by Canadian criminal courts. *Duke Law Journal*, 1030–1054.

White, P. (2004). The costs of injury from sport, exercise and physical activity: A review of evidence. In K. Young (ed.), *Sporting Bodies, Damaged Selves: Sociological Studies of Sports-related Injury*. Oxford: Elsevier Press: 309–331.

Whitson, D. (1991). Gendered identities: Discipline, power and pleasure. Paper presented at the North American Society for the Sociology of Sport. Milwaukee, WI, 6–9 November.

Williams, J. (1985). In search of the hooligan solution. *Social Studies Review*, 1: 3–5.

Williams, J., Dunning, E. and Murphy, P. (1984). *Hooligans Abroad: The Behaviour and Control of English Fans in Continental Europe*. London: Routledge and Kegan Paul.

Williams, J. and Goldberg, A. (1989). *Spectator Behaviour, Media Coverage and Crowd Control at the 1988 European Football Championships: A Review of Data from Belgium, Denmark, the Federal Republic of Germany, Netherlands, and the United Kingdom*. Strasbourg: Council of Europe.

Wilson, B. (1997). 'Good blacks' and 'bad blacks': Media constructions of African-American athletes in Canadian basketball. *International Review for the Sociology of Sport*, 32, 2: 117–189.

Wilson, B. (2007). New media, social movements, and global sports studies: A revolutionary moment and the sociology of sport. *Sociology of Sport Journal*, 24, 457–477.

Windeatt, P. (1982). *The Hunt and the Anti-hunt*. London: Pluto Press.

Winer, A. (2011). The worst sports fan. *GQ*, April: 102–106.

Wolfgang, M.E. and Ferracuti, F. (1967). *The Subculutre of Violence: Toward an Integrated Theory in Criminology*. London: Tavistock.

Yaeger, D. and Brown, J. (2002). Prisoner of conscience. *Sports Illustrated*, 15 April: 54–57.

Yang, J., Peek-Asa, C., Allareddy, V., Phillips, G., Zhang, Y. and Cheng, G. (2007). Patient and hospital characteristics associated with length of stay and hospital charges for pediatric sport-related injury hospitalization in the United States, 2000–2003. *Pediatrics*, 19: 813–820.

Yardley, J. (2007). Beijing is rosy about the games, but activists see abuse behind the rings. *International Herald Tribune*, 7 August: 4.

Yates, R., Powell, C. and Beirne, P. (2001). Horse maiming in the English countryside: Moral panic, human deviance, and the social construction of victimhood. *Society and Animals*, 9, 1: 1–23.

Yeager, R. C. (1977). Savagery on the playing field. *Readers Digest*, September: 161–166.

Yesalis, C.E. and Cowart, V.S. (1998). *The Steroids Game*. Urbana-Champaign, IL: Human Kinectics.

Young, K. (1983). The subculture of rugby players: A form of resistance and incorporation. Unpublished MA thesis, McMaster University, Hamilton, ON, Canada.

Young, K. (1986). The killing field: Themes in mass media responses to the Heysel stadium riot. *International Review for the Sociology of Sport*, 21, 2/3: 253–264.

Young, K. (1988). Sports crowd disorder, mass media and ideology. Unpublished doctoral dissertation, McMaster University, Canada.

Young, K. (1990). Treatment of sports violence by the Canadian mass media. Report to Sport Canada's Applied Sport Research Program. Ottawa: Government of Canada.

Young, K. (1991a). Sport and collective violence. *Exercise and Sport Sciences Reviews*, 19: 539–587.

Young, K. (1991b). Writers, rimmers, and slotters: Privileging violence in the construction of the sports page. Paper presented at the North American Society for the Sociology of Sport, Milwaukee, Wisconsin, 6–9 November.

Young, K. (1993). Violence, risk, and liability in male sports culture. *Sociology of Sport Journal*, 10, 4: 373–396.

Young, K. (1997). Women, sport, and physicality: Preliminary findings from a Canadian study. *International Review for the Sociology of Sport*, 32, 3: 297–305.

Young, K. (2000). Sport and violence. In J. Coakley and E. Dunning (eds), *Handbook of Sports Studies*. London: Sage: 382–408.

Young, K. (2001). Sociological reasons for expanding the terrain of sports violence research. First World Congress of Sociology of Sport, Seoul, Korea, 20–24 July.

Young, K. (2002a). Standard deviations: An update on North American sports crowd disorder. *Sociology of Sport Journal*, 19, 3: 237–275.

Young, K. (2002b). From 'sports violence' to 'sports crime': Aspects of violence, law and gender in the sports process. In M. Gatz, M. Messner and S. Ball-Rokeach (eds), *Paradoxes of Youth and Sport*. New York: State University of New York Press: 207–224.

Young, K. (Ed.) (2004a). *Sporting Bodies, Damaged Selves: Sociological Studies of Sports-related Injury*. Oxford: Elsevier Press.

Young, K. (2004b). The role of the courts in sport injury. In K. Young (ed.), *Sporting Bodies, Damaged Selves: Sociological Studies of Sports-related Injury*. Oxford: Elsevier Press: 333–353.

Young, K. and Reasons, C. (1989). Victimology and organizational crime: Workplace violence and the professional athlete. *Sociological Viewpoints*, 5: 24–34.

Young, K. and Smith, M.D. (1988/1989). Mass media treatment of violence in sport and its effects. *Current Psychology: Research and Reviews*, 7, 4, Winter: 298–312.

Young, K. and Wamsley, K. (1996). State complicity in sports assault and the gender order in twentieth century Canada: Preliminary observations. *Avante*, 2, 2: 51–69.

Young, K. and White, P. (1995). Sport, physical danger, and injury: The experiences of elite women athletes. *Journal of Sport and Social Issues*, 19, 1: 45–61.

Young, K. and White, P. (1999). Is sport injury gendered? In P. White and K. Young (eds), *Sport and Gender in Canada*. Toronto: Oxford University Press: 69–84.

Young, K. and White, P. (2000). Researching sports injury: Reconstructing dangerous masculinities. In J. McKay, M. Messner and D. Sabo (eds), *Masculinities, Gender Relations and Sport*. Los Angeles: Sage: 108–126.

Young, K., White, P. and McTeer, W. (1994). Body talk: Male athletes reflect on sport, injury, and pain. *Sociology of Sport Journal*, 11, 2: 175–195.

Young, S. (1990). *The Boys of Saturday Night: Inside Hockey Night in Canada*. Toronto: McClelland and Stewart Inc.

Zickefoose, A. (2011). Ringette coach faces sex assault charges. *Calgary Herald*, 20 April: B1.

Zimmerman, R. (2011). Goldy goes down after weekend fan assault. *Minnesota Daily*, 9 March. Internet source: (http://www.mndaily.com/2011/03/09/goldy-goes-down-after-weekend-fan-assault).

Website sources

http://news.bbc.co.uk/hi/english/education/newsid_2053000/2053233.stm

http://www.newsday.com/sports/unc-study-heat-related-deaths-steadily-rising-1.446105

http://www.canada.com/Courts+wrong+place+deal+with+hits+lawyers/4424603/story.html

http://www.huffingtonpost.com/2010/10/21/m16toting-fan-got-inside-_n_771369.html

http://sportsillustrated.cnn.com/baseball/news/2002/09/19/fan_violence

http://www.mirror.co.uk/sport/tm_headline=lampard--never-again&method=full&objectid=18784809&siteid=89520-name_page.html

http://sportsillustrated.cnn.com/football/nfl/news/19/06/04/lewis_agreement/

http://archives.cnn.com/2000/LAW/10/columns/cossack.carruth.10.23/

http://www.cbc.ca/sports/indepth/danton/

http://www.independent.co.uk/news/uk/crime/rio-ferdinand-stalker-jailed-2281475.html

http://cbc.ca/canada/prince-edward-island/story/2008/01/18/anderson-sentence.html

http://www.cbc.ca/sports/hockey/story/2008/03/25/roy-suspension.html

http://www.ctv.ca/servlet/ArticleNews/story/CTVNews/1106308011832_81/?hub=TopStories

http://www.independent.co.uk/sport/tennis/wimbledon-officials-relent-on-equal-pay-437390.html

http://www.calgaryherald.com/sports/Lingerie+Football+coming+Canada/4610463/story.html

http://www.bbc.co.uk/news/uk-scotland-13368945

http://www.drf.com/news/federal-regulation-could-cripple-horse-racing

http://cbc.ca/news/story/2003/04/24/Nike_030424.html

http://www.cbc.ca/sports/story/2004/03/04/olympicgear0303.html

www.unep.org

http://www.theuiaa.org/news_300_Eco-Everest-Expedition-2011-underway

http://news.bbc.co.uk/2/hi/americas/8176865.stm

www.stopconcussions.com

www.cdc.gov/concussion/sports

http://www.nytimes.com/2008/12/17/sports/football/17vecsey.html

http://news.bbc.co.uk/sport2/hi/funny_old_game/7067348.stm

http://today.msnbc.msn.com/id/35327155/ns/today-today_in_vancouver/t/lindsey-vonn-reveal-serious-injury-shin/

http://www.cbc.ca/news/canada/saskatchewan/story/2009/12/12/sk-head-injuries-don-cherry-charles-tator-91212.html

Media sources with no author

BBC (1993). 'Secrets of the Coach.'

Boston Globe (1996). 5 October: 72.

'Bullpen Protection' (2001). *Stadia*, Issue 9, May: 5.

Calgary Herald (1999). 1 November: C6.

Calgary Herald (1999). 8 November: C8.

Calgary Herald (2003). 29 January: F4.

Calgary Herald (2005). 19 October: E1.

Calgary Herald (2005). 5 November: E2.

Calgary Herald (2008). 'Olympic Stadium deaths covered up.' 30 January: A12.

Calgary Herald (2008). 29 March: A6.

Calgary Herald (2009). 8 October: F2.

Calgary Herald (2010). 10 July: E5.

Calgary Herald (2011). 'Kobe fined $100,000 for gay slur.' 14 April: F2.

Calgary Herald (2011). 16–18 June.

Calgary Herald (2011). 19 June: A4.

Calgary Herald (2011). 19 June: E5.

CBC, *The Fifth Estate* (1993). 'Crossing the Line: The Sexual Harassment of Athletes.' 2 November.

CBC, *The Fifth Estate* (1997). 29 October.

CBC News (2006). '"Fight Club" in Corner Brook drew 150 teens, police allege.' 26 September. Internet source: (http://www.cbc.ca/canada/newfoundland-labrador/story/2006/09/26/fight-club.html).

CBC News (2010). 'Whistler's homeless relocated ahead of Olympics.' 8 January. Internet source: (http://www.cbc.ca/news/canada/british-columbia/story/2010/01/08/bc-whistler-homeless-olympics-relocate.html).

CBC News (2010). '3 people hurt in post-game melee – minor hockey fight spills into parking lot.' 5 February. Internet source: (http://www.cbc.ca/news/canada/nova-scotia/story/2010/02/02/ns-hockey-fight-oxford.html).

CBC Sports online (2001). 'FIFA tells South Koreans to stop torturing dogs.' 6 November. Internet source: (http://cbc.ca/sports/story/2001/11/06/fifa011106.html).

CNN Education (2004). 'Rioting: The new campus craze.' 26 February. Internet source: (http://www.cnn.com/2004/EDUCATION/02/26/life.rioting.reut/index.html).

Daily Mail (2000). 21 June: 27.

Dateline NBC (1995). 'Dying to Win: The Christy Henrich Story.'

Globe and Mail (2008). 'Punches, pushes and tackles in WNBA brawl.' 23 July: R7.

The Guardian (1994). 'Violent players face clampdown.' 12 December: 17

The Guardian (1995). 'Prop banned until 21st century.' 10 May: 21.

The Guardian (1997). 'Injury pay out puts soccer on the spot.' 15 October: 9.

The Guardian (2002). 12 November: 5.

Hooligan (1985). Thames Television, England. Producer Ian Stuttard.

The Independent (2000). 3 October: 11.

The Independent (2001). 'Jockeys cleared of ending rival's career in fall.' 2 February: 13.

The Independent (2001). 26 January: 28.

Independent on Sunday (2004). 15 February: 16.

Los Angeles Times (1986). 25 November: 3.

Maclean's (1995). 30 January: 17.

Maclean's (2002). 21 January: 11.

Maclean's (2009). 'Suffering in silence no more.' 26 October: 64–65.

McMaster University *Silhouette* (1982). 28 October: 5.

National Post (1999). 6 September: B2.

Newsweek (1974). 17 June: 93.

Newsweek (2001). 13 August: 53.

News of the World (2002). 10 February: 64.

New York Times (1999). 6 June: 35.

Sports Illustrated (1980). 13 October: 29.

Sports Illustrated (1983). 28 November: 27.

Sports Illustrated (1993). 8 November: 60–65.

Sports Illustrated (1995). 17 July: 18–26.

Sports Illustrated (1996). 5 August: 58–65.

Sports Illustrated (1996). 19 August: 58–63.

Sports Illustrated (1996). 4 November: 20.

Sports Illustrated (1999). 13 September: 91.

Sports Illustrated (1999). 1 November: 91–107.

Sports Illustrated (1999). 13 December: 27.

Sports Illustrated (2001). 10 September: 74.

Sports Illustrated (2002). 29 July: 97.

Sports Illustrated (2002). 9 September: 97.

Sports Illustrated (2003). 22 December: 99.

Sports Illustrated (2004). 1 October: 18.

Sports Illustrated (2005). 2 May: 102–118.

Sports Illustrated (2005). 30 May: 102–122.

Sports Illustrated (2006). 9 January: 104.

Sports Illustrated (2008). 11 February: 108.

Stadia (2001). 'Winter Olympics will go on despite terrorist attacks.' December: 8.

The Sun (1996). 23 February: 42.

The Sun (2001). 'Crippled rugby lad sues ref for £1 million: Scrums "were not safe".' 16 April: 15.

Sunday Times (1997). '£1.5 million injury claim threatens football.' 12 October: 5.

Time (1994). 24 January: 34–38.

Time (2001). 13 August: 54.

The Times (2007). 'I like hitting women.' 21 October: 19.

Toronto Star (1995). 22 January: A6.

Toronto Sun (1996). 28 February: 5.

USA Today (1995). 14 July: 3C.

USA Today (2007). 'Human rights groups pressure China.' 8 August: 1B.

Vancouver Sun (2004). 9 March: E3.

AUTHOR INDEX

SUBJECT INDEX